Born Wild

The Extraordinary Story of
One Man's Passion for Lions and for Africa

TONY FITZJOHN
with MILES BREDIN

VIKING
an imprint of
PENGUIN BOOKS

VIKING

Published by the Penguin Group

Penguin Books Ltd, 80 Strand, London WC2R ORL, England
Penguin Group (USA) Inc., 375 Hudson Street, New York, New York 10014, USA
Penguin Group (Canada), 90 Eglinton Avenue East, Suite 700, Toronto, Ontario, Canada M4P 2Y3
(a division of Pearson Penguin Canada Inc.)
Penguin Ireland, 25 St Stephen's Green, Dublin 2, Ireland (a division of Penguin Books Ltd)
Penguin Group (Australia), 250 Camberwell Road,
Camberwell, Victoria 3124, Australia (a division of Pearson Australia Group Pty Ltd)
Penguin Books India Pvt Ltd, 11 Community Centre,
Panchsheel Park, New Delhi – 110 017, India
Penguin Group (NZ), 67 Apollo Drive, Rosedale, North Shore 0632, New Zealand
(a division of Pearson New Zealand Ltd)
Penguin Books (South Africa) (Pty) Ltd, 24 Sturdee Avenue,
Rosebank, Johannesburg 2196, South Africa

Penguin Books Ltd, Registered Offices: 80 Strand, London WC2R ORL, England

www.penguin.com

First published 2010

1

Copyright © Tony Fitzjohn, 2010

The moral right of the author has been asserted

Set in 13/16.25pt Bembo
Typeset by Palimpsest Book Production Limited
Falkirk, Stirlingshire
Printed in Great Britain by Clays Ltd, St Ives plc

A CIP catalogue record for this book is available from the British Library

HARDBACK ISBN: 978–0–670–91891–1
TRADE PAPERBACK ISBN: 978–0–670–91892–8

www.greenpenguin.co.uk

Born Wild

To the Creatures of the Wild

Contents

List of Illustrations

Section Four

Aerial photograph of elephants on page 187 from Peter Beard, *The End of the Game*, copyright © Peter Beard/Art + Commerce

Front endpaper: With Gigi, Freddie and Arusha overlooking the camp

Back endpaper: George at sundown, Christian's Rock

All photographs, unless otherwise indicated, are copyright © the author

List of Maps

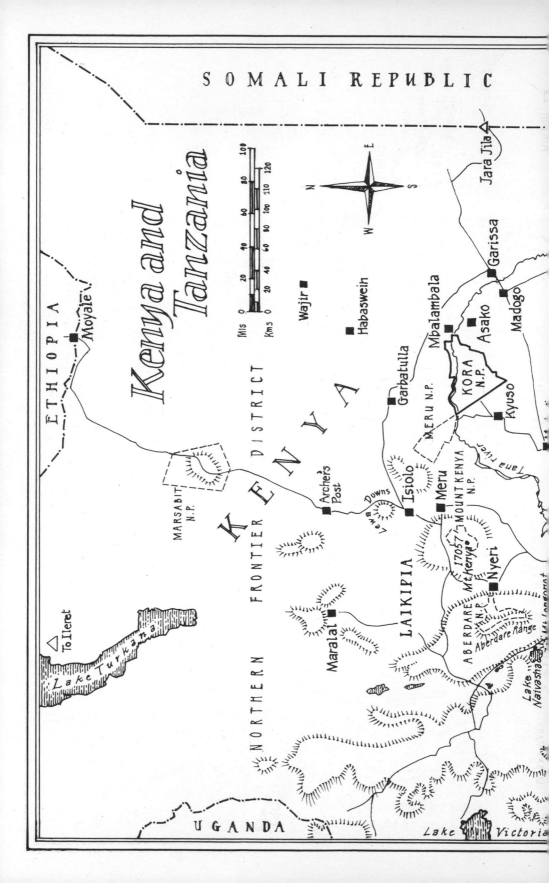

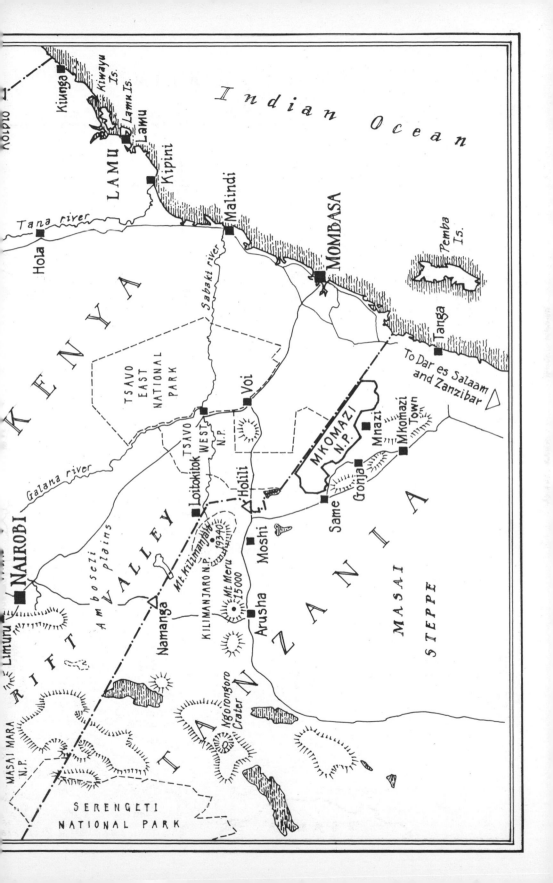

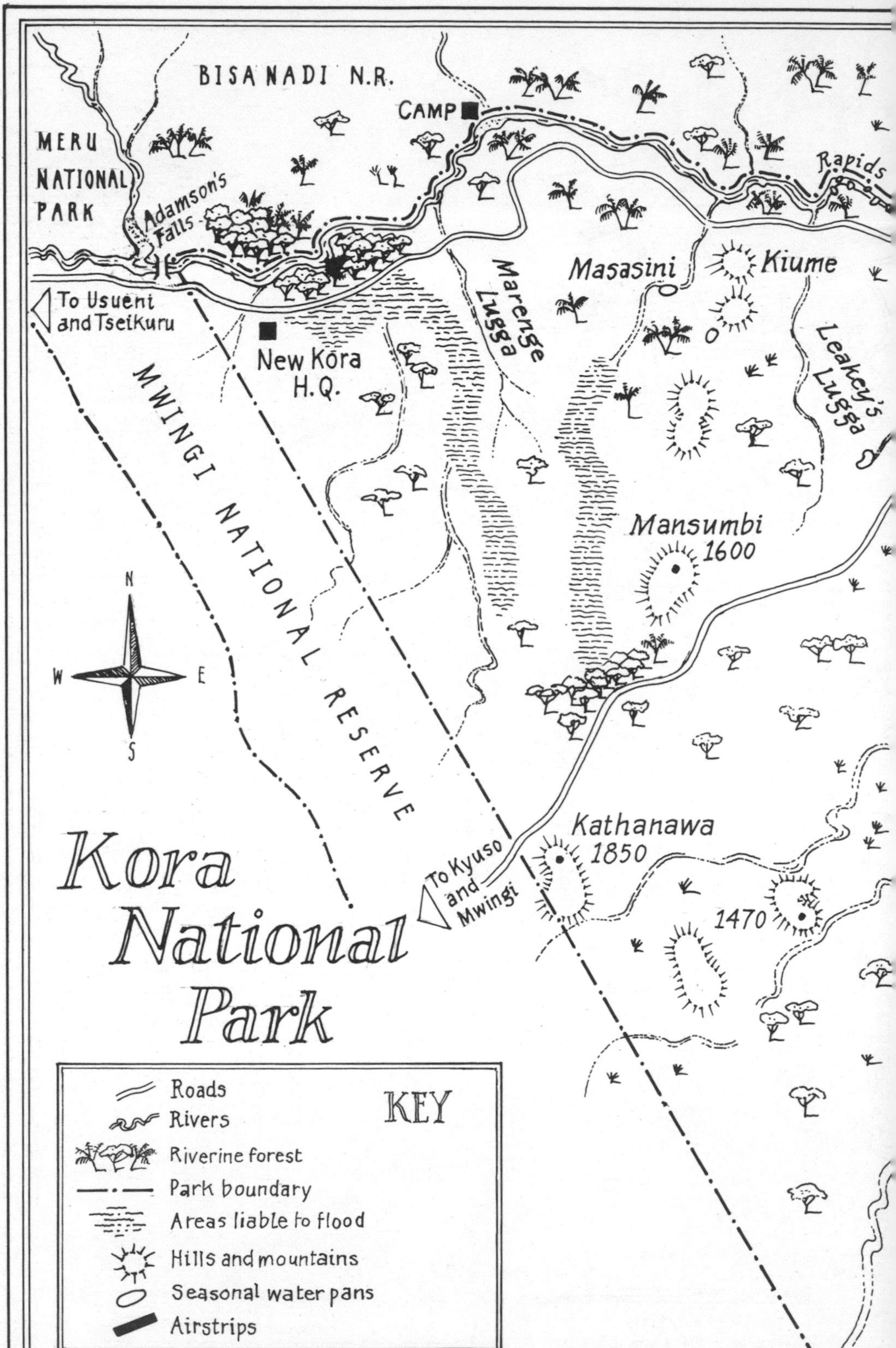

BISA NADI N.R.

CAMP

MERU NATIONAL PARK

Adamson's Falls

Rapids

To Usueni and Tseikuru

New Kora H.Q.

Marenge Lugga

Masasini

Kiume

Leakey's Lugga

MWINGI NATIONAL RESERVE

Mansumbi 1600

N
W · E
S

Kora National Park

To Kyuso and Mwingi

Kathanawa 1850

1470

KEY

Roads
Rivers
Riverine forest
Park boundary
Areas liable to flood
Hills and mountains
Seasonal water pans
Airstrips

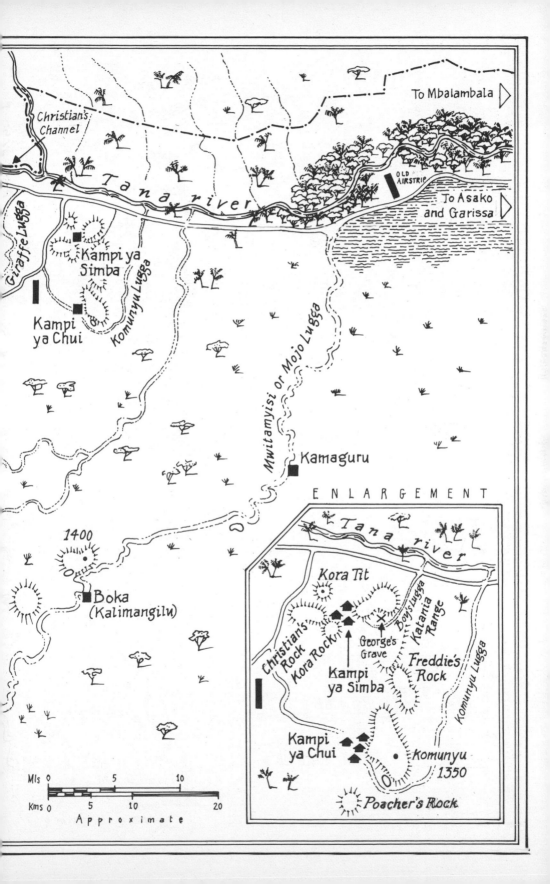

Christian's Channel

To Mbalambala

OLD AIRSTRIP

To Asako and Garissa

T a n a   r i v e r

Giraffe Lugga

Kampi ya Simba

Kampi ya Chui

Komunyu Lugga

Mwitamyisi or Mojo Lugga

Kamaguru

1400

Boka (Kalimangilu)

ENLARGEMENT

T a n a   r i v e r

Kora Tit

Boys Lugga

Katania Range

Christian's Rock

Kora Rock

George's Grave

Kampi ya Simba

Freddie's Rock

Komunyu Lugga

Kampi ya Chui

Komunyu 1350

Poacher's Rock

Mls 0   5   10
Kms 0   5   10   20
A p p r o x i m a t e

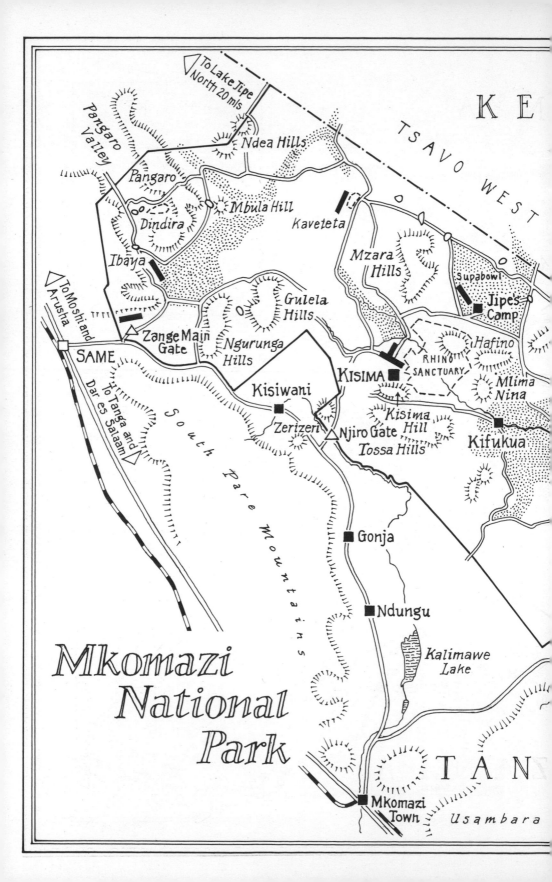

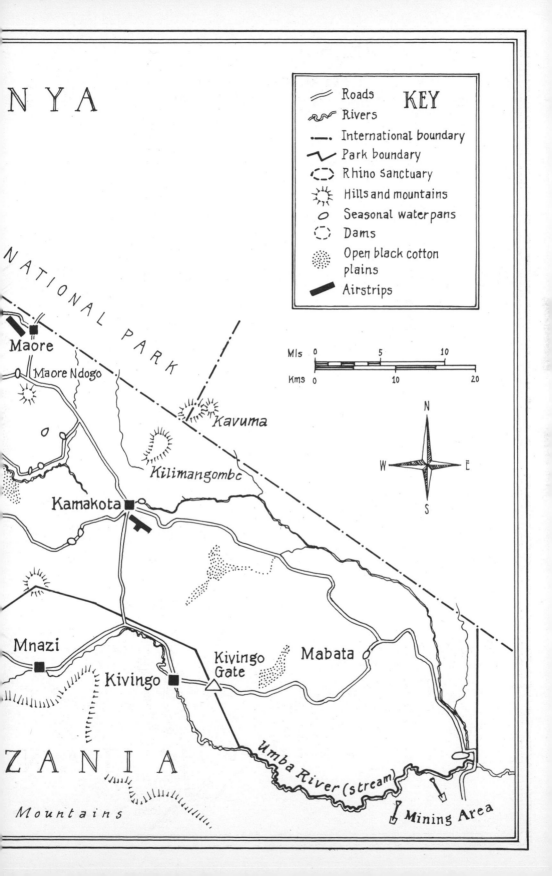

1. End of the Line

The funny thing about being chewed up by a lion is that they don't bite chunks out of you — they suffocate you. All that firepower and they use a pillow. I suppose I should be glad of it: two hundred kilos of fully grown lion pouncing on my back had already knocked the breath out of me. And when he put my head in his mouth and started to squeeze it wasn't long before I began to lose consciousness. Only when he clawed at my stomach did I wake up and my will to live reassert itself. It was just like that moment when you've been tumbled by a big wave and lost your surfboard: abruptly the light pierces the swirling water and, realizing you want to live, you kick towards the surface. I pushed my fist above my head and into the lion's mouth. But I wasn't strong enough: he was going to kill me, the bastard. I can remember wondering, as I faded away, Which one was it? A wild lion or one of ours?

It was one of ours, Shyman, and it was another of ours, Freddie, that saved me. I had raised Freddie from a cub, but unlike that big thug Shyman, whom we'd never handled, he liked me. Freddie charged Shyman and distracted him just long enough for me to regain a bit of consciousness and get into the foetal position. Freddie went for Shyman at least four or five times as Shyman came back to grab some other part of me. Even then the bigger lion got me round the neck and started to strangle me. I went through the '*Reader's Digest* tunnel', my life ebbing away — the festering rubbish dump at the camp gates my last view of the world. I knew what was happening. And as the rest of me gave into the blackness I was furious about that rubbish.

I had been working with George Adamson – the Kenyan game warden who reintroduced lions to the wild, as described in his wife's book *Born Free* – for the past four years and it was he who dragged me from the lion's maw. Alerted by our foreman, Erigumsa, he came charging out of our camp armed only with a short stick. He found Shyman dragging me off in his mouth, my body trailing between his front legs, blood pouring from holes in my neck, shoulders and body. I was dead, as far as the Old Man was concerned. George charged at the lion and, with Freddie, managed to see off Shyman and pull me away. Without Freddie, I wouldn't have stood a chance. I'd been attacked by one lion and saved by another. I'd lost a tooth and one of my ears was hanging off. A hole had been bitten in my right shoulder and neck, which was large enough to put my fist through. It would be a couple of painful weeks before I was back on my feet but I consider it my closest shave yet and not much to have paid for the privilege of living with animals since the day in 1971 that George Adamson had taken me on.

Mine was a long journey to George's camp in northern Kenya but I feel as if it wasn't until I arrived there in 1971 that my life really started. That said, I was actually born in 1945, rather freer than I would have liked – on the wrong side of the tracks, at the end of the line. I was raised in Cockfosters, the very furthest north you can go on the Piccadilly Line. My mother was a bank clerk; my father abandoned her before I was born. One of tens of thousands who met a similar fate during the Second World War, she tried to bring me up on her own but it was very hard to do when there was no work, little food and a hatful of stigma attached to dragging around a small boy without a father. When I was about seven months old she gave me up for adoption at the Church of England Children's Society. I don't know what happened to her and have never seen her again. I don't know either who my father was. I've been told he was highly decorated, married and in the RAF, but I'm really not sure; I can't remember whether that's true or wishful thinking, and I can't find out now because most of the Society's records have disappeared. My adoptive parents, though, I know all about. Leslie and Hilda Fitzjohn came and got me when my age was still measured in months. They took me to Cockfosters where they lived the kind of life I've been trying to escape from ever since.

My dad worked in a bank. He got on a train every day and went off to places like Greenwich, Covent Garden and Tooting. He had been in the Supply Corps of the Desert Rats during the war and had seen some pretty unpleasant sights during his five years in Egypt. When he got back, I'm told he just sat and drank for six months, staring at the fire and refusing to talk. Today you'd call it post-traumatic stress disorder but back then there were no words for it. Soon after he had recovered my parents had a tragedy. They had adopted a baby who settled down well and upon whom they doted. Six months later his mother appeared on the doorstep and asked for him back; she had just married a man who had lost his wife and four children in a car crash. My parents thought it was the only fair thing to do and handed the baby over, but they were shattered.

By the time I arrived on the scene, they were in much better shape. Dad was doing well at work and getting on better with my mum. She was an inveterate charity worker and always off doing something that involved wearing a hat – Mothers' Union, Townswomen's Guild or going to church. I suppose we were your everyday emerging middle-class family, the kind of people who appeared in those old black-and-white educational films, holidayed on the south coast and went to the Festival of Britain in home-knitted jumpers. We lived in a small semi-detached house in a road with hundreds of similar houses. Ours was smarter than the ones on the other side of the street because you could only just see the electric flash of the tube lines from our side, but they were all much of a muchness and there wasn't much of it I liked.

When I was two and a half or so we went to the orphanage again and, according to family legend, I picked out a sister, Margaret, who now lives a much more respectable life in the UK than her brother. We don't know why my parents adopted. Maybe there was some physical problem or they just didn't have enough sex. I certainly never saw them at it but this was the 1940s and 1950s: sex was not something one discussed with one's parents. Ours was quite a strict and repressed household and our parents might have quarrelled but they loved us and the good far outweighed the bad.

Back then the end of the Piccadilly Line was also the start of the countryside. I used to go for long walks with our dogs Trudi and Judy in the fields that began just a few hundred yards from our house. I'd play in the woods and climb trees with my friend Alex Duncan, the local vicar's son. We had an air pistol and we'd go up to the top of his house and shoot at women's bottoms as they tottered by. Inevitably we were caught. I've got one of those faces that has difficulty concealing the truth: I worked that out at an early age and have always behaved better than I would have wished. I hate to think what I'd have got up to with a more innocent face.

One of my greatest loves was Scouting. It doesn't have a good image these days – all paedophiles and sandals – but in the fifties it was a great way to escape and learn about the outdoors. By the time I finished school I had more badges than Idi Amin had medals. I loved Scouting and I kept on doing it right up until I left secondary school. We always had excellent Scoutmasters and the freedom of the outdoors was wonderful after the tight discipline that prevailed at home. All that practical stuff – knots, rope courses and the like – were fun at the time and have proved extraordinarily useful. I tie knots every day of my life and I knew most of them before I was ten. Although it's a dying pastime in England, Scouting remains hugely influential in Africa. Like so many other things here, it's just like it used to be in England in the fifties. It's taken very seriously: ministers will happily be photographed in shorts and woggle. They're always having jamborees, and Lord Baden-Powell even went so far as to die in Kenya. His grave was made a national monument by Kenya's Chief Scout, Daniel arap Moi, when he was president. One of my oldest and most respectable friends is Kenya's Chief Scout today.

When I wasn't Scouting I was at school, but almost the only thing I recall about primary school is the rabbits. I don't know whether they were being bred for fur, the table or as pets but I loved looking after them. I didn't go so far as preparing them for release into the wild but I do remember that even then I liked animals and dares as much as each other. Indeed, in an unhappy combination of the two, I caught typhus after drinking from a puddle in the school playground and had to spend months in bed, staring at a naked bulb as the sweat poured off me. It was during this time that I came across a book that inspired me to go to Africa and work with the animals that I had already begun to love.

Absurd as it may sound, in this age of the Discovery and National Geographic Channels, the book that stirred me was Edgar Rice Burroughs's *Tarzan of the Apes* – one of the most inaccurate books ever written about the 'Dark Continent'. We only had a small bookshelf at home and it was full of condensed reads and books about war in the desert, containing black-and-white pictures of men with their hands in the air. But hidden away at the back of the shelf was a paperback copy of *Tarzan* with a colourful cover. I read it over and over again. These were the days of Johnny Weissmuller and Cheeta down at the picture house, but it was actually the book that inspired me rather than the celluloid, although I always had a liking for Maureen O'Sullivan as Jane.

Tarzan fascinated me and inspired a lifelong love of Africa, its people and wildlife that endures to this day – even though I've eaten Africa's dirt, been shot at by its inhabitants and gnawed upon by its wildlife. I still find it hard to define what it is that I love about this place – the freedom, the challenge or the responsibility – but I know I love it with an almost painful intensity and I hate spending too long away from it. When I first read *Tarzan*, going to Africa became an imperative. And I also wanted desperately to be able to communicate with animals like my hero did. Rice Burroughs never set foot in Africa (in fact, William S. Burroughs has probably been a more reliable guide to me) and his descriptions bear no relation to what it actually looks like or what it's like to live here.

The first school I remember properly was Enfield Grammar, a couple of miles' bus ride from home. I must have driven my parents crazy when I was there: I was reasonably quick-witted but I did no work whatsoever. What I really concentrated on was stealing. I'm told that I was personally responsible for the installation of shoplifting mirrors in the local Woolworth's because we were always down there nicking stuff when we should have been at school. It wasn't because we wanted the things we stole. It was the buzz and excitement we yearned for – Enfield was tedious beyond measure, Cockfosters with more dirt, black-and-white to my Technicolor imagination. At first my petty larceny had been pretty harmless but it was fast aggrandizing, fed by my constant urge for excitement and my unwillingness to turn down a dare. Borstal and prison were becoming ever more likely.

It was at about this time that my life began to change. My father had worked hard at the bank and had been able to buy our first car – a Vauxhall 10 I loved and whose engine I used to play with when I was not out in the fields with the dogs. He washed it religiously at weekends and it always sparkled like new. Having a car in those days was a big deal and that consciousness of their worth has remained with me all my life. The Trust that George and I set up has loads of vehicles now and I keep them on the road way longer than I should because of some inbuilt sense of thrift: every vehicle we've ever had in Tanzania is still in use, an absurd source of pride until I was told how much it was costing us.

Rationing in Britain didn't stop until 1954 when I was nine, and life wasn't easy even then. Nevertheless, Dad's grafting at the bank paid off when he was offered the managership of a new branch. We moved to nearby – but much posher – Southgate, and Dad joined the Rotary Club, an event that set me off on a completely new path. Instead of going to Borstal, I was packed off to Mill Hill, a smart boarding school on the outskirts of north London. They had an assisted-places scheme through which the school and Middlesex County Council would help to pay the fees of a few boys each year. A Rotary Club member had tipped him off about it. I don't know why they took me but I'm so lucky they did. Almost all of my trustees in the UK are Old Millhillians to this day, including my oldest school-friend, Bob Marshall-Andrews, who was one of our founders and is now chairman of the George Adamson Trust.

It's fascinating to imagine how my life could have gone without out the influence of Mill Hill. Would I have carried on looting Woolworth's and ended up in jail, or would I have got a proper job and kept off the booze in my middle age? Mill Hill taught me many great things but it was a way of life I was after, not a salary; I haven't received a salary since the day I met George Adamson in 1971. Bob said in a speech when I got my OBE that the idea of Mill Hill was to take people from very different backgrounds – the wealthy, the *nouveau riche*, the middle classes and the poor – put them through the system and spit them out as useful, serving, articulate members of society. Then he turned to me and said, 'With you, Fitzjohn, it all went terribly wrong.' I may not be quite what they were planning but I knew from the moment I got to Mill Hill that I had to make it work for me.

Mill Hill was an amazing place to arrive after thirteen years on the grimy streets of north London. It's set in 120 acres of parkland and has views as far as the Chilterns in one direction and much of London in the other. The school buildings were like nothing I had ever seen before – towering ceilings with intricate plaster-work, polished wooden floors and panelling everywhere. It was like something out of a film. The school had gymnasiums, theatres and science laboratories – all things that would be impressive today, but in the 1950s I'd been used to having very little indeed. I was terrified. It was all so alien: I had to fag for someone, making his bed and cleaning his shoes, and I had to put up with a bit of bullying – but who doesn't? It didn't last for long. I was in the lowest class when I got there and right from the beginning I knew I had to get out of it and up to the next level. I had a great sense of privilege but was also conscious that this was my one chance. My schooling was virtually free but even having to pay for the textbooks and uniforms was a burden for my parents, who had to scrimp to make sure I had what I needed and that my sister's fees at a convent in Whetstone could still be covered. All around me other children had things that I wanted. I decided what I had to do was: change my accent, get three A levels and play rugby for the First XV. The first two weren't too hard but I was a weedy little squirt, and although I could jump like a Masai on a pogo stick – very handy at line-outs – getting into the First XV was quite a struggle.

I really threw myself into the school. I worked hard at my studies and outside the classroom I was like someone trying to join the Marines. I did cross-country running, pull-ups in the gym, rope climbing, anything – as long as it hurt. Boys fill out naturally at that age but I was also very athletic – something that's stayed with me, which is lucky or I would never have been able to do half the things I've done. Tracking lions and chasing after leopards all day is exhausting work and I really needed to be strong.

The academic work was a struggle. I've always had problems remembering things, and although I was good enough to pass my A levels, universities weren't exactly clamouring for me to attend and there was no way I was getting into medical school. I did chemistry, zoology and physics with all the future medical students. My chemistry teacher put me in touch with the personnel director of Express Dairies, who took me on as a management trainee before I'd even left school. Most of my contemporaries walked straight into jobs too, but I didn't have the contacts they had so this was a lucky break, even if it wasn't Africa.

As in Cockfosters, I devoted plenty of time to the Scouts. We had the option of Scouting or the CCF at Mill Hill – an easy choice. Play around outdoors, doing what I'd always loved, or wear reject Second World War uniform and march around in circles while being shouted at by a retired sergeant major. I must have got every single badge they ever made but I never became a Queen's Scout. I have always had a problem with authority and becoming a Queen's Scout required following rules.

By the time I reached my last two terms I'd achieved what I needed to get out of school and, with the Express job in the bag, I was able to play a little. Bob, who had left a year earlier, used to come and pick me up on Saturday night in his father's old Hillman Minx and we'd go cruising for girls. Unsuccessfully. But it was freedom.

I had loved Mill Hill but casting off the shackles of authority was still a great feeling. I went on a motorbike trip round Britain with a school-friend. We got into all sorts of trouble but it was a short holiday rather than a gap year so very soon I started work at Express. I travelled all over the country doing a variety of jobs as part of my training, from hotel management to a milk round in Muswell Hill, like Matt Monro who sang the Oscar-winning theme song for *Born Free*. 1963 was a great time to be young and in London and I had the best of both worlds. I was a management trainee in a huge and respected company at the forefront of Harold Wilson's 'burning white heat of technology' and I was also knocking on doors in a little blue cap in the early mornings. I soon learnt that all the clichés you hear about milkmen and housewives are true. I was having the time of my life.

As I stumbled from party to good time, Express were beginning to see the error of my ways. They battled away for two long years as I turned up late for work, took too much time off at the weekends to play rugby, grew my hair too long and showed a marked lack of interest in the dairy industry. Eventually they sent me on an Outward Bound course in a last attempt to get me to show some leadership qualities. It was to be an eye-opener both for Express and myself.

On the course, we were divided into patrols named after polar explorers – ours for Lawrence 'Titus' Oates, known for his honourable death when, aware that his ill health was jeopardizing his companions' lives, he told them, 'I am just going outside and may be some time,' before walking out into a blizzard. Being in the Oates patrol was another lucky chance akin to getting into Mill Hill. I've been such an ass all my life, chewing at the hand that feeds me and always getting bored, but every now and then I meet some incredibly good person who sees past the pain in their hand and totally changes my life. The man in charge of Oates patrol was one such. Campbell Whalley was just the man I needed to meet at the time. A former game warden in the Serengeti, he had lived the life I had always wanted to lead since reading *Tarzan* – an ambition I had let slide through laziness and a willingness to go with the flow. He was just the kick up the backside I needed. He told me fabulous stories about his life in the bush, the animals he had known, the battles with poachers, the solitary but hugely rewarding life. Blithely unaware of Macmillan's 'wind of change' then sweeping across Africa, I wondered what he was doing running an Outward Bound course on Ullswater for a bunch of misfits like me instead of running around the African plains. Early on in the course, he told me I should go to Africa if I felt I had to but added that I was thirty years too late.

Reading Campbell's assessment of me at the time is a chastening experience. He was extraordinarily prescient, recognizing all the faults I have carried with me through life. He immediately spotted the way my nervousness makes me bluster and show off and, of course, that I had that knee-jerk horror of rules:

Tony can, however, be very nervous as he showed when giving a lecturette that nevertheless was clear in its presentation and easily understood by the audience . . . He only spoilt a good course for himself by being very critical of the staff in his first few days and not keeping his opinions to himself. He was also inclined to pull the rules of the school to shreds . . . [he] gave an unfortunate first impression which we feel he must not give again no matter where he goes.

However, he also saw a good side somewhere, commending me for leading by example and being kind to the weaker boys. Not good enough for Express, though, who fired me as soon as they read the report: 'Well, thank God for that,' said Campbell, in 2009, when I met up with him forty-six years later.

I was enthralled by Campbell's tales of his time as a game warden and, although it took a while to happen, this was a significant watershed. My life in milk was over! I would run a game park in Africa. I would work with animals and, in honour of Titus Oates: I would work outside and I would 'be some time'.

Deciding to go to Africa and actually going took a bit longer than I had hoped. I worked my way through a bizarre collection of jobs over the next couple of years that brought me into contact with everyone from former colonial governors to the Beatles. I loved the rock and roll, the rugby at the weekends and, most of all, the dolly birds, but it was the old game wardens and colonial administrators who appealed to me most. To me, they embodied real freedom and adventure, not the manufactured Carnaby Street variety. But what a time to be in London . . . I had the best of it but my ultimate goal lay ahead of me.

In 1968 my opportunity came. Forget the Summer of Love, I was off to Africa with my maiden aunt Alice.

I first came to Africa by boat – the *Transvaal Castle* from Southampton to Cape Town. It was a proper old liner with all sorts of different forms of entertainment, and although it had just become a 'one-class' ship, the social dividing lines were still there until I met some of the wonderful 'White Africans' – the last hurrah of the Raj now working in independent Africa. Many would look after me and give me beds and a warm welcome in the years to come. I slept in a four-berth cabin – in steerage, right next to the propeller shafts – with a smelly and largely unintelligible group of Zambian tobacco farmers and miners, alcoholics to a man. It was a glorious trip. Of course I spent all my money before I even got to Grahamstown whence my aunt had relocated from England.

Bizarrely, I met the prime minister, John Vorster, on my first day there. He had just inherited the bloodstained helm of apartheid South Africa following the assassination of Hendrik Verwoerd and he was opening the museum in which my aunt, an artist, had been commissioned to paint murals. It was quite brave of him, considering it was the hated British 1820 Settlers Museum and he was a hard-line Boer. Vorster was just one of many apartheid-era South African leaders that I met in the next year or two. I'm afraid to say they were all disconcertingly nice. Reading about their exploits today, it is hard to equate the private people with their political actions. Vorster, for example, was a corrupt Nazi sympathizer responsible for the brutal suppression of those who opposed his rule, but he was a charming host and made a lovely cup of tea.

Alice had never recovered from the death of her brother, who was executed by the IRA in 1921 – a great shame as she was full of fun and truly kind. Whenever I'm feeling particularly sorry for myself I read the letter he wrote on the night of his death.

Dear Mother, Alice and Dad,
When out walking to-day, Toogood, Glossop and myself were captured by the I.R.A. and have been condemned to be shot to-night.

The O.C. I.R.A. and his men have been very civil to us throughout and have treated us well. It is terrible to have to leave you all so early in life but it is fate and a soldier's life.

Always remember I died smiling, and believing in a life to come.
A thousand kisses and a last farewell. Au-revoir, Rob
Don't let this worry you too much.

It always humbles me.

Back in 1968, I was not feeling sorry for myself at all but I was in pressing need of a job. I took my HGV licence and eventually found work as a bus driver in Cape Town, sometimes serving black areas and at others white. It was while I was there that I was shot at for the first time.

I had been having an affair with a lovely girl called Jane who, in a fit of madness, had confessed all to her husband. I was persuaded by a doctor friend, Richard Arnot – a 'chap' who was always getting people to do the decent thing – to go round and apologize. Never listen to a 'chap'. I arrived to find Jane lying on the floor in a silver lamé jumpsuit, her husband John pointing a revolver at me. Obviously I apologized. But having been forgiven, I couldn't resist shouting at John as I left. He fired out of the window, then ran down the street after me. Escape came in the form of a bus driven by one of my colleagues, who pulled over and yelled, 'Hey, *soutpiel*. In trouble again?' I sat on the back seat, panting like a dog and smiling broadly like Dustin Hoffman, but there was no Katharine Ross with whom to share the joke.

This was one of many events that encouraged me to get on with my life. I was in Africa and – rare in apartheid South Africa – I'd even made friends with a few Africans, but I was still very much in 1960s English mode and I might just as well have been back in the UK most of the time. I needed to make a move and decided to hitchhike up to Kenya where some friends were touring with a rugby team. This took longer than I'd expected but Kenya entranced me from the very moment I arrived. At last I had reached the Africa of my imagination. Even Nairobi National Park took my breath away.

The first place in Nairobi that I really felt at home was, inevitably, a bar. A long, narrow room, the Long Bar at the Stanley Hotel had a huge mural of the turn-of-the-century Nairobi rail-head behind Abdi's forty-foot bar. Everyone went there at lunchtime – hunters, tour guides, businessmen, actors from the Donovan Maule Theatre, off-duty pilots, minor European royalty, people up from the coast, upcountry ranchers, polit-icians, polo players, police informers, con men, drug pushers and even a few bemused tourists.

There was no racism and no privilege there. Prince Alfie Ausch-berg rubbed shoulders and shared stories with Jimmy Kariuki, an engineer with East African Airways, and Bunny Allen, a genu-ine Romany with an earring who would talk to anyone – as long as she was a she. If you wanted a lift to the coast, someone was flying down. Never been on a hunt? Someone would take you. Short of a few bob? 'Never mind – it's on us.' Need a tie for the Stanley Grill tonight? 'Take mine.' Problem with Immigration? 'Talk to Macharia over there.'

The Long Bar was one of those defining places – like Carnaby Street or Haight-Ashbury and Woodstock. It perfectly encapsulated a time and place. It was a hard-drinking outfit, the Long Bar – in the daytime as, for some reason, it was always a bit seedy at night when we would follow the BOAC hostesses back to the Grosvenor. And it was in the Long Bar that I first met Ian Hughes. A tough, broken-nosed Welshman with a brain to match his courage, he invited me on my first safari. Unbelievably, after all this talk of *Tarzan* and wanting to run a game park, I'd been in Africa for almost a year and never been out in the real bush. Ian was in charge of a specialist anti-poaching unit based in Maralal that had responsibilities across northern Kenya. I jumped at joining him. Just getting to Maralal, a one-camel town on the edge of the Northern Frontier District (NFD), was an adventure but from there it got better and better.

No one was allowed into the NFD in those days unless they had a permit and an armed escort. But for us it was different: we were the armed escort. We set off from Maralal with a Land Rover and an old two-wheel-drive truck full of game rangers, a great rooster of dust billowing up behind us. We headed north up the eastern shore of Lake Turkana to Ileret on the border with Ethiopia. I had hitchhiked across Africa but had stuck to main roads and aircraft. This was my first time out in the wild and I already knew I was home – the sight of faraway herds of oryx shimmering in the desert air, the taste of the dust and the noise of the howling wind. The hot desert air smelt of battles and sex and a time long gone. I loved everything about it.

Ian taught me a huge amount about the bush and its inhabitants: how to interpret tracks, which animals made what noise and when to climb up the nearest tree (which, in the NFD, could be miles away). It would be years before I knew what I was talking about but it was Ian who set me on my way. I vividly remember hearing my first lion – that deep, deep sound with which I would become so familiar but that is not at all as you would expect. Lions do not often roar *à la* MGM (that lion is yawning) but their resonant grunting makes the hair rise on your neck and completely fills the African night. 'WHO is the lord of this land? I AM, I AM, I AM . . .' He roars, then grunts. Then listens.

It wasn't just Ian's knowledge of natural history that I absorbed. He knew all the tricks for keeping vehicles on the road – how to use a high-lift jack and fix radiators with tea leaves (not that it works! It took me ten years to find out that curry powder was best for small leaks). I loved it all – it was Scouting for grown-ups. Everything went wrong: we ran out of food, we got stuck, our vehicles broke down and we sorted it all out because we had to and it was fun. There could have been no more perfect intro-duction to the bush.

When we got back to Maralal, I met the great explorer Wilfred Thesiger at his house there; he would become something of a thorn in George Adamson's side in later years but was very help-ful to me when I first arrived in Kenya. He asked me for a lift down to Nairobi and I almost killed him in the driving rain. The murram road south was a river of red mud, and after we had just hurtled off it sideways for the umpteenth time, he peered down his enormous nose and said, 'I haven't driven for over thirty years but if you'd like me to take over. . .' Thesiger told me how Kenya was not as it used to be, that it was sad I hadn't arrived before the internal combustion engine ruined everything.

There were a lot of unemployed game wardens and former colonial servants around at the time, who would all tell me the same thing. Following independence, many of the old European wardens took early retirement or were not so gently squeezed out of their jobs so that Africans could be promoted. At first these were properly qualified people who deserved advancement. But as things got more corrupt, and the government became increasingly desperate to let fall a few of the fruits of independence on which its members were gorging, people were promoted on no merit at all. The national parks and, indeed, everything else suffered terribly as a result. One of the outcomes of the policy was the poaching wars of the 1980s and the wholesale slaughter of Kenya and Tanzania's wildlife.

One of the still-employed wardens I met was a wonderful man called Rodney Elliot, who kept an eye on me and fought my corner for years. Ian's boss in the NFD, he was an old-school gentleman, famous for his upright character and iron toughness. It was extraordinary that he talked to me at all. I was a long-haired albeit charming lout with questionable language but there was obviously something in me that he liked. He always defended me when I was up against the authorities and he wrote me a wonderful letter when I first arrived at George's camp, saying, 'I'm very glad that you've found a new assistant. I think you will find George Adamson to be an enterprising and reliable young man.'

On the strength of my success at Ullswater I had managed to swing a job at the Loitokitok Outward Bound School at the foot of Mount Kilimanjaro. I was bowled over by its beauty. I can see the mountain from where I write today but I'm on the opposite side here in Tanzania. Kili rises out of the plains near Loitokitok with a drama that I've never seen equalled, a huge solitary volcano with a ruff of snow so perfect it looks fake. In those days, the Amboseli plains thronged with elephant, giraffe and all sorts of plains game. It was the Africa that I had always imagined. We used to get chased by the rhinos there, our hearts going like jackhammers as we cursed them for looking like rocks. You'd pay a king's ransom to be chased by a rhino in Amboseli today. Up on the mountain there were buffalo and bushbuck in the forest, Colobus monkeys in the canopy and all sorts of iridescent birds flitting among the branches. And always the sentinel mountain in the background. I even ran to the top of 19,340-foot-high Kilimanjaro with a friend – we were three-quarters of the way back when my legs gave up and I couldn't move for five hours. We would have smashed the record but for that.

The Outward Bound School was fun too but, typically, I managed to have a fight with a well-connected student and was soon on my way back to Nairobi and the Long Bar. In Kenya at that time you could do anything you wanted and we did. There was almost no population pressure and the economy was booming. There was a wonderful feeling of freedom and hope then, one that fifty years of misrule has done its best to wipe out but which still lingers on as an impressive credit to the resilience of ordinary Kenyans. But all this fun required a bit of cash and I was no nearer to finding a job that I wanted to do. So when Ian asked me on safari again, of course I agreed.

Ian, a game warden pal of his and I set off in a £50 Volkswagen Combi for points north. We had a spectacular time, doing everything the hard way. We traversed the NFD and crossed the border into Ethiopia near Mega, where we decided to go through the bush rather than take the dirt road. We soon found ourselves lost in the elephant grass with only first and third gear on the van working. It's a long, hard climb from the deserts of southern Ethiopia to the highlands around Addis Ababa and we did them all at crawling speed. Indeed, we went so slowly that semi-naked tribesmen with huge Afros and ancient rifles ran faster than us. We scared them off by waving pistols in the air. At the top of the hill and seven hundred kilometres away was Addis Ababa, the hundred-year-old town built by the Emperor Menelik. It was a funny old place – Haile Selassie was still in power and the whole country was run on feudal lines. His modernization programme hadn't caught up with the eighteenth century let alone the twentieth, and it was no surprise when he was overthrown a few years later. No one would help us mend the Combi because we had neither the right papers nor enough money – until we went to see Brigadier Sandford, to whom we had a letter of introduction from Wilfred and whispered the magic name, Thesiger. Suddenly the Combi was being mended, spare parts became miraculously available and taxes were waived. We drove on through the Simien Mountains and the highlands of Ethiopia to Asmara in modern-day Eritrea. This fabulous little town could have been on the shores of Lake Como, all pastel colours and gentle curves. The Italians had colonized Eritrea and built streets lined with glorious art deco buildings in its highland capital – even the garages were works of art. I remember it most for ice cream, espresso and beautiful girls. Those, and the insane journey down to Massawa we took in a tiny little train that drops around 2,500 metres in 56 kilometres (as the crow flies). There we found an Italian trader who offered to put our VW bus on top of his load of green peppers as it made its way along the Red Sea to Alexandria. Initially we balked at this as too easy, but after further mechanical disasters we took him up on his offer – in the end another of his boats took us to Venice. By the time we reached Paris we were freezing cold and only had one gear left. We made the last stage of the journey with a Primus stove keeping us warm between the seats, then some madman stole the bus and set it on fire. It had been a great safari but once again I hadn't really thought things through.

I had agreed to go on safari. That we would eventually arrive in England hadn't dawned on me until we got there. Ian had a job in Kenya. I had nothing and was back in the place that I had managed only recently to escape. It was a bit bleak. I ended up back driving trucks between Covent Garden and the airport, picking up goods being imported from Kenya. Occasionally I would get a short job at the Outward Bound School in Devon. I wrote to all my friends and acquaintances in Kenya asking for jobs and news, and even to Joy Adamson, whom I had met when doing a quick building job at the house next door to hers in Naivasha. She said she was looking for a secretary, a job I declined. No one else had anything they could offer me.

When I received a letter from Dawie du Plessis offering to fly me back to South Africa, I was amazed. I had known him in Cape Town but not very well. Nevertheless I accepted without hesitation and was soon on a BOAC Comet to Johannesburg, clutching a bag of rare records that he'd asked me to bring. We went out to his father's farm in the Orange Free State and were soon riding around bareback, mustering cattle and living a healthy life in the sun. Dawie's father was Sand du Plessis, the administrator of the Orange Free State, one of the most powerful men in South Africa. A lovely man, he said he'd get me a job in the South African national parks, but I told him I'd lost my heart to Kenya and turned him down.

One morning out at the farm I woke up hung-over and sore. I walked down to the kitchen where I was shushed into a chair and told to listen: there was a church service from the Bloemfontein Groote Kerke (Big Church) on the radio. I looked around as I listened quietly and realized I was sitting with more concentrated influence and raw power than I ever would again. The administrators of all the other South African states were on one side, with Sand du Plessis, Prime Minister John Vorster and President Jacobus Fouché opposite. It was that kind of house.

Later that day I discovered why Dawie had invited me out in the first place. He confessed as we were riding in the cattle: 'You know that trouble you had just before you left Cape Town? When that man tried to shoot you because you'd slept with his wife? That was my fault. I was having an affair with Jane, but because of my father's position I couldn't be seen to be the cause of her divorce. I've felt guilty for ages. I'm really sorry, *boetjie*.'

I couldn't have cared less. I had loved my time with lamé Jane and I was back in Africa again. Neither would it be the last I heard of my friend Richard Arnot, who had obliged me to do the right thing. A few years later he became front-page news when Nurse Helen Smith and a man with his underpants round his ankles fell to their deaths at a party Richard was giving in Saudi Arabia. I suspect it was a Foreign Office cover-up because there had been influential Saudis at the party.

I loved my time with the du Plessis, but now I was back in Africa, I knew that I had to get to the best bit: Kenya. It was with regret that I said goodbye to South Africa. I had stayed at the heart of Afrikaner country and found my hosts welcoming, gracious and fair. Prime Minister Vorster had been charming and generous on both the occasions I had met him. The people I couldn't stand in South Africa were the English-speaking whites who thought they were so much better than everyone else – the *soutpiels*. It was a relief to be returning to Kenya where in the post-independence euphoria, blacks and whites got on well, and there was an emerging black elite with whom one could drink and play.

I set off in May and hitchhiked my way up through Malawi, Rhodesia, Zambia and Tanzania, arriving broke and thirsty at the Long Bar in July. I still couldn't find a job doing what I wanted but there was plenty of little stuff that I fitted in between safaris and having fun to keep me solvent. I worked at the Djinn Palace on Lake Naivasha, a fabled old *White Mischief* haunt that had fallen into disrepair. It had been bought by a Dutch family who employed me to fix up the boats and get everything going again. I worked on a farm for a while in Timau near Mount Kenya and visited Ian Hughes again in Isiolo. He was living in George and Joy Adamson's old house where they had raised Elsa the lioness. But I wanted to be out in the bush working with animals.

1969 was possibly the worst time to have such ambitions. Mwai Kibaki, Kenya's current president, was then the finance minister. In need of some popularity and well aware of the effect it would have on the economy, he was making life hard for non-Africans, particularly Asians, and it was becoming impossible to get a work permit without the right contacts.

I was chasing a job in Maralal and another with Glenn Cottar, one of the old hunters, but nothing was coming up, so when some friends said they wanted an extra pair of hands on a 'cruise' from Lamu to the Seychelles in an unsuitably gaff-rigged Arab dhow, I accepted at once. Even today Lamu is a fabulous island despite all the Eurotrash cluttering up the beach and a huge new port being built there. Back then it was paradise on earth. Before it became a stopping-off point on the hippie trail it was a small island surrounded by powder-sand beaches; its coral reefs were home to myriad species of tropical fish. Marlin, barracuda and sailfish patrolled the deeper waters. An important trading port and seat of Islamic learning for centuries, Lamu has a unique architecture and there are still no cars on the island (except, of course, a Land Rover for the district commissioner that doesn't really go anywhere). Back in 1970 it was like stepping back in time. Almost all of the boats were classic lateen-sailed dhows, and it's a pity ours wasn't. Barry White, whose boat it was, must have known a bit about sailing but I certainly didn't so it was something of a surprise when we pointed the boat south only to find ourselves swept up by the powerful current and deposited a hundred miles off Mogadishu to the north. We had to beat our way back south, nipping in and out of the reef that protects the coast of southern Somalia and northern Kenya. I spent my time on board reading *Bwana Game*, George Adamson's autobiography about his time as a game warden in the NFD. I loved it and knew I must meet him.

It was ten long days before we got back to Lamu and I decided enough was enough. There was the chance of a lift back to Nairobi so the next day found me drinking at the Long Bar with Hector Vaughan Ryall. I was complaining about being unable to find a job and telling him how I wanted to be George Adamson.

'I know what we'll do,' said Hector, whom I'd just met that day. 'We'll go to Naivasha and I'll introduce you to Joy.'

So, we bought some cold beers, jumped into his car and drove off to Naivasha. In those days it was a wonderful trip: you drove 1,500 feet up past Westlands and Limuru into the Gatamaiyo forest, then dropped down on to a road that had been built by Italian prisoners during the Second World War. They even built a tiny church there. But it's not the architecture that's so astonishing: it's the view. Fifty years later it still makes my jaw drop when I take the kids back to school nearby. There comes a point when you turn a corner and you can see the Rift Valley stretched out below you. Mount Longonot volcano rises from the valley floor and just along from it Lake Naivasha sparkles in the sunlight. It's immediately apparent why it's called the Rift Valley on that road – there's a sheer escarpment and the valley is marked by a series of lakes stretching north: Naivasha, Elementaita, Nakuru, Bogoria, Baringo, all the way up to Turkana, Ethiopia and its own Rift Valley lakes. There was no pollution then, no flower farms with their plastic greenhouses, no people. The sight sobered us a little but we were still pretty drunk by the time we turned up at Joy's house, Elsamere, on the southern shore of the lake.

We parked the car and walked around to Elsamere's lakeside aspect. Joy was on the lawn with a monkey on her shoulder and an unsure smile on her face. She greeted us in her strong German accent and I asked her again for a job. She looked at me and Hector as if we were from another planet. 'I have nothing going,' she said. 'But I know my husband is looking for someone. His previous assistant has just been killed by a lion.'

2. Meeting George

George Adamson's brother Terence and I arrived in Kora after a long and uncomfortable journey. It had been a hundred-mile drive on which we had seen hippo crossing the sandy track as well as a few startled elephant and cats that are only seen at night. Terence had collected me off the Malindi bus at Garissa and driven for hours in silence. At Kora, a musky perfume scented the still air, the silence broken only by the ping of the manifold and the wheeze and crack of the broken exhaust as the Land Rover cooled down. A lithe young lioness called softly as she paced up and down outside the twelve-foot-high chain-link fence that surrounded George and Terence's camp. Soon the calls of frogs, nightjars and black-bellied bustards began again, piercing the all-enveloping darkness of the moonless night. A white-haired old man walked out of the mess hut, his head haloed by a hissing Tilley lamp. 'Hello, I'm George Adamson,' he said.

After supper, George poured himself a small White Horse whisky and I had a beer as we sat under the lamp. Terence, two years younger than George, grunted at the drink on the vinyl-covered table and took himself off to bed. I can't remember what was said but I'm sure it wasn't much. Everything was pure and simple. No adoring public, no colonial DCs, no sign of any wealth, no pictures and photographs, not a touch of pretension or vanity anywhere – just sand underfoot, enamel plates and mugs, some old packing cases and those hellishly uncomfortable fold-out camp chairs. I was hooked. I went to bed in a rickety old camp bed under the stars and stared at the heavens. As far as I was concerned, those heavens had come to earth and I had just discovered them. But how was I going to pull it off? I knew damn-all about lions, nothing about tracking, Somalis or Kiswahili, and in spite of having been an Outward Bound instructor, I knew nothing about surviving in a place like this. I had fibbed a bit to Joy about my experience and now I had met George I felt a bit guilty. At least I was fit, I thought, as I fell asleep. I was going to need to be.

I woke up before dawn to hear George pottering around and getting ready for the day. Not much was said so I just followed along. His camp was extremely basic, just a few thatched huts built on sand and surrounded by the tall, chain-link fence. After a cup of tea, George opened the big gate and I saw the point of the fence. A lioness jumped up at him, laying her vast paws on his bare shoulders; unnerving as it looked, Lisa knew what she was doing. She kept all her weight on her back legs and never extended her claws. Terence and Erigumsa had hacked a route up from the river three miles away and George walked down it to the Tana, the two-year-old lioness playing at his heels and Juma, her wilder and much shyer playmate, following at a cautious distance. I trailed them slowly in the rattling and ancient Land Rover pick-up.

Having arrived at night, I had not taken in the stark beauty of Kora. Kampi ya Simba (Camp of the Lions) was very basic indeed. There was one mess hut surrounded by three sleeping huts in which it was way too hot to sleep: we all slept under the stars in cots with mosquito nets. Showers were of the bucket variety and water was in very short supply. The camp lay at the foot of a great series of sandstone gneiss rocks, or inselbergs. They change colour as the light upon them alters, from orange and ochre to pale yellow in the fierce heat of the day and a rich red at sunset. The camp was in harsh, dry country, surrounded by flat-topped acacia, *terminalia*, *commiphora* and a swathe of stick-like bush, but down by the river there is a totally different environment. Lush riverine forest lines the perennial waters of the broad and muddy Tana, Kenya's longest river. Often sticky and humid under the doum palms, huge *Acacia eliator* and Tana river poplars, the land along the riverbank is cooled by the flowing water and breeze, a welcome contrast to the scorching heat in the bush and at camp. Temperatures at Kora consistently top 100 degrees Fahrenheit by ten in the morning, and by two o'clock the bush is dead quiet. Even the birds save their energy. That was why we took our walks with the lions at dawn and dusk. In the heat of the day it was impossible to get them to move.

I remember thinking then that it was a long walk down to the river for a sixty-five-year-old, but George was the same age then as I am now and I, too, feel like I can take on the world when I get up in the morning. As we reached the river a large, short-maned lion charged out of the bush and came bounding up to greet George.

George turned to me. 'Come and say hello to Christian,' he said.

I screwed up my courage and stepped out of the car. Christian took one look at me with his unreadable yellow eyes, growled loudly and crouched, ready to pounce.

'I think you'd better get back in the vehicle,' said George. 'He's a bit frisky today.'

I obeyed his instructions, feeling somewhat ashamed as the Old Man talked to the three lions and sat down to smoke a pipe and watch the river with them. So this was the famous lion man whose attempts to reintroduce lions to the wild had been immortalized in Joy's multi-million-selling book, *Born Free*. And this was the lion I had heard about that had been bought from Harrods as a cub by Ace Bourke and John Rendall, a couple of Australian hippies, and had lived on the King's Road until he had become too big to handle. I looked at the fine young beast, not fully mature but still huge and powerful, his muscles rippling clearly under his loose skin. I found him hard to equate with the Chelsea furniture shop where he had been raised: a bull amid crockery would have been much easier to handle.

Crocodiles lolled on the banks of the Tana while herons and egrets waded in the shady shallows as the heat of the sun built up. I looked across at the Old Man, who was already inspiring my loyalty. Shirtless, in a pair of tattered old shorts and Afghan *chapli* sandals, he held a rifle loosely in his right hand. His long white hair contrasted with the neat Vandyke beard that emphasized the point of his chin. His strong shoulders were a rich reddish brown after a lifetime spent in the sun – in India where he was born and in Kenya, to which he had devoted his adult life. There was a quality of peace and stillness about him that clearly put the lions at ease. Everything he did, he did competently, deliberately and calmly.

I had just finished reading George's book *Bwana Game*, which speaks of the years he spent patrolling the NFD, protecting its people and animals. George had tried his hands at many things – gold prospecting, road haulage, hunting and farming – before he joined the Game Department. He had led a solitary and independent life, even during his marriage to Joy, a twice-married Austrian painter with whom he had fallen hopelessly in love in 1942 when she was on a safari through Garissa, soon to be my home town. Theirs was a tempestuous relationship, whether they were living together or apart in a marriage that was so unlike its celluloid re-creation that it was a standing joke among their friends and acquaintances. The fact that George was one of the most famous people in the world at this time was the unlikely outcome of his shooting a lioness in 1956 when out in the bush with his successor and colleague as warden at Isiolo, Ken Smith. The film of *Born Free* (1966), Joy's book about bringing up the lion cub he had orphaned and then returning her to the wild, had been a stunning success. Starring Bill Travers and Virginia McKenna, it had broken all sorts of box-office records, won two Oscars and made George, Joy and Elsa into household names. Since then people were always trying to meet George and asking him to speak at events: in vain. He was the most taciturn of men, who communicated mainly in grunts. His harrumphs, however, spoke volumes.

I've only met one person who spoke less than George and that was his brother Terence. I think they must have gone weeks without talking before I arrived on the scene. He had a crumpled face with huge bags under his eyes and was much given to scowling. A perpetual rather than confirmed bachelor, Terence was one of the strangest men I have ever met. After a lifetime of building houses and working as a game warden in a subordinate rather than leading role, he had ended up at Kora, living with a brother who quietly and unconsciously dominated him. They camped miles from anywhere in an environment Terence himself had designed entirely for the welfare of his brother's lions. Kampi ya Simba was split in two – one part for the humans, the other for the lions, with a simple system of gates and chain-link fences dividing the two. The lions' comfort and safety always came first. When George first moved there with Christian and Boy all he had needed to say to Terence was 'Build me a camp for my lions,' then turn up when it was ready. The road system that Terence designed and his team of labourers hacked from the bush with machetes remains unchanged to this day: Kora would not function without it. The airstrip he sited ninety minutes away, paced out and cut, remained for years the only one for miles and was in the only place it could be: there was no other suitable ground. In short, without Terence, George and I would have been completely unable to do our work with the lions we both adored. Yet Terence would have absolutely nothing to do with them: he built a complicated infrastructure for them but actively disliked living with lions. He thought George and I were quite mad.

George was easier to read. There was something about Kora and about George that gripped and inspired me. I couldn't be him but from the moment I arrived I knew that this was it. This was how I wished to live my life. I want some of that, I thought. To get a part of it, though, I was going to have to prove myself first. I wasn't going to be much use to George if I couldn't even make friends with Christian. The next morning we followed the same routine – up before dawn, then the slow drive down to the river in George's footsteps. There was Christian again, tail swishing, an unfathomable look in his eye. I thought, If the Old Man can do this, so can I. I walked straight across and said, 'Hello, Christian, I'm Fitz.' Christian got up, rubbed his head against me and just sat there on my feet while I scratched his head. It was the beginning of one of my life's most valuable relationships.

The feeling of tranquillity and unity with nature that we experienced when we were out walking with the lions was a major part of why I loved my life so much. It was a feeling and code of behaviour that went entirely unexpressed, indeed would actually dissolve if I thought about it. Integral to everything we did was that the lions came before ourselves. We lived very simply and would go hungry rather than ration the lions; we wouldn't sleep if we needed to watch out for them; we wouldn't leave camp so that they were always protected. I had been living a pretty dissolute, aimless and selfish life since leaving England, yet within a few weeks of being at Kora I was a better human being. I felt spiritually and morally refreshed. That's not to say I didn't behave badly and have a lot of fun when I was away from camp but the core of my life now had some meaning.

We lived a life of quiet routine at Kora, punctuated with memorably disgusting meals cooked by Hamisi, a Sudanese cook who had been with Terence for decades. We didn't give him much to work with – tins of carrots, bits of goat and posho, Kenya's staple maize meal – but even with better ingredients he was no

Escoffier. Every morning George and I would take the lions for a walk down to the river. There was always something to do as we walked along – the lions would follow trails and George would show me what to watch out for and which tracks were made by what animal. He was a shower, not a teller, and by this method he taught me a huge amount very quickly. I soon recognized the songs of birds and the tracks of animals; it would be a while longer before I could recognize individual animals but it came with time. When we reached the river, the lions would lie down with explosive sighs and we would sit with them, shaded by the palms and giant figs, to watch the river go by. At eleven o'clock or thereabouts George would make himself a pipe and pull out his battered Stanley flask. Then we would have a cup of gin and Treetop orange squash before walking back to Kampi ya Simba for lunch.

The camp Terence had built did the job but that was all. The fence kept the wild lions out and allowed those that needed a safe place to stay inside. Life for us revolved around the sand-floored mess hut, with its thatched roof and three cement-covered hessian walls. Where the fourth wall should have been, a sandy area led to the fence and, beyond it, the bush. George's ancient typewriter sat on the table, much as Ruark's or Hemingway's must have done, the litter of books, papers and *objets trouvés* that surrounded it shuffled to one side for meals. He was a great correspondent and was always writing to some old friend or dealing with the council or Game Department. Rough bookshelves housed his collection of photographs, novels and reference books and quite often a snake or two looking for a quiet place to rest. The sand floor displayed the spoor of George's menagerie of guinea fowl, ravens and seed-eating birds, which to Terence's disgust would beg at meals or at the very least clear up afterwards. I'm sure George did most of it to tease his brother, but he also had a definite St Francis of Assisi streak that allowed him to hand-feed even the shyest creatures, like the hornbills, ground squirrels, dik-dik and vervet monkeys. It was one of the reasons for his great success with the lions.

The lions ate rather better than us. I bought them fresh meat in Asako, our nearest village. We usually lived off corned beef, camel, maize meal or rice and tinned vegetables. Pudding was tinned fruit and evaporated milk – just like school dinners back in Enfield. Because of this we didn't usually linger over our meals. This left more time for a siesta in the brutal heat of the day, something I insist upon to this day. Little goes on at midday: the bush is still, sounds are dulled and only the most intrepid lizards move around. At about four o'clock we would get up, have a cup of tea, go out into the bush again and look for the lions. If they were nearby they would come to George's call but if they were tired or had killed and eaten too much we would have to go and find them. This was hard work and not always fruitful. The baked earth around camp and the rocks were hard for tracking so we often had to cut through the *nyika* bush on buffalo paths to the narrow *lugga*s (dried-up riverbeds) that ran down to the Tana and flowed only when it rained heavily every twenty years or so. Picking up tracks on the sand in the *lugga*s was a much easier proposition and often met with success, particularly when the sun was not too high. Sometimes, though, the lions would cross rocky outcrops and we would have to circle through the thick bush at their base to see which way they had gone.

Hard to believe now, we used to have to watch out for the numerous rhinos when we were tracking. They can go at quite a pace when riled, and relying on their poor eyesight is not always a successful tactic when trying to avoid them. If you literally have your nose to the ground, looking for small signs and indications of what has passed that way, it's very easy to miss the large and obvious signs like the vast elephant leaning against a tree, dozing in the heat. We had many lucky scrapes on coming face to face with the larger wildlife but usually they were just as surprised as we were.

The lions were all old enough to hunt a little but they still needed a lot of looking after and protection from the wild lions in the area so in those early days we still tried to keep them in camp at night. The bush was thick and the game wary, so the lions had to adapt to hunting by sound first, smell second and then a sighting when they were already in full pursuit. Christian, who was of a similar age to Lisa and Juma, was still learning to hunt well. Nevertheless, he was independent and would usually meet us down at the river from which we would try to coax all three back to camp to avoid encounters with older, smarter and already established wild lions.

George had discovered that walking with the lions was the best way to get them acquainted with the bush and ready for a self-reliant life. As we strolled along they would head off into the surrounding country as dogs do when you take them out, following scent trails and searching for excitement. We found that by watching the lions we observed much more than we would on a normal walk as their ever-watchful eyes scanned the bush like snipers', their bodies stiffening as they spotted anything strange or unnatural. Christian, with whom I became ever more friendly, was particularly rewarding to watch. I think he saw similarities between Ace and John, who had loved him so much in England, and myself; it was very much as if we were growing up together. Soon he and Lisa began to bounce up and greet me as they did George, but Juma was always very wary of everyone – even the Old Man himself. We thought she had been mistreated on capture and she was never really able to look on humans with the warmth we felt from Christian and Lisa. At times she tried to be like the others, but it was too much for her. The damage had been done and she was always careful with Man.

Every week or so I would drive for about an hour and a half

to Asako, the closest village to our camp at Kora, and buy meat for the lions. Almost inevitably it would take longer – a leaf spring on the Land Rover would break, I would get stuck or have a puncture or two. The Trust that George and I created has done a lot of work in Asako over the last twenty years, but forty years ago there was nothing there except a few huts and some mangy livestock. There was no dispensary, no school, no security, no Land Rover 'taxis' to our main town Garissa, no shops even, just a crocodile-infested river crossing to Mbalambala on the far bank and three islands, famed for their enormous elephants. The people of Asako are from a small tribe called the Korokoro. No one really knows their ancestry. Terence was convinced they were the indigenous people of that area, others that they are a subset of the much more numerous Oromo people of Ethiopia. For years they had been subjected to raids from both the Oromo and the Somalis. Scattered throughout the length of Kora are large stone mounds, supposed to be thirteenth- or fourteenth-century Oromo, or Galla – an ancient tribe from the Ethiopian border – graves.

The Maalim, or spiritual leader, of Asako was a great supporter of George and our lion project and, along with the village chief, would encourage his people to sell us livestock, which we would feed to the lions. This was an expensive way of doing things, but although we had permission to shoot for the pot outside the boundaries of Kora, we had all developed a distaste for killing wild animals – George and Terence after a lifetime spent working on game and predator control. Buying our meat from Asako had the advantage of providing the Korokoro villagers with a little extra money, which they desperately needed. The meat also helped a great deal in luring the lions back to camp in the evenings and meant that we could supplement their diets when they were learning how to hunt.

Maalim Shora Dirkicha, to give him his full family name,

would look around for likely cows for us. He still lives there today and, although pencil thin, can walk thirty miles a day in intense heat without batting an eyelid. We looked for beasts that would cost as little as possible. Even though they were for feeding to the lions, we always had them killed by the village in the Muslim way before taking them back to camp for butchering.

Butchering was a messy process at which I soon became expert. First I would remove the skin from the cow and the meat from the bones. I chopped the meat into two-kilo chunks and the skin into squares, then hung the meat overnight. If the lions weren't about we would put the carcass into the back of the Land Rover and drive around with it in the hope of attracting them. If they were near camp we tied it to a tree with all the guts and lungs hanging out, a strong chain through the pelvic girdle. This allowed us to have a good long look at the lions as they were interacting with each other and meant that wild lions were unable to steal the carcass. Over a very long period this had the effect of bringing the wild and introduced lions together. There's nothing like meeting for a meal to kick-start a relationship.

The meat went into the elderly propane gas fridge that we shared with the lions. Incredibly temperamental, gas fridges were the only way to keep things cool at Kora; thank God we have solar fridges today, which are so much easier to deal with. Each gas fridge has its own personality, seldom pleasant, and must be lit and fuelled with great care. As with the even more dangerous paraffin fridges, if you get it badly wrong, the fridge blows up and burns down your camp – this happened to Joy ten years later, when she was living in Shaba. More usually they allow your meat to go off or they freeze it solid. The lions used to lick the frozen chunks like lollipops, their sandpaper tongues gradually wearing down the flesh until it became chewable by their back molars.

Over many years we found that feeding the lions like this did not – as many suspected – give them a taste for domestic stock and break down their fear of man, but it did give them a reason to come back to the safety of camp and encouraged a certain tolerance of man, which meant they didn't attack humans. Although there were issues about them eating domestic stock, we never had a problem with them attacking people out in the wild in my whole eighteen years at Kora. Where we did have difficulty was around camp, the centre of their territory, where they were often hungry and expecting food. A hungry lion is an angry lion, as all three of us discovered over the years. We had to be very careful with the blocks of meat we gave them as a reward for coming back to camp. These often triggered an attack reflex, of which we had to be aware. The lions loved butchering days and they were always a cause for celebration with George, Terence and me. Our one concession to our own stomachs was to cut out the fillets and eat them ourselves rather than give them to the lions. When we changed to camels we had to forgo even that treat.

Our evenings were spent under the Tilley lamps in the mess, reading the *Encyclopedia Britannica* and the old Penguins Terence bought by the yard when he was at his house in Malindi, or talking quietly about safaris of the thirties, forties and fifties. Terence would occasionally join in and tell stories of elephant he had saved from sink holes and swamps or of his work for the Game Department when he had shot buffalo by the hundred to protect crops from wildlife. George would chuckle quietly and match Terence's stories with his own. When we could still afford batteries, and before the news being broadcast became too depressing, we used to listen to the BBC World Service on a battery-powered short-wave radio. Nixon was the American president and the war in Vietnam was raging; he had devalued the dollar, which had knock-on effects in Kenya, as did the accession of Idi Amin in neighbouring Uganda. Nonetheless, everything reported seemed very otherworldly while I was living in these simple, severe conditions with two men old enough to be my grandfathers.

There was no generator for electricity at Kampi ya Simba so keeping the lamps in working order was an important knack I had to learn. They had to be primed every evening by pumping a little piston on the fuel tank to build up the pressure within. They ran on kerosene but had to be ignited with a small amount of methylated spirit as part of a complicated sequence that required a great deal of patience. The key was never to touch the mantle, the 'bulb' of the lamp. Fiddly to replace, they were made of thin silk net. As soon as they had been lit, they took on the consistency of ash and became extraordinarily fragile. The white-flamed Tilleys were an essential part of our lives and far superior to yellow-flamed hurricane lamps for reading by. Getting them organized was a chore we had to remember to do before we'd had a drink.

Gin was George's daytime tipple. By night he was a whisky man. He collected the plastic white horses that came around the necks of his whisky bottles, a habit that irritated Joy so much that he hid the ever-growing stable whenever she visited. Once, on a visit to Nairobi, I found hundreds of these horses and hung them up in camp, leading Joy to think George had become a raging alcoholic. Joy did not like me at all – or Terence, with whom she had been fighting for thirty years. When I first went to Kora she looked on me as a potential ally and spy: 'I'm sure George keeps women up there,' she had said. 'I want you to tell me about them.' I had refused – not that there was anything to tell her for we led the most blameless of lives in camp. But when I heard her voice on the HF radio at the end of my first week at Kora something about it immediately made me feel apprehensive.

'You must get rid of that boy, George,' I heard her say, through the hiss of static on the radio. 'He wastes money and crashes cars.'

'Hmph,' said George. 'Sorry about that, Tony.' He switched off the radio.

This vast contraption, which ran off a car battery, was our only access to the outside world. It was linked to a central controller in Nairobi who used to listen in and join people up with telephone calls and other radio callers. It still functions today in a slightly modified form, although there are now satellite and mobile telephones to augment it. Back then radios were pretty primitive with big glass valves and they often broke down; ours was always needing new parts that were expensive and fragile and thus took weeks to fix. When it worked, we were able to get in touch with people across the country but it was a very public means of communication and we usually used it only for resupply lists and emergencies. As there was just one channel the whole country could listen to anything that was said. I used to ache for George as Joy harangued him about this or that, imagining the hundreds of people listening in on the frequency before or after making their own radio calls.

It seemed then as though I was one of the few people in the world who had neither seen nor read *Born Free*. I had read *Bwana Game* but it was mainly about George's earlier years as the warden of the Northern Frontier District so I was still not sure of the philosophy behind his lion-release programme. It was not the sort of thing he discussed so I had to work it out for myself. As a hunter and a game warden, George had shot hundreds of wild animals, large and small, and had come to realize in his forties that it was not something he or anyone else should be doing. I think Adrian House described it just right in his joint biography of the Adamsons, *The Great Safari*. George believed:

If it is wrong to thrash a human being, draw his nails, subject her to involuntary medical experiment, to lock him up or kill her without trial, it is morally wrong to treat an animal in this way. The more evolved the animal, the greater its

potential to suffer, and since it is handicapped by the double disadvantage of not
speaking our language or possessing a vote, we have a double duty to protect it.
Its unnecessary injury, captivity or death diminishes each one of us.[1]

George devoted his later life to assisting as many animals back
into the wild as he could. Having started with Elsa, he continued
with the lions that were used in the filming of the movie *Born
Free*. He was on the set in charge of the only lions that could
interact with the actors, Boy and Girl. They had previously been
mascots for the Scots Guards based in Kenya, and went off after
the movie to the Meru Game Reserve with George, where he
started his pioneering work of training them for release. There
followed a series of incidents, the most far-reaching and influential being that Boy bit the warden's son, Mark. Warden Pete
Jenkins and George's assistant had met on the road and stopped
to chat one day and Boy had taken the opportunity to bite Mark's
arm.

The resulting injury had little lasting effect on Mark (who
became warden of Meru himself many years later) but it lost
George a lot of support for his lion project from old colleagues,
many of whom believed that all lions habituated to man inevitably became man-eaters. Pete Jenkins and George didn't speak
for years afterwards. Indeed, it took Joy's death to bring them
together again. Despite Mark's mauling, George had been allowed
to stay, but when Meru was promoted from a game reserve into
a national park, he was obliged to leave. With nowhere else to
go he took Boy, who had broken his leg, to Elsamere, Joy's house
on Lake Naivasha, an area he hated, where the lion had to be
caged rather than roaming freely. Boy spent months recovering
before George was able to move him to Kora in 1970. But by then

---

[1] My thanks to Adrian House and Collins Harvill for permission to quote from *The
Great Safari*. *My Pride and Joy* and *The Great Safari* were very helpful for checking
the chronology of my life with George.

Boy had company in the form of a tiny female cub called Katania and permission had been given for Christian to be brought out from England. It was Christian who speeded up the search for a new area, and had it not been for him, things might have gone very differently for George, Boy and Katania. We all had a lot to thank Christian for.

Everything at Kora had started well. It was almost perfect lion country – sparsely populated and remote, if a little low in hard-to-catch prey species. Boy had reacted well to the move. He had charged at Christian with stunning violence when George had first introduced them, but with the help of Katania, who was still a small cub of which both were fond, they had soon become friends. The process was memorably filmed by Simon Trevor in the documentary *Christian the Lion*.

Just before I arrived on the scene everything had gone badly wrong. Boy had killed Stanley Murithii, one of George's long-standing employees, who had known Boy since he had first come to Kenya as a nine-month-old. No one will ever know why it happened. Stanley was outside the chain-link fence near the rubbish dump against George's express orders. He might have been looking for honey or tidying rubbish. We don't know why he was outside or what he was doing but even then Boy had known him for years – yet he killed him. Maybe Stanley ran away from the huge lion or fell over, two actions that trigger lion attacks.

George heard Stanley's screams while he was eating lunch. He rushed from the camp, forcing Boy to retreat, then stepped across Stanley and shot Boy through the heart. He carried Stanley back to camp where the young man died in his arms. This incident was a tragedy for all who knew Stanley. It also prompted much debate over George's lion project, which was nearly closed down. Instead George was given another chance and allowed to continue for a short while: there were to be no more lions, and feeding of the existing ones must be phased out as soon as possible. It was also made patently clear by the wildlife authorities that if anyone else was harmed by one of George's lions, the experiment would be brought to an immediate close.

When I arrived George was down to just three lions but they still needed constant care. They roamed free but were in danger from all sorts of threats, including wild lions, crocodiles, snares and poachers, particularly Christian, who was always being beaten up by other lions trying to keep him off their occasional territory. George and I had to do our best to protect him without hurting the wild lions, a never-ending and often dangerous struggle. Most nights Terence and I would go to our cots and sleep soon after supper while George stayed up reading and writing, but I would soon be up again, woken by roaring fights going on outside the fence. In later years my experience of nocturnal existence made me a useful father. Even now I am up most nights, saving tents from marauding elephants or dealing with fence alarms in the rhino sanctuary and it doesn't affect me at all. But I do stick with an afternoon siesta whenever I can.

When roused, George and I would pick up our rifles and run outside the fence, clutching torches that never seemed to work. We often ended up on the rocks above the camp, trying to work out what was going on around us. With lions roaring on all sides, strange crashes and howls from the undergrowth, it was extremely frightening as we stumbled around in the dark. And not just for us. Christian would hear us and come bursting from the bush, having shat himself he was so scared. At speed and in the dark, a lion charging towards you for safety looks much the same as one with homicide in mind and is always a terrifying sight to behold. One night when we had forgotten the bullets for our rifles (my fault!), we found throwing stones around the wild lions strangely effective. It distracted them at crucial moments but was a tad nerve-racking. At such times, it was essential to stay upright and stand up to the lions both wild and semi-wild. To crouch on the ground was an invitation to attack, even for Christian – a lesson George had learnt the hard way on the set of *Born Free*.

In my early months at Kora, Christian was constantly being clobbered by the wild lions and would come hobbling back to camp, his hindquarters scratched and bleeding. It was hard to know what to do. Lions are fiercely territorial and Christian had to be able to fight his own corner – Kora Rock – and defend it against all comers. The fact that he was brilliant at football, which he used to play with Ace and John, was of no use to him now and there was very little that George and I could do to improve his boxing and wrestling skills. I remember the gratification we felt when it dawned on us that his wounds were now all on his front. Christian was wandering ever further and taking on the wild lions, asserting his territorial dominance. Poor boy, though, nothing we could do would help his balls to drop any faster.

Lionesses reach sexual maturity before their male peers. This meant that Lisa and Juma, Christian's constant playmates, came on heat before he knew what to do with them. Tough for Christian, this was nonetheless wonderful news for the lion project. Like learning a foreign language, adjusting to life in the wild is best done through sex. When Lisa and Juma came on heat they attracted shadowy males from miles around Kampi ya Simba. Eventually they mated with the wild lions and ended up spending most of their time in the bush with their new boyfriends, learning to hunt and fend for themselves. Once George and I sneaked up when Lisa was mating. We could only have been ten yards or so away. My heart sounded as loud as the male's ecstatic roars. It was one of the most exhilarating and frightening times of my life – especially when the wind changed!

Soon the girls were coming back to Kampi ya Simba only if they were sick, thirsty, hurt or hungry. This was a glorious success, vindication for George and his methods. Christian, though, took much longer to adapt. He was doing very well, disappearing into the bush for days at a time, but always coming back because, as yet, he had nowhere else to go.

In this respect he was a little like me. I was living the dream I had nurtured since reading *Tarzan* under the bedcovers in Cockfosters. I loved the atmosphere in camp, those peaceful regular days of happy routine, but I was twenty-seven years old with a raging thirst. Occasionally I would go into Garissa, five hours and a hundred miles away, to stock up on tinned food for us, fill the forty-four-gallon drums with petrol for the Land Rovers and buy rations for the staff. Garissa was a real frontier town. Just three streets on the edge of Kenya's North Eastern Province, it was where the government's writ ran out. Garissa boasted the only bridge over the Tana for hundreds of miles so it was a natural meeting place for Arab and Kikuyu merchants, Somali herdsmen or anyone else who was trying to trade between cultures. Since independence the new Kenyan government had made Garissa into a major administrative hub and had drawn a line in the sand there. South of Garissa was Kenya proper, north was no man's land, home to ethnic Somalis and a buffer against Somalia itself. Convincing the Somalis to respect the line was the unenviable task of a young generation of Kenyan civil servants, from soldiers to teachers.

The Kenyan government's treatment of its Somali citizens had been consistently bad but it must also be said that Somalis are an expansionist people, who have been pushing south for genera-tions in search of a 'Greater Somalia'. Lawless and independent, they make great friends and implacable enemies; they will laugh as they kill you and cry as they listen to a poem. Many didn't really understand what the government meant when it imposed law and order upon them, and those who did were having none of it. One of the people obliged to urge this new regime upon the Kenyan Somalis was one himself, Mahmoud Mohammed, the head of the army in Garissa. He was a great ally of ours in the early years at Kora and would never interfere when our friends in the police helped us out with the poaching and banditry in later years.

Garissa was a town of extraordinary characters. If you weren't one when you got there, the heat and the flies would drive you into characterhood before too long. One of my best friends there was Brother Mario Petrino, a former nightclub owner from Chicago. A portly man with a Hemingway beard, he would sit in the police mess sipping warm Tusker beer with me and telling tales of when he had driven a powder-blue Cadillac and drunk champagne all day. A truly good man, he built a school for orphans in Garissa where he taught them carpentry, mechanics, welding and agriculture. He transformed the town in his short time there, setting up a pipeline and water-purification system, building a school, a fuel station and the orphanage. A few years later, when he was moved on by his order, the Consolata Fathers, there were howls of outrage from his resolutely Muslim flock.

Like many Kenyan towns in Muslim areas, Garissa's police mess and the Kikuyu-run dives were the only places, until quite recently, where you could get a drink. The latter were a hotbed of debauchery where all the heathens would meet. Dark, tin-roofed shacks that never seemed to close, the bars were normally a raw wood counter protected above by the same wire mesh that we used for discouraging the lions from sleeping on our beds. I don't think those shebeens were ever cleaned and they always smelt of warm beer and Rooster filterless cigarettes but they were home and I loved them.

I once burst into the Catholic mission to tell Mario a pretty risqué political story. Halfway through I realized he was looking at me rather oddly. At the next table sat a Gammarelli-socked cardinal sent from Rome to ensure that Brother Mario was making the right sort of friends. He must have been hard of hearing because apparently he approved of me.

It was in the police mess that I first met Philip Kilonzo, who became a true friend over the years and a great and worthy success in Kenya's ever more corrupt police force. The fact that Garissa bred so many notables is a testament to how hard it was to work there. New York it was not, but if you could make it there, you could make it anywhere. Philip helped us enormously when we were under threat from the gangs of poachers and the Somali bandits who were soon to infiltrate the area, but back then Garissa was relatively peaceful. I would buy a crate of beer and work my way through it as I drove back along the sandy dirt road to camp. The main danger then was driving into a ditch or shunting an elephant rather than being ambushed.

Keeping the Land Rover on the road was a constant challenge both literally and metaphorically. Old and knackered, it was always breaking down but the fact that there were so many of them about helped a lot. Now everyone drives Toyotas in the bush but in those days it was all Land Rovers. I became as fast as a Formula One team at removing bits from laid-up government vehicles and swapping them with broken parts from ours. Always when I was in Garissa I was on the hunt for carburettor needles, seals, springs, mountings or other parts as there was inevitably something wrong with our engine or a steering rod about to break. We needed the car for resupplies from Garissa but its most crucial function was ferrying water from the river. We lived off the Tana's heavily silted water for eighteen years but it needed treating before we could drink it. Watched by highly opportunistic crocodiles and wallowing hippos, I would collect the water in big drums, then add alum to get rid of the worst of the sediment. After a few days Hamisi boiled it over an open fire, then filtered it through diatomite candles (which was the classic way of filtering water) to further reduce the sediment. It was a lot of

1. Leaving Southampton, 1968. *From left*, Dad, Mum, my sister Margaret, Tony Hill, Mark Stewart

2. Kora Hills from the air. *From left*, Kora Rock, Christian's Rock, Kora Tit with Boy's Rock in the foreground. Kampi ya Simba is at the foot of Kora Rock

3. Kampi ya Simba

(a) Kora Rock with the camp in the foreground

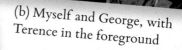

(b) Myself and George, with Terence in the foreground

(c) Shared breakfast in the mess

(e) Waiting for the lions

(d) George does office work in the mess

5. Growing up with Christian

(a) With George by the Tana river, looking at tribesmen on the opposite bank

(b) Sharing a quiet moment

(c) Early days with Christian

(d) On Christian's Rock

(e) Tracking on Boy's Lugga

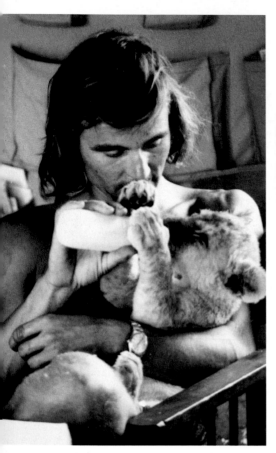

6. Freddie was bottle-fed until he was five months old

7. With Freddie

8. Freddie and Leakey (foreground, far right) pause for a drink on Boy's Rock after the rains

9. Doum palms along the river road

10. Fishing on the Tana in spate

11. The waterpoint on the Tana river, three miles from Kampi ya Simba

12. Resting with Freddie and Arusha

13. Playing is always important: Gigi and Arusha in the rear, Freddie in the foreground

14. Freddie gets a lift and Gigi tries to join in

15. Arusha, Freddie and George on the Tana river walk

16. I was here to stay

17. Keeping up
appearances – outside
the hut where I lived
for ten years

effort to go to for a glass of water but, given the heat at Kora and the lack of sodas, we needed it for mixers. George used to mask its taste with Treetop orange squash. To carry the drums from the river to the camp three miles away we really needed the Land Rover to be working.

I learnt everything there was to know about that vehicle. I took it to pieces and put it back together again, modified parts and replaced others with ones I made from scratch. It makes me hell to work for today as everything that needs doing in our workshop now I can do myself. I started on my dad's Vauxhall 10, moved on to his Singer SM1500, then the Land Rovers; now I can even work out the hydraulics on the JCBs that Anthony Bamford sends us from England. For the wiring on our Dutch-donated Suzuki Grand Vitaras I need a bit of help from the computer.

The Land Rover's worst enemy at Kora was a natural one: the vicious thorns that grew around the camp. *Commiphora* myrrh trees are very beautiful but the thorns that protect their buds and fresh shoots from rhino, elephant and other browsers are death to tyres. We had punctures the whole time and seemed to spend half our lives repairing them. When I first arrived at Kora, we didn't have a proper workshop so mending a puncture was a major performance. First we would have to break the bead – the part where the rim meets the tyre. We did this by jacking the whole weight of the car on to the sidewall of the tyre. This had to be done very carefully so as not to damage the wall. Tyres were very expensive and we had no money. Bead broken, we took the tyre off the rim with a couple of tyre irons, pulled out the inner tube, located the hole in water and mended it with patches vulcanized to the tube. After levering the tyre back on to the rim came the fun part – forty-five minutes to an hour of hard work with a foot pump to get pressure back into the tyre. It was back-breaking labour, often required on drives to Asako, the small village twenty-six miles away.

Kora lies a hundred miles to the east of Mount Kenya, the stately mountain that stands snow-covered and alone on the equator, its silhouette unmarred by foothills or ranges. Snow has never fallen on Kora's yellow soil where the low altitude ensures that the temperature is always high. Waterbuck, lesser kudu, giraffe and eland were all common then, as were the predatory hyena and caracal. Elephant and rhino were ever-present and widespread – the rhino almost common. We always had to watch out for them on our walks, as we did for buffalo. There were also decent numbers of zebra and oryx, Grant's gazelle and bushbuck. There were, however, no leopards: they had been hunted out when the fashion for leopardskin was at its height in the 1940s.

Neighbouring Meru had suffered a similar fate – but it was a neighbour only on the map. There was no bridge between the two banks of the Tana river for hundreds of miles so for us to get to the other side opposite our camp it was a ten-hour drive. Because of this isolation Kora was more protected and did not fall victim to poachers until later than Meru, which became a notorious poachers' lair in the years to come. That's not to say there was no poaching at all.

We had the occasional visitor. The Wakamba, who live in the area to the south of Kora, are famously good hunters and used to come into Kora whenever they wished. But they used poisonous *acocanthera*-smeared arrows to hunt elephant for ivory, and wire snares for the herbivores. They failed to make much of an impact on the elephant and rhino population: that privilege fell to the AK47-armed Somalis in the years to come.

There was also licensed 'sport' hunting in Kora until it was banned in 1977 and often the commercial hunters would come and visit us if they were old friends of George's or even if they weren't. I can see little justification for game hunting today, but in those days there were many good people who had lived their lives in the bush, hunting on foot and to a certain extent protecting the wildlife as their livelihood. Many of the early game wardens, like David Sheldrick, Bill Woodley and George himself, had been hunters before joining the national parks or Game Department. These visits from hunters were often the only contact that we would have with the outside world for weeks at a time and they were usually welcome. Most who turned up at camp had done us the courtesy of learning our tastes so would bring supplies of whisky and beer with them – a sure-fire way to be invited back.

Other than that, it was very quiet at Kora. Until Terence cut five hours off the journey by hacking a back road in, it was a nightmarish ten-hour journey to Kora from Nairobi unless you had a plane. This kept visitors at bay and ensured a peaceful camp. George would occasionally be dragged off to Naivasha by Joy, or to Hola, two hundred miles away, by the council – our land-lords – leaving Terence and me in camp. Before Kora was made a national reserve it was a tribal trustland and George had to pay £750 a year to rent it. This didn't leave much for Terence to pay his crews or for any of us to have any pocket money. We always did it for love. To this day, I have never managed to get the Trust to pay me – I live in Trust property and drive Trust cars but have nothing of my own. I feel genuinely privileged to have lived the life of my choice and find it much easier to fundraise because I can say that none of the money is spent on paying me.

Terence and I didn't have much to say to each other, not that he ever said much to anyone. He was a grumpy old sod who disapproved of me and thought I encouraged George in his wilder schemes. He was right: I loved George's wilder schemes. But I think the key problem between us was that we were both compet-ing for George's affection. A self-taught engineer, architect and road-builder, Terence didn't drink or smoke. He loved elephants and knew a great deal about their habits, and he was brilliant on plants and regeneration cycles, but none of that made him any easier to live with. When we found ourselves in camp alone together I would go on long walks around Kora, ostensibly in search of the lions but really to get away from Terence and enjoy the bush. I bitterly regret it now. He was a good man and I should have treated him better.

I would often climb to the top of Kora Rock, at 450 metres above sea level the highest point in Kora, from which you could see hundreds of square miles of real wilderness. The bush has a strange rusty hue that comes from iron in the ground. It can look dramatically red in the right light. The course of the river stands out as a slash of bright green in the distance with the far bank rising away to higher ground. George had asked Terence to build the camp at the foot of Kora Rock for a reason, not just for the view. He judged correctly that it was excellent lion country and easily defendable. If Christian could mate with wild lionesses, they could take control of the Rock, George thought, and it would make a great place to bring up a family. There were all sorts of nooks and crannies where cubs could be hidden safely, lairs where lions could hide and rest by day. I often took Christian up there on walks with Lisa and Juma as our relationship developed. It was obvious that the more we went there, the more he thought of it as his. He was not the only one. Mine was a strange life for a hot-blooded twenty-seven-year-old to be living but I knew it was the right one. I felt I was doing something useful at last. I was enormously stimulated and I was incredibly happy in those halcyon days at Kora.

After I had been living at Kampi ya Simba for about three months, George and I set off for the river in the early morning as usual. The car was out of action so we walked down together and were soon sitting by the Tana drinking our gin from the flask. Christian, Lisa and, at a distance, Juma dozed quietly beside us. Suddenly Christian's ears twitched up and his body tensed. We followed his gaze and saw a large herd of elephants emerging silently from the forest downstream. Crocodiles slipped into the muddy waters of the Tana to avoid their enormous feet, outraged hippos lurched out of the way, spraying shit with their tails. The elephants marched stolidly across the beach, waded through the shallows, then swam the hundred yards across the river to Meru, shepherding the younger ones and protecting them against the current. It was one of the most beautiful sights I had ever seen. George turned to me and said, 'How long do you think you can stay?'

'About ten or fifteen years,' I replied.

3. One of the Pride

From the moment Christian sat on my feet and licked my hand on my second day at Kora I was hooked for life. I soon discovered that if you treat lions with respect, understanding and love they respond with their trust and affection. Once they've given you that they don't take it back and neither shpould you. I loved being with the lions like nothing I had ever before experienced. It wasn't entirely from self-interest that I was enraged when, a few months after I'd arrived, Ken Smith came into camp and said he was closing George down. Ken was the warden of Garissa and one of George's oldest friends. As such, I always felt that he should have given us more support than he did. He had helped George to find Kora for which George had given him some of the earnings from *Christian the Lion* so the fact that he always caved in to pressure irked us both. The problem was that he was white with a government job and, back then, very few Europeans dared rock the boat. We found over and over again that Europeans and white Kenyans would support us with words, but it was the black Kenyans who helped us with action. With this in mind, I headed for Nairobi to see John Mutinda, who had just been appointed chief game warden.

John's office was in one of those crazy old falling-down colonial buildings that never seemed to get repaired. Up on stilts with a warped veranda and a leaking corrugated-iron roof, it had a temporary air that belied its age. John was a Mkamba, a member of the tribe whose lands bordered Kora. An academic, he always seemed rather bemused by but fond of the old colonials he had inherited as game wardens. He presided over the Game Department's later merger with the National Parks Authority but the resulting body's passionate embrace of corruption did not occur on his watch. He had the power to close us down at any minute but instead, after only a little persuasion, he allowed us to continue with our controversial project to reintroduce lions to the wild. This was my first interaction with the wildlife authorities – and a rare good one. Beating the system and actually achieving anything would become harder and harder. Back then it was easy. John had a few words of warning for me as I left the Game Department: 'Just keep it safe, Tony,' he said, as I skipped out of his office, like a schoolboy who'd been let off a detention.

I went out and celebrated long into the night and was back on the road to Kora at dawn. I arrived home in triumph, eleven bone-shuddering hours later. George harrumphed his approval; Terence harrumphed his dismay. And we settled back into our routine as if nothing had happened.

In Nairobi I had bought food and drink to last us a few weeks and was intent on getting better at tracking the lions. These were the days before radio collars and it was no easy task keeping tabs on them, even when we only had three – they could comfortably travel eight or nine miles between dusk and dawn. The key thing was getting up before the sun: the shadows in the early morning and evening help you to see faint impressions that you miss when the sun is overhead, and the slightest breeze, as the heat of the day starts to move the air, can rub out even the most distinct tracks. Once I was up it was just a matter of watching George. He never actually said anything but he would point at some bent grass or a patch of urine or gesture at his nose, encouraging me to smell.

After a lifetime spent in the bush, George had the most extraordinary knowledge of animal behaviour. It was almost as if he knew what they would do before they knew it themselves. A great many ill-informed words are spoken by people who 'know it's a mock charge because the elephant's ears are waving' or because the lion isn't swishing its tail vigorously enough – words that are often wryly recalled at their hospital bedsides, or over the mahogany by friends at their funerals. George didn't talk about it and he didn't have any tried and tested rules but he *knew*. Always armed, he never had to shoot a charging animal in the entire time I knew him. And we were charged a lot. By the time I met George he always avoided killing animals: memories of shooting game by the thousand to feed the British Army during the Second World War haunted him. But it wasn't just repugnance that put him off shooting charging beasts. He seemed to know what was going to happen and reacted accordingly. He seldom got it wrong.

In my early years at Kora there were still a great many rhino and they charged us regularly. It's quite easy to avoid rhinos if you keep your cool and you're not hemmed in, not because it's a mock charge but because they have lousy eyesight. George was a master at avoiding them with minimum effort but even he needed to see them first. When Christian's playmates, Lisa and Juma, were out hunting and I was still very green, we were once out looking for them in thick bush when George held a finger to his mouth to hush me. He came back to me very quietly, then moved to one side and I stepped forward. I had a rifle but I didn't have a bullet up the spout as it's too dangerous when you're walking in thick *nyika* bush behind a friend. We could hear a crunching sound so we thought Lisa and Juma had made a kill and were enjoying the spoils. We stopped and listened again because it's always dangerous being around lions and their food, then I moved up once more. I came face to face with a two-ton rhino just six foot away from me. It snorted in shock. I snorted back, then turned and ran, holding the gun above my head to load it without snagging it on the ground. I turned to fire and, as I did, the rhino veered away from me and went straight for George. Everything happened very slowly and clearly as the adrenalin kicked in. Christ! I've killed the Old Man, I thought, as I watched the rhino thunder down upon him. I couldn't shoot because the rhino was between George and me. I was utterly powerless. Horrified, I watched as George lowered his rifle, held it across his chest like a guardsman and jumped sideways two feet over a small bush. The rhino roared past him, followed at pace by a calf, and smashed away through the undergrowth. George looked up with a smile. 'Nice calf,' he said, and carried on tracking the girls.

Another time Christian, George and I were walking down a sand *lugga* towards the river when George stopped and pointed in front of us all. The lion and I looked ahead, our eyes scanning the ground for tracks. We saw nothing. We then raised our eyes from the ground to see a huge cobra, its hood extended and much of its body raised, moving fast towards us at four foot above my head height. The look on my face and Christian's kept George amused for weeks.

One of the many things George taught me was to use my sense of smell. George smoked a filthy old pipe and I smoked filterless Roosters, but despite our healthy tobacco intake, smell was still one of our most useful senses. But it's the sensory landscape that you construct with *all* your senses that allows you to become good at following spoor and finding animals. George had been doing this for fifty years so it was second nature to him to smell the air and recognize odd sounds. Christian and I were both from London so we had to learn it, although Christian was by far the quicker student. I managed it by trying to think like a lion, or if I was looking for a waterbuck, trying to think like a buck. Because Christian was the age he was and had been brought up under such strange conditions, we learnt together. He would assimilate things from me and I would acquire skills from him.

Christian was developing well and he soon became very big. Not big enough, however. As Lisa and Juma became ever more attractive to the wild lions, Christian was obliged to make himself scarce if he wanted to avoid a fight. It took him a while to work this out and there were a good many tense nights when George and I had to help him fight them off but he gradually learnt, giving himself enough time to reach sexual maturity and grow even bigger. In July 1972, when Lisa and Juma came on heat, all hell broke loose. Christian was still too young to do anything about it but the two wild lions who claimed Kora as a distant outpost of their territory had been prowling around for months, waiting for the girls to show they were ready. Lionesses can decide when they want to come on heat but once a lion has decided he wants to mate they don't have much choice in the matter: males are twice the size of females, particularly in Lisa's case – she was tiny.

Lions mate for days on end. The actual act itself is very quick – a couple of minutes at most – but each time the males ejaculate, they let out an earth-shattering roar, roll over and go to sleep. So far so human, but then they repeat the routine every half-hour for four or five days! The reproductive science behind this is: the males have barbed penises that must pierce the lioness's vaginal wall, triggering ovulation. One particularly tatty-looking beast we named Scruffy was a big hit with both the girls. One afternoon George and I crept up when Scruffy and Lisa were mating and got to within ten yards of them before we lost our nerve. If distracting a lion while eating could prompt an attack, distracting one while he was on the job didn't bear thinking about. And we knew Scruffy was a hard nut because he was always beating up Christian.

This constant violence against Christian brought about a dilemma for George and me. There came a point when Lisa and Juma were both pregnant and the wild lions became rather more territorial about our obscure corner of their range. Christian got the message and would spend days away from Kampi ya Simba but he would always come back, covered with scars after another assault. The scars were now on his shoulders but it was usually two against one so he was still taking a beating. It was hard for us to bear as he had done so well – he was hunting on his own now, not just with the girls, and George had seen him mating down by the river with one of the lionesses from across the Tana. Everything pointed towards his release into the wild being an unlikely success. Scruffy and his friend Shaggy's attacks on Christian became ever more ferocious as the girls got closer to giving birth and we were terrified that they would either drive Christian away before he was quite ready to look after himself or kill him in a fight.

George and I debated what to do for hours and hours and reluctantly decided that we had to let nature take its course. To go out and shoot a lion would be wholly unethical and against everything we stood for: Christian was on his own. It was a hard conclusion to stand by as we both loved Christian and he trusted us to look after him. By declining to defend him, had we just signed his death warrant? A few days later we walked up on to the rocks with Lisa and Juma to find Christian and Scruffy lying side by side, looking out over Kora towards Meru. They had made friends at last; the wild lion had accepted Christian and his weird relationship with the future mothers of Scruffy's cubs. It was a great moment and a vote of confidence in our philosophy but it was also a warning for the future. Christian was accepted but there was no real place for him at Kora any more: he was going to have to find his own territory and maybe it would be on the other side of the river where we couldn't reach him.

Christian now went off on ever-longer safaris along the banks of the Tana and across the river into sparsely populated Somali cattle country. I spent most of my time looking for him and trying to keep track of his movements. He roamed far up and down the river, often coming perilously close to human habitation and its easy pickings. A couple of times I saw him swimming back across the Tana into Kora, his nose and ears just above the hippo- and crocodile-filled waters as his paws thrashed in an undignified doggy-paddle that seemed only just to keep him afloat. For the first time in my life, I felt the acute anxiety of a parent as I watched his reckless flirtation with danger.

At times like these I felt like a father to Christian but most of the time it was more of a fraternal relationship. We'd go on adventures together, following tracks through the bush, getting chased by rhinos and looking for dik-dik, lesser kudu and ringed waterbuck for him to stalk. We used to play games, seeing how close we could creep up on animals before they noticed us; this soon developed into real hunting. He got better and better and wanted to leave me behind because I spoilt his chances with my clumsy movements and horrible smell. Still, though, we spent long siestas lying by the Tana, Christian with a huge paw on my chest as I read a book or me leaning against him, watching the river flow by. We were lying in our favourite spot under the poplars by the *mswaki* and henna thickets one day when George turned up in the Land Rover: Joy had come to camp with some guests so Terence and I were both keeping a low profile. Christian woke up and prepared to greet George, then did a huge stretch and fell off the bank into the river. He scrambled up and raced off into the riverine forest and for the next two days refused to greet George, slinking off when he saw him because he was so embarrassed.

I know anthropomorphism is disapproved of but we did become extremely close to the lions and I could feel Christian's embarrassment just as easily as his fear and excitement. Never, though, have I shared his eyesight – I've worn spectacles since I was a child. A few weeks later we were all in the same spot when Christian became quite agitated and crouched, flicking his tail, as he stared at the far bank of the river. After a short while we saw an upturned canoe being swept down the river; we hadn't seen any strangers for weeks and were amazed when we had caught the canoe to see a small figure waving at us from the opposite bank. It was the leader of a party of people from the World Bank who had chickened out at the rapids and lost all their kit. We managed to rescue them the next day and indeed to recover most of their kit. One of them wrote a book about it and called it *Your Lion Saw Us First*.

In this period I wasn't just learning from Christian and George. Other friends, too, had to put up with my insatiable quest for knowledge of the bush and animal behaviour. Ian Hughes taught me a huge amount. That summer of 1972 I went on two trips with him, one with his anti-poaching unit from Isiolo and another up to Lake Turkana with my girlfriend, Susanne Turner. In those days poaching was only just starting to be a problem but even then the anti-poaching units had to be made up of tough men who could track all day and ambush a poaching camp at the end of it. It was an exciting safari. I remember thinking that this really was the life I had dreamt about when I had first met Campbell Whalley, instructor of the Oates patrol back in Ullswater.

Lake Turkana has about as much in common with Ullswater as Garissa does with New York. Known as the Jade Sea, it's a 290-kilometre-long lake in the middle of harsh desert. It's the world's biggest alkaline lake so there is nothing gentle or pretty about it. Wordsworth would be stymied to describe it but a few people have managed to convey the brutality of the landscape, the independence of its people and the inhospitable beauty of its rugged shores. Bursting with fish, its shores carpeted with crocodiles and wary flamingos, Turkana is a mysterious place where rock paintings and archaeological finds made by the Leakeys and others show that people have lived there since the earliest of times.

George and his old friend Nevil Baxendale had been stranded

on one side of Lake Rudolf – as Lake Turkana was then known
– when, in their twenties, they were looking for the Queen of
Sheba's gold. They had sent their donkey off with their porters
and cook to walk around the bottom end of the lake while they
had planned to sail across in an old canvas canoe. During the night
jackals ate the leather thongs holding their boat together, leaving
them stranded with no food. George had solved the food problem
by shooting the head off an Egyptian goose on its eggs with his
9.3mm Mauser rifle at a hundred yards. With this and some
tree bark they had found on the barren shore, they had managed
both to eat and fix the canoe before making it to safety a few days
later. I own that gun now and carry it whenever the occasion
demands.

I envied them the gold search, but even in the 1970s there were
still adventures to be had at Turkana. It was fabulous to see the
places George had talked about still in much the same state as he
had remembered them. So much of Kenya was changing so fast
that it was good to visit the areas like Turkana that seemed for
ever stuck in time. It was also great to get out of the camp every
now and then and go off with some people of my own age. It
wasn't long, however, before I began to worry about George and
the lions. In between the two trips we flew over Kampi ya Simba
in Ian's Super Cub and parachuted a crate of food and whisky
down to George and Terence but it wasn't enough and I soon
decided I had to get back.

Christian was becoming ever more independent of George,
me and the girls. He would go off on long walkabouts and not
return for weeks on end. He had killed a couple of cows when
the opportunity presented itself, a new departure that we couldn't
allow to form into a habit or he wouldn't survive for long in the
wild. Under normal circumstances there was no opportunity for
him to take cows because there were none in his radius. It only
ever happened when illegal grazers moved their animals into the

area we rented from Hola County Council – but the fact that grazing in Kora was illegal didn't mean Christian's behaviour wasn't a problem. Whenever we knew there were illegal grazers around we had to watch him very closely day and night or he might have been poisoned or shot. It was also essential that we knew when the grazing happened so that we could do something about it. The people who lived near Kora – in Asako and further afield – were incredibly tolerant of the mad white folk who lived with lions. They could have caused us enormous problems and had us closed down at will, but instead, although they were shockingly poor, they were immensely supportive and helped us whenever they could. It was important that we did not abuse that tolerance and reciprocated their trust by ensuring that our lions didn't eat their livestock.

The Somalis who came down from the north were another matter entirely. They didn't know or care about our work: they just wanted to use our pasture and would poison our lions without hesitation. Like the Masai in Tanzania and southern Kenya, the Somalis would push their stock on to anyone's property and die defending their 'right' to do so. The residents of Asako suffered terribly from this and the Wakamba continue to do so.

As soon as we realized that Christian had killed a cow down on the river, George and I set off in opposite directions. George went to meet the police and I went off to babysit Christian. I found him and prepared to spend the night in the back of the pickup while he prowled nearby. It was a beautiful night and I lay watching the stars and listening to the sounds of the bush as I fell asleep in the flatbed. When I woke up in the morning Christian was nowhere to be seen but I could see his fresh tracks in the soft sand by the river so I wasn't concerned that he had moved off in the night. I went down to the Tana to splash my face and brush my teeth, examining Christian's tracks at the same time.

As I walked across the beach, Christian came bounding out

from behind a rock and jumped up at me. He flattened and winded me. Then he grabbed me by the shoulder and shook me. I shouted at him to stop but he took no notice. There was nothing I could do and soon I was really scared. He put my head in his mouth, rolled on to his back and started kicking me with his back legs, like a leopard does. After all this time growing up together, I suddenly grasped – too late – how powerful Christian had become and I was terrified. As quickly as he had jumped me, he dropped me and bounced away. Then as I was getting up he knocked me down again and shook me. I stood up again, legs shaking, heart pounding, and shouted at him again to stop. He didn't listen and came for me again. I punched him on the nose as hard as I possibly could and he went bounding off into the bush as if nothing had happened. I was seriously shaken. Still holding my toothbrush, like an idiot, I stumbled back to the car, screaming at him when he came at me again. 'Don't you fucking dare!' I shouted, as he charged at me again. And I slammed the door in his face.

I was too rattled to deal with him there and then so I sat in the cab of the pickup, trembling and sweating until I had calmed down a bit. This was my first big fright with any of the lions and I realized I had been getting a bit lazy and complacent. It dawned on me then that Christian had grown up a lot since I had first met him eighteen months earlier and he wasn't going to be with us for much longer. He was almost a fully grown lion: he needed to get away from our protection and to fend for himself in the wild. George had seen and heard him mating a couple of times and we knew he could kill big game as well as livestock, but he had always come back to camp for a drink, to see the girls or to say hello to George and me. I loved him, but if our programme could ever be judged a success Christian would need to set up his own pride independently of us. If he failed to do so it would be an indictment of our project, proof for the nay-sayers that you

couldn't take a lion from SW3 and expect it to thrive in the NFD.
I sat in the car for two hours, pretending to read a book as Christian made greeting sounds and nudged against the car. At last I
got back my courage, climbed out of the car and gave him a hug;
he had been playing and there wasn't a mark on me, but he'd
given me a hell of a shock.

While Christian had yet to produce a litter, Lisa and Juma were
both heavily pregnant and spending a lot of time up on the rocks
near camp. Juma was still hard to approach but Lisa was always
a darling. She was so easy and funny and affectionate. She always
had a silly smile on her face and would come and greet me with
a head rub the moment she saw me. Sometimes she would jump
right over our heads, like Tigger in *The House at Pooh Corner*. Lisa
and Juma had been much more independent than Christian and
would go off for long periods at a time, hunting up and down
the river together and swimming the channel to the other side,
but they always came back for some meat or to have any wounds
tended. They roamed up to eight miles inland, so providing water
after they had been away from the river allowed us to keep an
eye on them even when they were almost entirely independent.
We first had to find them and then give them a drink in a cut-
down oil drum, which we filled with water from jerry cans.
Unless it had rained, the river was the only source of water
nearby, so if they wanted a drink it was much easier for them to
come to the camp. When they did, they would always greet us.
Lisa would jump up like Christian and give us a proper hug, but
after Juma had acknowledged us, she hung back and skulked in
the bushes. She was perfectly safe to be around but she just didn't
have the faith in us that Lisa had. We had been tremendously
proud when they both became pregnant by wild lions, even more
so when Juma showed us her cubs in November.

As George had predicted, Kora Rock was an excellent place
to raise cubs. Lionesses like to find good hiding places for their

cubs, which are born totally blind and helpless, and they move them every couple of days for safety. Baboons, leopards, hyenas, eagles, almost anything will kill a lion cub if it gets a chance so they require good parenting if they are to survive, and moving them is of key importance. We first saw Daniel and Shyman, Juma's cubs, in late November 1972. We didn't go close, but it was wonderful to discover that they had survived and were thriving. Lisa gave birth in December, and the two lionesses helped each other to bring up their families, suckling each other's cubs as lionesses in a pride will do. We named Lisa's cubs Lisette, Kora and Oscar and were almost immediately invited to come and meet them by their fabulously laid-back mother. They had just opened their blue eyes and were tiny spotted kittens, only weighing a kilo or two when we first glimpsed them. Juma's were slightly bigger and darker than Lisa's, Shyman with a personality very similar to hers and Daniel more relaxed. All the cubs were wild, so we avoided making any unnecessary contact with them.

We were very wary of going close to the girls with their cubs, but when we didn't approach Lisa she looked rather hurt. She would lick us and head rub us even when she was suckling. We could get nowhere near Juma and didn't try: she was still wild as hell, which, given that restoring the lions to the wild was our ultimate aim, was a blessing rather than a problem. That Christmas we felt very pleased with ourselves. Here was the complete vindication of our methods. Both Lisa and Juma had mated with wild lions, given birth to healthy cubs and were entirely capable of living freely and independently of us. They were not vicious man-eaters, as many had predicted they would become; neither did they require us to feed them. Lisa and Juma had been hunting very successfully for some time now and it seemed that, as long as they were able to support each other, they would be all right whether we were there or not.

They had other ideas – independent as they were, we still had our uses. When the cubs got a bit bigger, the girls started dumping them at camp for us to babysit while they went off hunting each night.

George had told Joy about our success so she brought some friends from England to witness George's triumph when she came to Kora for Christmas. Of course Terence and I were chucked out of Kampi ya Simba for the duration and set up a rival camp on the river close to where Christian and I used to sleep in the afternoons. I jumped on a bus in Garissa and went off to the coast for Christmas itself. I had a great time with my friends PA and Agneta – I had been staying with them in Malindi when I'd first heard of the job with George so it was wonderful to be back with them. I could see how much my life had changed, and that New Year I reflected that I really seemed to have pulled it off. Despite my lack of skills on arrival, I was now a useful member of George's team and one of the pride. Months earlier he had written in my copy of his autobiography *Bwana Game:* 'To Tony Fitzjohn, Latest of the Pride, George Adamson, Kora, Sept 1971'. (It was stolen from camp in the eighties by a souvenir hunter.) Now I could look after the lions and track them. I kept the vehicles on the road and dealt with the local authorities when George was too fed up to do so. With help, I had even set up a little twelve-volt darkroom, which enthralled George who loved photography.

Kenya had just banned elephant hunting, so for the professional hunters who were on the coast that Christmas, the writing was on the wall. All game hunting would follow: they were soon to be out of a job. Although I had many hunter friends, I'm afraid I felt little sympathy for them then – but we soon found out that they were much better than what replaced them in the years to come.

When I got back to Kora I still had to stay out of Joy's way so George and I used to meet up on the rocks before we went to look for the girls and the cubs. We had great trouble keeping them away from Joy and her guests but we managed. The cubs were wild and we wanted them to stay that way; the last thing we wanted was another Elsa. We soon found that it wasn't just us who had been introduced to them. By checking the *luggas* in the mornings to read the tracks in the sand from the night before, we could tell that both Scruffy and Christian had met them. Around that time, when everything was going so well, George and I would often talk about how much help we should give to the lions after they had reached a certain level of independence. George – who had experience of it – was keen to keep them around, continuing to feed them and putting out water for them so that there was always something to encourage them back. I saw their leaving us as a sign of success and something we should be striving for at all times. But neither of us was prepared for the shock when Lisa disappeared with her cubs in early 1973.

We searched all over Kora. I went way inland into Ukambani, then headed off to the other side of the river and drove high up into Meru, looking for spoor and asking people if they'd seen a small lioness with three cubs. Just getting to the other side with a vehicle was a major safari – it took almost a day with the nearest bridge in Garissa, a hundred miles downstream. George searched on the Kora side of the Tana and we would meet every couple of days and shout across the river to compare notes. Sometimes I'd take the little dinghy with its hopeless three-horsepower engine on the back. But there was no sign of Lisa. After about a week on the Meru side of the river, I had found nothing and set off back to Kora.

George and I took to following Juma when she went hunting in the hope that she might lead us to Lisa but by the end of three weeks we had run out of ideas. We didn't know what to do. We'd been to all her favourite places, checked the *luggas*, stayed up all night calling her through a megaphone but we had never seen the slightest sign of her. We had even taken to driving around

Kora with an increasingly smelly dead goat in the back of the pickup and calling her every mile or so. We were doing this one afternoon a few miles from camp when I saw a small lion cub walking across a *lugga* and into a bush.

I looked across at George and said I thought it might be one of Lisa's. George harrumphed his disagreement but I jumped out to investigate. The sand in the riverbed was covered with the tracks of cubs – a good sign – so I pushed on further. The tracks led to a bush into which I gingerly stuck my head. There was an earth-shattering roar and a blast of hot breath hit me full in the face. I toppled over, falling flat on my back. I returned to the car, knees shaking and breath coming in panicked pants. George was chuckling happily and pointing behind me. It was Juma and we had disturbed her with her cubs. We hadn't fed her for a while so I chained the carcass to a tree and we sat down to watch what would happen. They were all shy so we had to wait for a while, but after a few minutes Daniel and Shyman poked their heads out of the bush and tottered over to the carcass. Then Juma's big head came out again. She looked around suspiciously. Suddenly, behind her, came Lisa's three cubs – Kora, Lisette and Oscar – but not a sign of Lisa.

We couldn't work out what had happened. The cubs were very small and emaciated but they were alive and there was no way they could have looked after themselves and survived for almost a month on their own. We knew they hadn't been with Juma because we'd been tracking her and her cubs. And they hadn't been with Christian either. It was a mystery: one that remains unsolved as we never saw Lisa again and never found out what had happened to her.

We were devastated. Lisa's disappearance left a big hole in our lives. She was a lovely lioness – so friendly and trusting. But Juma was wonderful too, if in a different way. She immediately adopted Lisa's cubs and looked after them from that day onwards. It was

hard work for her. She was a brilliant hunter but it was much
harder hunting without Lisa, and five cubs were a lot for her to
bring up on her own. In a normal situation she would have been
part of a pride and the extra burden shared between a group of
lactating lionesses, but Juma was alone. We helped out with
babysitting duties while she went hunting and also with a bit of
meat and cod liver oil every now and then. Amazingly it worked.
Lisette, the weakest of Lisa's cubs, had a hernia and died young
but the others grew up to be strong and resourceful.

Whenever George got a bit of money – from his publishers, his
pension or supporters of the lion programme – he would give
some to Terence to hire people from Asako to cut more roads.
Terence and Erigumsa Dirkicha were utterly tireless and their
expansion of Kora's road network was fast, efficient and long-
lasting. Terence could make a little money go a very long way.
We all had to. We did most of our vehicle maintenance in the
bush, sometimes making spare parts out of wood and used inner
tubes. Keeping old cars working on bad roads is extremely hard
work but the police and provincial commissioner's workshops
in Garissa were extraordinarily helpful. They would take our
cars into their workshop when I was in town and let us cannibal-
ize parts from their crashed vehicles or borrow parts until we
could replace them.

Police Superintendent Philip Kilonzo was a constant support
when we had illegal grazing and would send in patrols to move
the herds out of Kora whenever we needed him to. In return we
would always help his patrols with food and fuel when they were
moving through Kora. One such patrol came through when
George and I had been out with the lions. They had set up their
tents too close along the road near Kampi ya Simba. The fence
was there for a reason: we returned to find all the men lined up
behind their officer being inspected by a group of curious young

lions. The officer in charge was insisting to his men, 'Don't worry. Tony said these lions were really nice.' We dispersed the lions and got the police inside the fence as quickly as we could.

We were always invited to official celebrations in Garissa or Madogo, our District HQ, and made a point of attending them. I had to sit through many a sports day and even more speech days in the searing heat – once I was the only European at a district commissioner's event to mark Independence Day. I made some great friendships then that lasted for many years. One such was with Noor Abdi Ogle, a young Kenyan-Somali, an assistant game warden. Over the years Noor and I had some terrifying adventures together. He would help us during the worst of times and I accompanied him on some fairly hair-raising anti-stock-theft and poaching patrols. He was incredibly tough and hard, one of the bravest men I've ever met. A couple of patrols I went on with him ended in heavy gunfire and Noor never ducked or even flinched. As a result his men would follow him anywhere. A few years later he was fired: twenty-three elephant tusks and sixteen prisoners in his custody had gone missing. He hadn't been paid for six months. He survived the scandal to become an MP a few years later, but died young of diabetes, the curse of so many Africans. It was a great loss to me.

Occasionally one of us would have to go to Nairobi for some administrative reason. Almost always it was me and I quite welcomed the break. George hated Nairobi and Terence was such a stick-in-the-mud that he only left Africa once in his entire life. I loved it in the bush at Kora but every now and then I liked to go to Nairobi for some fun. I loved Nairobi in those days but only for a short while. I would let errands stack up until a trip became necessary, then head off to the big smoke and indulge myself. After living such a quiet life on such a bland diet for so long, I invariably got sick after a few days of late nights and hard living. Changes in altitude can also bring on malaria so trips to

Nairobi usually took much longer than they should have done. A lot of George's money was spent at Cooper Motors where I would drop off a Land Rover for a bit of care and attention. There was never much left for beer.

When I was in town I would always meet up with Mike Wamalwa. A young professor at Nairobi University, he had been to the LSE and Cambridge. He was a scion of a very political family from western Kenya. Mike was a brilliant speaker, in public and private, and, married to the spectacularly beautiful daughter of Foreign Minister Njoroge Mungai, he was half of one of the great power couples of the time. Their marriage had been a terrible scandal as Gathoni, a member of the Kenyatta family, was Kikuyu royalty and he was Abaluhya. Intertribal marriage was almost as shocking as interracial marriage had been years before.

Mike and I had a madcap idea in the mid-seventies: we would import that period icon Mateus Rosé to Kenya. With another friend, Ben Ng'anga, we managed to bring in a shipment of the weirdly shaped bottles that everyone used to make into candlesticks and got it past Customs with the minimum of fuss. It wasn't so easy to find a buyer, though, and we ended up drinking most of it before we could sell it. I used to take Mike to the Aero Club at Nairobi's Wilson airport, which, in those days, was a bastion of white supremacy. In later years, after he had become one of Kenya's youngest MPs, he would return the favour by taking me to Parliament where the only white face belonged to Richard Leakey's brother, Philip. Once, Mike introduced me to the then vice president, Daniel arap Moi, in the restaurant at Parliament. Moi had a startling presence even then. He shook Mike's hand, saying, 'And what are your plans, young man?' Mike's nickname was *kijana*, or young man, but he didn't like being called it to his face. He held Moi's hand, looked him straight in the eye, and said, 'I'm after your job, sir.'

In those days I slept on many people's floors and was the most

appalling houseguest. Kit and Sandy Dickinson put up with me
for years before they temporarily threw me out after a particularly
reprehensible evening when I brought back two young ladies
who were in need of a place to rest. I was at least able to return
a small part of their hospitality when Sandy and some friends
came up to Kora to see the total eclipse. They crashed on the way
but arrived on the night before the eclipse and set up camp within
the wire. None of us had ever seen an eclipse before and were
astounded by what we witnessed. Kora was always quiet and
peaceful – particularly after the organ-bruising drive from
Nairobi – but however quiet it is in the bush it's never entirely
silent. Crickets chirrup, babblers scuttle in the trees, superb star-
lings chatter to each other. There is always noise in the background
even in the very dead of night.

When the moon crossed the sun above Kora all that changed.
Croakey and Crikey, George's fan-tailed ravens, flew off to roost
on Kora Rock's sheer face. The hornbills took off for their night
trees, and the vulturine guinea fowl flew up on to the roofs of
the huts. Everything slowed down and stopped. All creatures
were still. No one spoke for the duration – at more than seven
minutes, it would be the longest eclipse for the next five hundred
years.

Jack Barrah had come into the Game Department a generation
after George and was now a senior adviser at Wildlife HQ. He
often came into camp in the early seventies and was invaluable
to us in dealing with the authorities. A former colonial game
warden, he was particularly valued by the new administration in
the Game Department for his fairness, knowledge and integrity,
and for his skill at getting the best out of often resentful and
cantankerous Europeans. He had seen how Kora was being
invaded ever more regularly by illegal herders and how the council did nothing about it. We couldn't rely on having supportive
police and army chiefs in Garissa for ever so he pushed for Kora

to be made into a game reserve. This would provide it with some protection, put the area on the map and de-gazette it as a hunting block. While still under the auspices of the distant Hola County Council, it would be given a warden and some rangers to show that it was an official wildlife area.

This was a brilliant and necessary idea and much more than George and I could have hoped for but it needed a lot of work. In August Jack made two trips with council members, in very rough flying conditions, to sell the idea to them, and it was only after he had delivered them all back that he revealed to us he had had a bug flying around inside his skull all night. He was in agony as the creature crawled around his ear canal, buzzing like a bench-saw. I suggested I box his ears but ended up shining a torch into his ear and out flew the bug. Just like that!

On 19 October 1974 his efforts and planning came to fruition and Kora was declared a game reserve, a change in its status that offered it much more protection than when it had merely been property rented from Hola County Council. It also gave us a bit more legitimacy that helped in attracting benefactors and freed us from paying the rent, which had gone up to £1,250 a year – a fortune for George at that time. The lions now had a real home that was recognized by the wildlife authorities – but there weren't many of them left.

Around the time that Lisa disappeared, Christian started going away for longer and longer periods. We were happy that he was finding his feet and daring to go on long walkabouts but were worried that he might stray towards human habitation or come across the increasingly frequent illegal grazers invading Kora from the north. I travelled all over Kora and Meru looking for him – long hard safaris on foot and by Land Rover. Everyone we knew was always keeping an eye out for him. Eventually, after he had been gone for three months, we reluctantly decided that he must have gone across the river with no intention of returning and had started a new life. We were upset that we didn't see him any more but it was tempered with gratitude as this, again, was an affirmation of our methods. The programme at Kora had been created with the express intention of introducing Christian to the wild and we had succeeded. I missed him like a severed limb.

By the end of 1974 Juma was the only full grown lion still at Kampi ya Simba. We were sure Lisa was dead. We hadn't seen Christian for most of the year although we did think occasionally that we had heard his roars over the river and seen his spoor so we felt he was still alive. Juma's cubs were growing up and would try to do a bit of hunting on their own but they were still too young to be fully effective and needed help from Juma and ourselves. We had stopped putting out Farex baby cereal for them but we often stayed up at night waiting for them to come home before we went to bed. All in all, it was a bittersweet end to the year. Juma and the cubs were thriving but where was the next generation? When John Rendall, one of Christian's keepers in London, came out for Christmas, we decided to give it one more try and go on a last search for Christian. He might be able to produce a litter that could mate with Juma's cubs.

I met John off the plane in Nairobi. He was all Bee Gees haircut and King's Road strides but he fitted in well with my reprobate friends, even though he was remorselessly un-bush. I had met Ace and John a couple of times when they had come back to visit the ever-growing Christian and watched the nervous look in their eyes as this enormous lion – who still loved them beyond measure – bounded up to greet them. This time, though, there was no Christian, and Joy had dragged George, kicking and screaming, to Naivasha, so I was worried about how we might get on – unnecessarily so. Forty years later, John is still on the board of the George Adamson Wildlife Trust, which he joined early on, and is one of our greatest supporters.

We had a wonderful Christmas together at Kora. John worked

on his tan while I did a lot of routine maintenance on the cars and the camp. We went for long walks in the mornings and evenings, often with the young cubs and Juma tailing us. Looking back now, it was strange how we were sure that Lisa was dead and that Christian was alive. We had scant evidence for either belief but that was very much the way we felt. We used the little rubber dinghy to thread our way through the hippos and cross the Tana rather than drive the ten hours around via Garissa. John and I made a couple of half-hearted searches for Christian over on the Meru side but we had no luck and didn't really expect any. Christian had gone for ever. He had moved from a Bentley in Chelsea to a Land Rover in Kora and now he had gone off to Meru, where they had the new Toyotas, to start his own lineage. We were proud of him but, God, I missed him.

4. Pride before a Fall

George received a call over Christmas from Perez Olindo, the first African head of the National Parks Service, urging him to go and see him at his office. In those days, Parks and John Mutinda's Game Department were separate but we needed to be friends with both in order to operate successfully. Perez told George that he had far too many foundlings at Nairobi National Park animal orphanage. He wanted to give George a young lion called Leakey, who was becoming too big to stay there.

John Rendall and I were elated when the news came through on the radio. We had spent Christmas discussing the problem of not having a lion to replace Christian and here was a late Christmas present landing in our laps. And from such a source! To receive a lion from the head of Parks gave us a nice official nod. We rigged the pickup for a translocation, then drove to Nairobi, where I dropped John at his plane, and scraped together some cash for more fuel so that I could collect George and the new lion. We were always operating on a shoestring at Kora but this was the time of the Yom Kippur war, and the resulting global fuel crisis, so things were worse than usual. The price of fuel in Kenya went up 500 per cent between 1972 and 1976 so we had to be very careful about how and if we drove. The same applied to the gas we used for the fridges, and the build-up of lions over the coming period meant we had to buy much more meat than we had in earlier years. It was a long time before we realized that thousands of people out there would be willing to sponsor us to get over such problems because they admired the work we were doing.

The orphaned Leakey had been named after Louis, the great archaeologist who discovered the origins of man in East Africa and was the mentor and friend to so many 'Monkey Women': the late great Diane Fossey (gorillas), Shirley Strum (baboons) and Jane Goodall (chimps). Louis and his equally talented wife Mary's children went on to be very influential in Kenya and indeed the wider world. Philip became an MP when no other white Kenyan dared join the political fray and indeed became a minister under President Moi. Richard made major archaeological discoveries, headed up the National Museums of Kenya, then took on the poachers and beat them when, many years later, he sat in Perez Olindo's chair. Yet more bravely, in the mid-1980s he used his position as CEO of the East African Wildlife Society to take on the minister, the directors and the government as a whole over poaching, corruption and law and order. He then went into politics himself. I have had many run-ins with the Leakeys over the years but I have always admired their balls while remaining keenly aware of their less shining parts. When most white Kenyans have sat on their butts, sure in the knowledge that they can reclaim their nationalities of birth at the drop of a hat, the Leakeys have embraced being Kenyan, involved themselves in politics and worked in the Kenyan civil service for the greater good of the country. They are almost alone in this regard and I admire them both.

Perez told us that Leakey had been badly treated on capture and that recently he had been put on display at a fair in Nairobi. At around one year old he was going to be difficult to integrate and reintroduce to the wild, but it was either take him or leave him in the orphanage. George and I were rather wary of what we might be letting ourselves in for but we took him without hesitation. Juma, too, had been treated badly on capture and was still very cautious and jumpy around humans. A distrust of humans is a healthy attribute in a wild lion – humans are their only predator – but dislike can be dangerous for both man and beast. George drove back to Kora with Leakey in a large cage on the back of the pickup and I followed in the station wagon in case of breakdowns. I saw some tremendous double-takes from passers-by as we made our way out of Nairobi on the main Thika highway. As quickly as possible we got him into the compound and stashed in the holding area within our camp, which Terence had reinforced while we were away. We need not have worried about Leakey being aggressive towards humans. He was a hopeless lion – he had a great deal in common with the one in *The Wizard of Oz*.

Hopeless Leakey might have been but he also had a lovely personality. He soon developed an incredibly endearing habit. In addition to nudging our thighs in greeting, as all the lions did, he took to nudging the front wing of the Land Rover as soon as we came home. We tried to take him out into the bush, as we had with the others, so he could learn about life in Kora, but he hated walks. There was one place he liked going just near camp. He would charge in and out of the thicket there for a while, then sneak back to camp when we weren't looking. It was maddening, particularly as, in the bush, a ready-made family was waiting to teach him the tricks of his trade. Lisette had died but Juma was doing a sterling job bringing up the other cubs and they were all about the same age as Leakey. We had to keep them apart from each other because – due to his incarceration at the orphanage – he had not even learnt how to play when the others were already hunting successfully. We had to drag him out of his compound by the dangerous method of pulling a piece of meat on a rope but sometimes he just wouldn't come. After a while we managed to get him to come on a long walk down to the Tana, and he gradually fell into the daily routine that we had worked up with Christian and the girls, but he was way behind his peers.

The routine wasn't to last for long. In late February, I drove into Garissa on a supply run and went to see Brother Mario, the former nightclub-owning priest. His latest project was growing melons in the desert, three miles inland from the river. It sounds like a biblical parable but he did it for real. And, like everything else Mario did, it defied logic but worked: he made Garissa melons famous. As soon as I pulled up, Mario told me that I had to go and find Fred Leminiria, the new game warden. 'He's hiding from you,' said Mario, 'because he's got a tiny lion cub from Wajir and he knows you'll want it.'

I charged around town – from the police bar to the shebeens by the river to Brother Mario's petrol station – until I found Fred hiding in the army mess, cradling a tiny cub whose mother he'd been obliged to shoot for stock-raiding. I stormed over to him – all dust and hair and shorts. Fred just said, 'OK, Tony, you can have him.' I gave him a Temptations tape and a T-shirt in return. And, of course, we called the lion Freddie.

Fred Leminiria would never have let me have him if the cub hadn't been so sick – he would have been sent to the orphanage like Leakey. Little Freddie was so weak I thought he might not make the journey home and drove the whole way back from Garissa with him on my lap. By the end of the journey it was love. He was my first lion cub and I was going to make sure he survived. He had terrible hookworm, one of the biggest killers of wild animals. We cured him of that pretty quickly and then he thrived on the Farex and cod liver oil we fed him before moving him on to solids. I was besotted with him and he would go nowhere without me. It was with Freddie that I really worked out how to communicate with lions; Christian and I had been close, but he had been brought up by Ace and John before he got to me. Freddie was less than a month old. I would have loved to show off and take him to the coast, to Nairobi and all the great places that George and Joy had gone with Elsa, but that wasn't the purpose of our project: our goal was to give the animals we brought up a real life as lions, to help them survive and be lions in their natural habitat. So, I had to stay with Freddie: he couldn't come with me. Everything went by the board – visits to Nairobi, girlfriends, trips to Garissa, even. I devoted my life to that cub.

At first he and Leakey had a very strange relationship. Although Leakey was much older than Fred, he was utterly goofy. He didn't like going for walks, he didn't know how to play; hunting was a faraway dream. Freddie, on the other hand, was a proper Somali lion: although tiny he was already good at playing and he loved walking. Leakey was useless but he knew that the smaller cub had to kowtow to him and was pretty rough with him, beating him up and forcing him to show subservience. It was hard not to intervene in those meetings, but I knew they had to learn to get on – as lions – or life would become very complicated. Our restraint worked and we were rewarded with the discovery that Leakey had a talent – even if he did hunt backwards. He was the Henry Kissinger of the lion world and could make friends with anyone. His diplomatic skills would become extremely useful as we tried to keep the ever-multiplying prides from fighting with each other.

Freddie was very gentle – like Lisa – but he was adventurous and brave as well. He and Leakey helped each other to learn about the wild as I guided them through the pitfalls. George and I would take them for walks and they became increasingly curious as they grew in confidence, setting off into the bush in pursuit of guinea fowl and dik-dik. It was quite some time, though, before they caught anything. The bush was starting to change: it became increasingly thick as the rhino that had browsed the shrubs and kept the roads and elephant paths open were systematically wiped out by Somali raiding parties. We met fewer and fewer rhino on our walks and we often heard shooting at night. For some reason the poachers kept out of our way but they were very busy all around us and we often came across vast grey carcasses with gaping holes in their snouts where their horns had been cut out. You could smell the rotting remains from miles away.

The fact that Kora had become a game reserve should have given it some form of protection but the Game Department was understaffed and inefficient, and the Somalis now doing the poaching were not like the Wakamba with their poisoned arrows. They had powerful semi-automatic rifles, easily good enough for shooting rhinos and even more so for killing anyone who tried to stop them. Vast as they are, rhinos are surprisingly easy to kill: you just follow their tracks and shoot them when they charge. You don't even need a heavy rifle as you do for buffalo or elephant. Within a couple of years there would be none left. No one understood why there was suddenly such an insatiable demand for rhino horn but after a lot of research – some of it very dangerous – our friend Esmond Bradley Martin discovered that, like everything else in the seventies, it was OPEC's fault. By pushing up the price of oil, Sheikh Yamani and his cohorts had multiplied the Yemeni GDP seven-fold. A rhino-horn dagger in Yemen is a symbol of manhood, so an entire species was all but wiped out in order that a load of newly oil-rich Yemenis could have them.

As the two Yemens moved towards unification the football authorities of peace-loving Kenya were at war with each other. The whole country had gone football crazy and Pele was visiting. I bought Freddie a football in Garissa. He soon caught the soccer bug and turned into an excellent dribbler although, with opposition like Leakey and me, he had no trouble looking good.

When I had arrived in camp with Freddie, George's first words had been 'not another male'. Juma was looking after three boys already and we really needed some girls to even things out. As if in answer to our prayers, Dr Aart Visee, a Dutch vet who would become a lifelong friend and supporter, got in touch to say he had a lioness he wanted to give to us.

In a world of strange coincidences Aart worked at Rotterdam Zoo, which had connections with both Christian and Elsa. He was desperate to find a home for a lioness called Arusha. Like Christian, she had once been a pet that had grown too big for its owners to cope with. These were the days before satellite phones and email so it took some feverish letter-writing to the Game Department and the ministry before we obtained permission to import the cub from Holland. Before I drove to Nairobi to collect her, I reinforced the holding compounds to put her in when she arrived. She would need a place of her own in which she could have time to adjust before being introduced to the other lions.

I pulled all the seats out of George's new long-wheel-base Land Rover to make more room, welded on a few ring-bolts so we could tie down the container and made sure everything was ready for the new arrival. George looked a bit forlorn as I modified his new car but understood that it was for the greater good of the project.

I set off first thing to pick up Aart and Arusha from that night's KLM flight into Nairobi. It was a spectacular day and the drive down was eventless. I met up with my girlfriend, Tina Aschan, for dinner on the way to the airport. We had a wonderful meal, then walked out to George's new car. It wasn't there. I thought it was a practical joke. I looked up and down the street; I interrogated the security guards. No joke: someone had stolen George's car and the flight from Holland was landing in forty-five minutes. We threw out the contents of Tina's VW Combi, gunned the engine and arrived at the airport, flustered, late and slightly drunk, a few minutes after Arusha had been unloaded.

We were taking coals to Newcastle and there were many raised eyebrows at the airport: no one believed we had permission to import a lion. The paperwork, of course, was in the stolen car. All those carefully sought permissions from the wildlife authorities were now in the hands of a car thief: I was going to have to talk my way out of it. I can't imagine what Aart must have thought as we tried to smuggle a large lioness through Customs. After a good few hours, I managed to blag our way past – but what were we going to do with the lion? I'll never forget Aart's face when he first saw the Combi. We squashed the crate into the back, then shoved Aart in on top of it and drove to Carol Bell's house in Langata on the outskirts of Nairobi. Carol had a big house and a garden shed so seemed like the obvious victim even if Aart had been expecting a holding cage at a wildlife veterinary clinic. We put a bewildered Aart in the shed with the lioness, Tina and I had the sofa – and Carol's kids slept on, unaware that there was a lion in their shed. It all came good the next morning. The car was insured so we were lent another Land Rover by Cooper Motors until we could claim. Only a short wheel-base, it was nonetheless more suitable for driving to Kora than the battered old Combi. Aart and I put the lion crate in the back, a beer crate between us, then drove the ten hours to Kampi ya Simba while working our way through it. George took it very well when I told him I had driven through a puddle and his new car had shrunk.

Fred was delighted with Arusha. She determined how their relationship would go and soon they were inseparable. Just a few months after she had arrived, the orphanage gave us another two female cubs, Gigi and Growlie, bringing our total up to a nicely balanced ten. There followed the most intense but enjoyable few months that I have ever spent, juggling the different needs of the individual lions and helping them to grow as a pride. From the sadness of losing track of Christian, and Lisa's probable death, things were suddenly going remarkably well for George, me and the lion project.

There had been a definite change in perception of our project from the authorities as the old-school colonial wardens were phased out and the new African leaders took over. Both Perez

Olindo at National Parks and John Mutinda, the chief game warden, were incredibly supportive. Perez kept us stocked with cubs from the orphanage and John gave us the authority to look after them. Both patriotic Kenyans, they valued the fame that George had brought to Kenya and its wildlife, and they got on well with him. Until Kenya had stunned the world with triple gold at the Mexico Olympics, almost the only thing most people knew about the country was the Adamsons and *Born Free*. *Born Free*'s contribution to Kenya's GDP must have been enormous. In the eighties, *Out of Africa*, the movie, doubled tourism earnings overnight and still brings visitors today – then, as now, Kenya's main income is from tourism. It took another movie to teach the world about Happy Valley, a sad story involving a tiny number of selfish people indulging themselves while the rest of the population was fighting a war.

George had retired just before independence so never suffered the integration problems faced by some of our friends, like Bill Woodley and David Sheldrick. Both men were excellent game wardens and had to adjust to having under-qualified Kenyans promoted over their heads. Like Jack Barrah, and unlike many others, they managed the change masterfully but there were times when it had not been easy. The fact that Perez and John had never worked under George in the colonial system or over him post-independence made the relationship much easier. It wasn't as if George was going to say anything to offend them because he never said anything! They could look upon him as a relic of colonial times, admiring the bits they liked and overlooking the bits they didn't. In turn, we felt a great responsibility towards them. They took significant personal risks in supporting us and we did not want to let them down.

It wasn't just the wildlife authorities at Headquarters who were supportive of our lion project at Kora. While the army sat in their barracks playing darts, because all Kenya's problems were 'internal' not 'external', the other men on the ground in Garissa always helped us when they could. When, as increasingly happened, Somali and Orma grazers invaded the reserve, Philip Kilonzo would always try to send his policemen to move them out. We had the run of the police and provincial authority's workshops and the Anti Stock-theft Unit always picked our brains for information. The support was a two-way street. We would always provide fuel and assistance if our neighbours needed a hand, and when elephants menaced crops at Asako we would help herd them back into the reserve. I once got called in to Rahole on the other side of the Tana to help out with a buffalo that had become stuck in the mud. Buffalo may look like large cows but they are actually one of the most dangerous animals in Africa, responsible for many more deaths than lions, crocodiles or elephants. I spent all day trying to pull it out with the Land Rover. This involved some very tentative lassoing and then some very careful pulling so I didn't inadvertently break its back or otherwise injure it. After hours and hours of this, it eventually popped out. The huge buffalo lurched to its feet, legs shaking and head nodding. It gave us a belligerent look, let out a massive bellow and dropped down dead.

Visitors from outside Kenya were beginning to see that our methods were working and to show their appreciation by donating money. We were incredibly bad at accepting donations, so bad in fact that we actually frightened away some donors by our 'frightfully British' reluctance. At this stage George, Terence, the lions and I were living off George's colonial pension and we needed all the help we could get. Luckily the pension was index-linked, but even so, the small cash injection brought in by the success of *Christian the Lion* made a significant difference. The whole world was in economic crisis and the price of everything – from posho, the Kenyan staple maize meal, to fuel and camel meat – was rising. It sounds a bit dramatic but away from the bubble of Kora it seemed that the world was going crazy. US

President Nixon resigned in 1974, Saigon fell a year later, marking the end of the Vietnam war, and closer to home, Haile Selassie's successor, Colonel Mengistu, and Uganda's Idi Amin were extremely scary neighbours, who laid claim to vast swathes of Kenya. After a while, we just stopped buying batteries for the radio and kept our heads down – completely immersed in the lions. We did, however, have an increasing number of visitors.

One of our most surprising and welcome guests was Henry Starkey, my old school chaplain who had saved me from expulsion dozens of times; he brought his whole family and seemed pleased that I had stayed out of trouble and done something useful. It was great to see them but even more exciting were the wildlife researchers who were taking an interest in our work. Hugh and Ros Lamprey from the Serengeti Wildlife Research Institute came and stayed for a few days. Hugh gave me a long lecture about hippo behaviour and a duck-like bird called the Peter's Finfoot while we were out on the river in the nine-foot rubber duck. As he delivered his talk a tiny pink hippo jumped off the riverbank and plopped into the water in front of us. Hugh described how hippos were fiercely territorial and protective of their young as I was feverishly pulling the cord on the ancient outboard like a maniac. 'What's up?' he asked. 'Why the engine now?' It coughed into life and we shot downstream just as the mother hippo charged towards us, mouth agape.

Nigel de Winser, who went on to be a very big cheese at the Royal Geographical Society, set up camp in Kora for his Tana River Expedition. He brought a small group of scientists from a London polytechnic to study the flora and fauna from Kora to Kipini on the coast. He was wonderful to have around and his crew taught us a huge amount about the area. A colleague of Hugh's, Bernard Grzmiek from Frankfurt Zoo, also visited and checked us out. Gratifyingly, he took one look at our project and said we needed to open up the reserve if we were to continue successfully. To that end, he gave us the money for a tractor, a road grader and two years of manning for them.

After a great deal of research, combined with advice from friends, I was despatched to Nairobi to buy the aforesaid tractor. We had decided on the most basic model we could find with absolutely no extras. The thinking behind this was that the simpler it was, the less likely it would be to break down in the harsh conditions of Kora — that, and the fact that I heartily disliked Terence's proposed tractor driver and wanted him to be as uncomfortable as possible. I went to pick up the tractor from CMC — a Massey Ferguson MF20 with a three-ton trailer — and was delighted to see that, although it was a beautiful piece of machinery, it was just as uncomfortable as I had hoped, with a thin metal seat and no suspension to speak of. Then it dawned on me that I was going to have to drive it the whole way to Kora. It took me three days, travelling in the baking sunshine at 12 m.p.h. and camping by its side at night. When I arrived Terence thought Christmas had come early and set off to play with his new toy. The equipment made a huge difference to our lives and those of the lions by speeding up all the lengthy processes, like getting to Asako to fetch staff, collecting firewood and water. Mainly used for road-building, it took the heat off the Land Rovers and meant we could track down the lions more quickly with fewer breakdowns. My intention might have been mean but my logic was correct. That tractor still delivers the water at Kora.

The people that utterly transformed our daily routine were Esmond and Chryssee Bradley Martin. Chryssee is a conservation writer and worked with Gloria Lowe at the Nairobi National Park to make sure all the orphans came our way. Esmond, with his working partner Lucy Vigne, is the world's expert on the illicit trade in ivory and rhino horn. They first came to visit us because Chryssee had worked with Leakey at the animal orphanage. Leakey had playfully nipped Esmond's leg when they were walking with George, a slight for which Esmond seemed to bear him no grudge even though it must have hurt considerably. Having seen the laborious methods we used to track the lions, Esmond told us that if we found out about radio collars he would find the money to pay for them. This was very new technology at the time and we didn't have the Internet to help us search but I was eventually put in touch with Barbara Kermeen at AVM Instrument Co. in California. She designed our first lion collars and still produces all our collars today. The original system was very primitive indeed and required a lot of trial and error because batteries were unreliable. We and AVM were learning as we went along.

The first collars came in a huge box with an H-shaped aerial – about the size of an old-fashioned television aerial, attached to a wooden pole – which connected to a radio set and a pair of headphones. The collars themselves were constructed from very strong webbing made of machine belting. They had to have holes drilled in them so that they could be bolted together at a point that fitted the lions' necks. Next to the holes lay the transmitter and the batteries, which had to be soldered together, then covered with pink dental acrylic so that the system didn't short-circuit when wet. This is a complicated and fiddly process for dentists, let alone in the middle of the bush. The next step was yet more challenging: getting the collar round the lions' necks without having an arm chewed off.

We decided not to immobilize the lions. We didn't have any experience of using anaesthetics – even now a very hit-and-miss science – and we were frightened we might kill a lion by getting it wrong. It fell upon me therefore to convince the lions, using my hands and my voice, that what I was doing was for their own good, and persuade them that it was the right thing to do. The first lion we collared was Leakey, who was a big boy now – standing above our waists and weighing close to three hundred pounds

– but had a gentle character and was very easy-going. George stood in front of him with a stick for him to chew and I moved towards him holding the collar in front of me. It was important to be very calm, relaxed and firm. 'This is good for you and needs to be done,' I said, as I moved towards him. I put the collar round his neck in one fluid movement, pushed through the bolts, put on the lock washers and nuts, then tightened them with a spanner. God, I loved it. I loved the fact that I could do it.

I don't know what it was about George and me that the lions allowed us to do this. We had conquered our fear and honed our understanding of them by practising on the likes of Christian and Lisa, but over the years we became able to co-exist alongside entirely wild lions without them attacking us or running away – indeed, we were only ever attacked by our 'own' lions. When I fitted the collars, I was putting my hand into the lion's maw and they understood and allowed me to do it. It felt great. And I had to keep on doing it, too. We did Freddie, Arusha and Gigi next, and after that we had to adjust the collars every few months for a couple of years. There was something magical about being able to communicate with the lions at such a level that I could get away with putting collars on them. And there was something magical, too, about what the collars did for our lives. It took a few weeks to discover what all the squawks and beeps meant on the headphones but once I'd figured it out our daily routine moved on to another plane. Instead of scratching about in the dust looking for tracks we could find the lions pretty much at will. George would drive the Land Rover while I stood on the back, holding the aerial and searching for spoor: we must have looked like a mad professor and his brainwashed disciple.

In mid-1975, after years of exemplary motherhood, Juma seemed to decide she was fed up with it. She had brought up her own cubs and Lisa's two with quiet competence and startling success. She had taught them how to hunt and look after themselves. They were now as efficient a bunch of killers as you could hope to meet. Then one day she crossed the Rubicon towards Meru and never returned. Independent and wild as the cubs were, George and I still had a paternalistic interest in their welfare. We didn't want them to get into trouble by eating domestic stock or straying too near villages. This was one of our worst fears as they were less scared of humans than a wild lion should be because we had babysat them as cubs and they had always lived near our camp. Nevertheless, they were completely wild so there was no way we could collar them without using an immobilizing drug and we wanted to avoid doing that if at all possible.

Leakey, the gormless but lovable lion who at two and a half was their age, was our best hope. Despite being a very slow learner, he was brilliant at making friends, a bullshitter of note who turned out to have more balls than we had ever imagined. George and I decided on a risky strategy to introduce Juma's older and more streetwise offspring to him, the Switzerland of the leonine world. We put out a camel carcass from Asako when we knew that the now big sub-adults were on their way to camp and allowed Leakey to get well installed on it. We held our breath as the four cubs swaggered up to camp and stopped dead, tails twitching as they stared at him. Instead of turning tail as we had feared, Leakey let out an earth-shattering roar at which the cubs came over all submissive. Then he invited them on to the carcass. This spectacular display of chutzpah worked. Leakey became firm buddies with Juma's cubs and they quickly taught him how to hunt and accepted him as one of their own. Now with Leakey's radio collar, as long as he was with them, we could always find them and steer them away from the ever-increasing dangers of Kora. As the prides grew to include wild lions, cautious lions and self-sufficient lions, there were always a few we knew well enough to collar without calling in the boys with the dart guns and the certificates.

The collars took a great load off our shoulders but there was a lot to be concerned about. We bumped into illegal grazers ever more frequently and there were no rhinos left. At the same time we had more surprise visitors as George's fame continued to grow. Among others, Ali MacGraw – then hugely famous following the success of 1970's *Love Story* – stopped over when the American tennis player Stan Singer was with us. They helped us to understand fundraising for the first time. They showed us what we should do to make sure the project didn't wither away. Stan went back to the States and set up the Kora Trust, the direct ancestor of the Tony Fitzjohn/George Adamson Wildlife Trust. Ali is still its president.

Around the time that we were first using the radio collars there was an example of how faithful and trustworthy the lions could be. But they were still lions. We always slept under the stars at Kora but we each had our own hut outside which we would hang our mosquito nets. One beautiful morning March I woke up early. The bloom of green that the rains had brought to Kora made it especially beautiful that year. I'm a desert man but it felt good to be alive as the desert came out of hibernation. I was very annoying in those days. Incredibly fit, I always woke up full of energy and raring to get on with the day. George hadn't surfaced so I put on my flip-flops, picked up my stick and ran with the lions the mile or so down to the *lugga*, across it and up the 300-foot Boy's Rock on the other side. I had reached the top and was enjoying the sight of the sun strengthening over Kora when I saw George coming up the hill behind me.

He started to play a game with Arusha who had been lagging behind. George hid behind a rock, poking his head out every now and then. Arusha pricked up her ears, went bounding down the rocks and jumped on to his back. She knocked him over and he fell awkwardly. Immediately I saw something was wrong and came barrelling down the rocks with Freddie and Gigi chasing after me. It didn't look good. George was lying on his back with

Arusha on top of him. With the strength of panic, I grabbed Arusha and flipped her over but she came straight back at George. She was playing but something was wrong. She didn't have her claws out and she wasn't biting George but she wasn't backing off either. George was still on the ground, groaning in obvious pain, when Arusha took another lunge at him. I saw red and threw her over my shoulder before punching and biting her. I gave her everything I could, which, given that she was almost a full-grown lioness, made little physical impact but she did understand how angry I was. She submitted to me as to a dominant male and slunk off into the bush. I put George over my shoulders and began to walk down the rocks but it was too painful for him; he had to lie down every few yards. I couldn't leave him there with Arusha prowling about and I couldn't carry him either. He had broken his pelvis and was in agony. I didn't know how I was going to get him back to the camp.

When there's a fight or a kill or some other kind of commotion, lions usually get very antsy and twitchy. It's not as extreme but it's a bit like sharks in a feeding frenzy: something instinctive and primeval takes over. Arusha had obviously been stimulated by George falling over, thus losing his dominant status, but with Freddie, the opposite happened. He knew George and I were in trouble and was keen to help. It was as if Freddie knew exactly what was going on and was talking to me. He sat down calmly by George and said, 'Don't worry. I'll look after the Old Man.' I believed him and I was right to do so. I ran back to camp and got the Land Rover and a bottle of whisky. On my return Freddie was still guarding the Old Man, and had already lashed out at Arusha a couple of times. I got some whisky into George, before the pain got too bad, and our old friend Jack Barrah managed to get the Flying Doctors up later in the day to take him to hospital. I don't know what I'd have done without Freddie. I'm sure I'd have worked it out eventually, but there had been an amazing moment of communication between us. I'd known it was safe to leave George because Freddie had told me it was.

The Flying Doctors, as ever, were fabulous and had George in hospital within hours. He was away for weeks and I was left on my own with the lions. I spent happy drawn-out days, working out how to use the new equipment and going on long walks with my pride. I milked every minute of sunlight, then slept the clock round before repeating the process. I soon became quite expert with the tracking equipment and could tell not only which direction the lions had gone in but also whether they were on high ground, in dense bush or nearby. Terence's new tracks, cut with the help of the Frankfurt Zoo tractor, made it easy for me to slip across by road to the closest point, pick up the lions' spoor, then follow them on foot.

Not long after George returned from hospital – and the stress of convalescing at Joy's house – we had another disaster, one entirely of my making. I had spent a long day in Garissa, doing a resupply and meeting up with my game warden friend Noor Abdi Ogle. It was boiling hot at four in the afternoon and I didn't look around as thoroughly as I should have. I had missed Freddie and the cubs so jumped out of the Land Rover to say hello to them as soon as I arrived. During the greeting Arusha killed a guinea fowl up against the fence. I went inside the fence to have a beer with George, who said he was having trouble getting the cubs in and was worried as he didn't know where Leakey and the big lions were. I went outside again and was crouching on the ground talking to Fred, when I felt a tremendous force hit me between the shoulder-blades and on my head. A lion whose strength was way beyond that of the cubs was attacking me. It sank its teeth into my shoulder and shook me like a shark with a seal pup. You know what happened next – it's how I started this book. The big lion got my head into his mouth and started to squeeze. There was nothing I could do and I blacked out for a moment; he was so powerful that everything I tried was fruitless. None of the fancy judo moves I had used on Arusha were any good to me now and I didn't seem to have any strength at all. I just didn't have the energy to fight him off.

Then I saw Freddie coming for me and thought, Oh, no. An incredibly close relationship and when push comes to shove I'm just another bit of prey. But Freddie wasn't coming for me at all. He was going for the big lion that had attacked me. The attacker must have been twice Freddie's size but Freddie attacked again and again with extraordinary bravery and the same loyalty he had displayed when Arusha had set upon the Old Man. And hard up behind Freddie came the Old Man himself. Alerted by Erigumsa, he came out unarmed, waving a stick and shouting at the top of his lungs. Astonishingly it worked. I owe my life to two incredible bonds – one with an old man I loved and who loved me, another with a young lion who would have laid down his life for me. The experience was humbling in countless ways and determined how I have spent the rest of my life.

I was incredibly lucky to survive. My attacker's teeth had come within millimetres of both my carotid and jugular arteries. There were holes in my throat I could put a fist through – and did. I opened my hand inside and my fingers came out of the tooth holes at the back of my neck. George and Erigumsa dragged me back into camp where I lay, blood pouring from my neck and shoulder.

'*Atakufa*,' said Terence, when he saw me. He will die.

This made me so angry that I started feeling better immediately. Terence poured neat Savlon on my wounds as George filled me up with whisky and veterinary Valium. It was a long wait before the Flying Doctors could collect me the next morning. People say you can't remember pain. Utter rubbish. It was the worst night of my life – I was in excruciating agony and I wasn't well psychologically either. I really thought I was going to die as I lay through the long night with George watching over me.

And so did George, he told me later. On top of the pain, I kept thinking, What will happen now? Who will look after the Old Man? Will they close the project down? Who will raise the cubs?

Daylight, and the promise of rescue, was a blessed relief but the long and bumpy drive to the airstrip was agonizing; it took George well over two hours going as carefully as he could. He had been working the radio during the night and had contacted Lindsay, my new girlfriend, in Nairobi. She had pulled every string she knew and had the Flying Doctors' plane in the air as soon as possible; it was with us by ten a.m. The relief of seeing her (and taking the pethidine the nurse had brought) was quite phenomenal. Indeed, I was able to laugh when the stretcher didn't fit into the brand new plane and they had to walk me in. From the moment Lindsay arrived, I was cosseted and comforted, cleaned up, then cured. It was testament to how healthy I was that I recovered so quickly. Thirteen days after being at death's door, Nairobi Hospital threw me out for making too much of a disturbance.

The lion had taken a chunk out of both my shoulders and bitten me in the waist. He had knocked out a tooth and ripped off one of my ears. I had scars all over my head where his claws had torn into me. All in all, however, I got off very lightly. When George had come charging on to the scene the battle had already been won: the lion had been dragging me off to eat me in the shade. As I walked out of hospital two weeks later, shaky but under my own steam, I saw John Mutinda coming in, a worried frown on his face.

'Who are you coming to see?' I asked.

'You, Tony.' He was lost for words at the sight of me, then smiled and said, 'I thought I told you to keep it safe.'

'Oh, don't worry, John. It was only me,' I said.

He smiled and helped me to the car. The lion project was safe for a while longer.

I had to stay in Nairobi for at least a month as various complications from the attack kept cropping up. There was something wrong with my spleen and I had a massive malaria attack, brought on by general weakness.

George sent me a wonderful letter that I have treasured to this day, telling me what had gone on after I left.

Kora
25th. June

Dear Tony,

      Getting chewed up by a lion is one of our occupational hazards, so there is nothing for you to blame yourself for. It could just as easily have happened to me. For the sake of the lions, one can be thankful that it was not an African ! What does a bloody mzungu matter ?! It is great to know that you are getting on so well and I hope the hospital has not been too much of a bore for you. I have not been able to find your tooth. Haragumsa says he saw it lying at the foot of your bed when he was helping Terence to clean you up. Perhaps Mad , Bad or Worse have gone off with it.

(George had a habit of mangling people's names, so 'Haragumsa' is Erigumsa. And 'Mad, Bad and Worse' were resident fan-tailed ravens.) George explained that the lion that had got me had disappeared, but then returned to camp thirty-six hours later. It was Shyman, one of Juma's now adult cubs. My blood was still all over his muzzle and paws; lions are just as obsessive about keeping clean as their domestic cousins so this was very unnatural behaviour, as was the attack itself. George studied him for a while and when Shyman drunkenly and nastily started going for the young lions with patently evil intent, he realized something was wrong, got between them and shot him in the brain. He was convinced that Shyman had been poisoned by the Somali poachers who were systematically killing all the rhinos in the reserve and poisoning the carcasses, an opinion informed by Shyman's uncharacteristic behaviour and the fact that a rhino had been killed nearby a few nights previously.

Shyman had always been a bit tricky compared to his brother Daniel and Lisa's cubs, with whom he had grown up. He took after his shy and wary mother, Juma, but I had known him almost since the day of his birth and had never had a problem before. This was one of the reasons why the murderous attack was so shocking.

When at last I got back to camp a couple of months later, I was nervous that things would not be as they were. I need not have worried. As soon as I arrived George and I went off to find the cubs. They looked at me with amazement, then hurled themselves at me. Arusha threw herself into my arms; Freddie, who had come off worst in a scrap with a wild lion, limped down from the camp rocks and hugged me; Gigi bounded up to join in and Growlie came close but was just too shy to say hello so sat down under a bush and forgot to growl. It was a great moment and allayed a lot of my fears. But, from the perspective of two months away, I could see that things were changing in Kora.

The fact that Kora had become a national reserve was having scant effect on the poachers and illegal grazers. I would say that storm clouds were gathering but, in fact, we longed for them. Kenya was suffering from a terrible drought so the nomadic Somali and Orma people were travelling long distances to find grazing for their massive herds. Occasionally the Somalis would move through Asako or one of our other neighbouring villages, daring the cowed inhabitants to protest. Their herds were like locusts, eating crops and fodder and anything else they could find. Kora wasn't much good for grazing cattle but they could still strip it clean, hastening the process of desertification. And the riverine forest along the Tana was perfect browsing for camels and goats so they cut down hundred-year-old poplars for an hour's feed. Lions and domestic stock do not make happy companions, however well-brought-up the lions, so the encroachment was of real concern. John Mutinda had told me to 'keep it safe'. He had allowed me to get away with being mauled myself but, as George had noted in his letter, if anything happened to an African – even one who was trespassing – there would be trouble. We owed it to John to make sure this didn't happen but it was a constant struggle and involved a lot of driving to Garissa to beg Philip Kilonzo to keep the illegal grazers away from us. He did the best he could but it was far from easy – and there was nothing anyone could do about the poachers. They were determined, motivated and armed to the teeth.

As Esmond had discovered, the origins of the poaching problem lay in the increased demand for rhino horn from Yemen, but the supply was met by the Cold War. Kenya's northern neighbours were fighting a particularly nasty war over a patch of grey bush that divides Ethiopia and Somalia. The war was made yet more unpleasant by the cynicism of the two countries' backers. Until 1974 the United States had supported Haile Selassie in Ethiopia while the Russians had poured arms into Somalia. Ethiopia had become less strategically important and Haile Selassie's successor claimed to be Communist, so when the Soviet Union started flirting with Ethiopia, the Americans swapped their support to Somalia overnight. During the war that followed, thousands of US-armed Somalis encroached into Kenya, looking first for rhino horn and then for elephant ivory. At Kora, we had none to spare but plenty of both. The ivory wars were in the future, but the rhino poaching was a clear and present danger. Early in 1976, we saw six Wakamba poachers with bows and arrows down on the river. By the end of that year, the Somalis were on the attack and the slaughter was gaining pace; we looked fondly back upon the Wakamba poachers as bucolic figures of a bygone era.

In spring 1976 I went to visit Bill Woodley in Mweiga on the slopes of the Aberdares where he was warden of the Mountain Parks, which included the Aberdares and Mount Kenya. He told me poachers were moving into Tsavo. Jack Barrah told us that further down the Tana from us, the Somali poachers were follow-ing 'a policy of total extinction'. Poaching on a major scale had not yet come to Bill's Mount Kenya National Park but he was having a problem with people getting lost or injured when climb-ing the mountain. He took me on a mountain rescue and discussed his plans for setting up a real mountain rescue team. As we were hurtling down a gorge in his Piper Super Cub he asked me if I wanted another lioness. 'Of course,' I replied, and returned to Kora a few days later with Jojo, who had been orphaned in the Masai Mara.

Kaunda, who had come to us from the Nairobi orphanage, joined Jojo as the newest recruits. We now had three separate prides. Daniel, Oscar and Kora were thriving without Shyman and Juma. We still tracked them and saw them occasionally but they were completely independent. Freddie, Arusha, Growlie and Gigi were moving around together and had started interact-ing with each other and with wild lions. Leakey continued his shuttle diplomacy, bouncing between the three groups and help-ing us to keep tabs on them with his collar. Keeping track of them all was exhausting work, particularly when George was away. George would get ill occasionally – pneumonia and malaria usually – and I felt a huge responsibility not to let any harm come to his lions while he was out of camp. In retrospect we probably had too many and I should have taken a break but I loved it so.

My life was totally, utterly and completely absorbed in Kampi ya Simba. I felt no need to go abroad: I loved Kenya, I loved George and I loved the job. And, of course, I adored the lions. It was startlingly hard work, though, and very intense. Deter-mining how the groups would behave, bringing them together or keeping them apart as we saw fit, required a lot of thought and then arduous work to put into practice. We were incredibly lucky to have Leakey's help with the diplomacy – we could always use him as an emissary between the groups.

Friends came and went, brought supplies and were fascinated by the lions and our relationships with them. We had to be very careful not to involve them with the lions: they were used to us but always got a bit twitchy when strangers were around. People used to drive hundreds of kilometres to see George with the lions and then be furious that we made them stay in the cage or, as we often had to do, pretended we didn't know where the lions were. We were lucky that Arusha was around when Jack Barrah arrived one day with two planes and Prince Bernhard of the Netherlands. Although she had a habit of knocking over George, she was incredibly friendly and easy to get along with. We fed the prince on corned beef and tinned fruit but he was so enthralled by Arusha that he didn't seem to mind the rather basic food.

After lunch we climbed up on to Kora Rock to look at the sky. It was blood red. A massive dust storm had blown up in Tsavo and stained the sky from horizon to horizon. George treated the prince just as he would anyone else and was astonished when he made an enormous unsolicited donation to help develop Kora. His money allowed Jack Barrah to start the rangers' base in Asako and man it for years. Donors who have vision enough to fund the boring things, like ranger lines, drains and roads, are rare indeed. Later that year, Frankfurt Zoo's tractor, another unglamorous but invaluable donation that Terence had been using daily, at last broke through to the Kyuso road on the main drag to Mwingi. The job would have taken years without it.

As ever, the lions were our *raison d'être* and we wanted to make that journey to Nairobi as seldom as possible. Adrian House, who was George's editor and biographer, came out at about this time to help George write *My Pride and Joy*. He asked me to work out the linkages between the different lions from which scrappy piece of paper he created the meticulous family trees (see the Kora Family Tree, page 318). I think we had done pretty well. By the end of 1976, Daniel, Oscar and Kora were living proof that returning lions to the wild was possible and sustainable. We hardly saw them but we knew they were still around. Arusha was pregnant again, having had an earlier miscarriage. Freddie and Leakey were increasingly independent and the cubs were growing up. On Boxing Day 1976, George and I took the cubs down to the river for the first time. It was wonderful to see their faces light up when they came through the forest and saw the Tana in all its glory. We were happy that Christmas.

5. Trial by Simba

A radio call came through on New Year's Day 1977 announcing the death of Gloria Lowe. A good friend and one of our staunchest supporters, she had campaigned for us at National Park Headquarters with Chryssee Bradley Martin and together they had made sure that the orphanage sent lions our way. It had been at Gloria's urging that we took on Leakey, a mark of official approval we sorely needed at the time. We then went on to prove the efficacy of our methods by reintegrating him successfully. It was a sad start to the year and, although we didn't see it at the time, Gloria's death stands out as a signpost of things to come.

On the rocks above Kampi ya Simba we toasted our departed friend and assessed how the lion programme was going. As we sat on the striated gneiss rocks, the view emphasized our isolation. The camp lies in the lee of three spectacular inselbergs, rising from a sea of thick bush: the huge rock outcrops soaring three hundred feet from the flat bush give parts of Kora the look of Monument Valley, where John Ford filmed all those old Westerns. From the rocks, the view stretched for hundreds of miles in which it was impossible to see anything man-made that we hadn't built ourselves. Even so, the wider world was beginning to encroach upon the idyllic life we led at Kora; the most apparent change was the smell. The stench of death was beginning to pervade every corner of the reserve. Drawn south by the lure of horn, the Somali poachers had wiped out all the rhino and were now setting their sights on Kora's elephant population. Given that they were AK47 sights it wasn't going to take them long. Many nights we were awoken by the sound of shooting and the first thing we saw from the rocks in the mornings would be teetering towers of vultures, spiralling down on to the latest victim. Nowadays there are few vultures left – they have all eaten poisoned carcasses left out by herders to deter predators.

There is something obscene and wasteful about the slaughter of a vast elephant, its tusks hacked out with axes, an enormous cadaver left to rot in the sun. In Kenya that year – as in most years – people were starving. The price of meat had soared 75 per cent; staples were less severely affected but the whole nation was suffering. The wasted elephant meat was particularly grotesque: if they were going to kill the animals, they could at least have used their carcasses efficiently. This was indicative of a larger change in the Somalis. Traditionally the herders had always dug wells in the dry riverbeds as they moved with their stock. Whenever they did this, they would always dig another well a few hundred yards away for the wild animals and never use it themselves. Custom and the example of the elders who led them dictated this. George, who had worked in the north of Kenya for decades, was well known to the elders: sometimes in person, always by renown. They respected his right to be in Kora. But the poachers and herders coming to Kora now cared naught for the Old Man, not a jot for the animals and nothing for the environment.

They were not pastoralists from northern Kenya, grazing their own animals; increasingly they were from Kismayu on the eastern Somali coast, Bosasso in the north of Somalia and all points between. A Western-primed population explosion was laying waste to East Africa. Young Somali men were herding for livestock barons, vast unsustainable herds that had to roam many hundreds of miles in search of forage and grazing. Simultaneously they established themselves to be the heart of the domestic and export markets for cattle throughout Kenya. Now, we noticed, there were no elders accompanying the young men and fewer families too. The herders never dug an extra well for the wild animals as they used to: they took only the most valuable parts of the animals they killed; they left poisoned bait in wide circles around their camps and burnt extravagantly wherever they went. The ancient doum palms, Tana river poplars and *Acacia eliator* that lined the banks of the river were being burnt by pyromaniac youths, merely for the hell of it – hundreds of years of growth destroyed in a matter of minutes. Such wanton destruction would never have been allowed under the elder system with which George had worked throughout his time as a game warden. And there wasn't much we could do to halt it. The forces of law and order in Kora consisted of George, myself and Terence. The warden and rangers confined themselves to Asako. We chased after the poachers with hunting rifles when we stumbled upon them but they played with us, always keeping one step ahead and, if we got too close, shooting over our heads with their modern automatic weapons. Bizarrely they never tried to kill us but neither would they go away. It was incredibly frustrating.

Five hours away in Garissa there was more formidable opposition but the poachers were well aware of its capabilities. My friend Noor Abdi Ogle and his anti-poaching teams did a grand job. I'm sure it was because of our friendship with him that the poaching gangs didn't just kill us outright. The police, General Service Unit (GSU) and army all fought brave battles against the invaders but they were neither equipped nor authorized to fight what was in effect an all-out war. The Kenyan authorities had to tread extremely carefully as the Somali government had ambitions upon Kenyan territory that they had no wish to provoke. Protecting us and the lions was not high on their list of priorities when held against maintaining peace among their neighbours in 1970s East Africa. These were tough days and they would only get tougher.

Nonetheless, despite all the poaching and the price rises, looking after the lions was so all-encompassing that it was only when we glanced over the parapet that we noticed such things. As always, our every waking hour was devoted to the care of our growing family of lions. Arusha, Growlie and Gigi were pretty independent by this time, coming and going at will but still bringing their cubs to show them off to us. Jojo and Kaunda were beginning their integration back into the wild and in January spent their first night out alone. We hadn't seen Daniel, Oscar and Kora for a couple of months. Freddie and Leakey, we accepted, were long gone – off to the other side of the river where game was plentiful among the open spaces and heavenly herds in Meru National Park.

Arusha was desperate for a mate after the failure of her first pregnancy and competed with the gunfire to keep us awake at night, roaring her availability from the rocks just outside camp. There is a peculiar note in a lioness's call when she is looking for a mate and it can be heard for miles. Many were the nights we listened to the wild lions scrapping over her, then mating endlessly as we three men lay on our camp beds thinking of England. It didn't stop at night either. I once walked up on to Kora Rock to find Arusha and a wild lion having a post-coital nap that I should never have interrupted. The male looked utterly outraged but was so shocked that, when I charged him, he backed down and slunk off into the bush. Luckily Arusha didn't expect me to take his place.

Even with Gloria gone, more lions continued to come our way and, like children in a sweet factory, we were unable to say no. And when Gigi gave birth we called the cubs Glowe and Growe in honour of Gloria and her husband Graham Lowe. Our vet friend Aart Visee was staying in camp when we received a radio call saying that Galana had a couple of lion cubs for us. We patched up the holding pen and set off to Malindi on the coast for some fun. I had been staying with PA and Agneta in Malindi when I first received George's call so I knew it well; Aart and I had a great couple of days, surfing, catching up with friends and lounging on the beach. It was the first proper time off I had enjoyed since Shyman had attacked me. After the harsh, dry heat of Kora, it was wonderful to be in the water, playing in the surf and diving on the reef. We made midnight excursions to the Gedi ruins and sailed up to Lamu with some easily impressed holiday-makers. It's hard taking a break when you're completely consumed by something you love and I had failed to do so for almost a year. As soon as I arrived, I could feel the tension in my back drifting away as I swam out to the break, opening my shoulders and powering through the surf. Our holiday was too short.

At eight months, the cubs were a little larger and a lot more rambunctious than we had expected so we stayed at Galana for a few hours while its wildlife manager, Ken Clarke, modified our capture cage to keep the two cubs separated on the journey back to Kora. He remade them as crush cages so that the lions would be held tight and wouldn't be able to injure themselves when the tranquillizers Aart administered wore off. Ken told us about the poaching problems he was facing on the million-acre ranch where elephant carcasses were turning up almost every day. Galana – like Kora – was being overrun by Somalis, keen to kill all of its rhino and elephant. The ranch was the last buffer zone left between the poachers and Tsavo National Park, the vast area whose elephant population would soon be left wide open to incursions from the north. Galana was a very successful operation so Ken had the financial muscle to run anti-poaching patrols by land and air but even then he felt he was receiving hindrance rather than assistance from the authorities and was probably fighting a losing battle. It was becoming increasingly apparent to him that, while the rhino poaching was mainly a foreign affair, the elephant poaching had local backing. It dawned on none of us then that the poaching could get any worse. But, in fact, it was about to enter a more industrial phase: this was the last time we would see Ken alive.

As Aart and I drove off towards Garissa, the lions turned right around in the tight crush cages Ken had made for them.

'My God, did you see that?' I said to Aart.

'They're cats, Tony,' said the vet, with a condescending smile.

Sheba was a captivating lioness, similar to Lisa in temperament and very beautiful. Suleiman on the other hand was an awkward SOB. Ken had killed his mother when she was attacking a cattle *boma* at Galana and one of the bullets had passed through her and into Suleiman. It was encapsulated in fat so we left it there as it was causing no harm – but it was a reminder that Suleiman was the offspring of a wild stock-killer rather than a store-bought hippie, like Christian or Arusha. We put the pair into the holding pens at camp and hoped they would adjust, but from the very beginning they didn't get on with the other lions at all – there were just too many. We weren't sure what to do. Every time Arusha, Gigi and Growlie came near they would charge the fence with spectacular ferocity. I remember being nervous that one day the mesh might not hold.

We needed Leakey to do some diplomacy but he'd gone off with Freddie and we hadn't seen either of them for ages. In the time being we kept walking Jojo and Kaunda and hoped that a solution would present itself as we immersed ourselves once more in the lions' world. We stayed in touch with the other world by playing host to a slow trickle of visitors who would bring us supplies, gossip and news. Despite the growing insecurity of Kora and Kenya as a whole we still had a good many. Father Nicky Hennitty, a wonderfully hyperactive and dedicated Irish Catholic priest who lived in Kyuso, came over often. He had a sixth sense about us and used to load up his new Toyota Stout and resupply us with fuel, gas for the fridges, food and whisky when he judged we were getting thirsty. The fact that we no longer listened to the radio led to odd juxtapositions of news. Eras ended simultaneously. We learnt, for example, that Elvis had died and 'sport' hunting had been banned on the very same day. The latter was of rather more significance to us.

Although George and Terence had stopped hunting long before they began working for the Game Department, many of their friends – and, indeed, mine – were professional hunters or had been, so it was with mixed feelings that we heard of the destruction of our friends' livelihoods. We had seen few hunters near Kora recently; the area had been famed for its elephants but elephant hunting had, of course, already been banned. Also, the bush around us was so thick that it was hard country for hunting anything smaller, and none of the licensed hunters would think of going after lions in the hunting block adjacent to us for fear of killing one of ours. However, the ban proved positive for some affected by it: Ben Ng'anga, with whom Mike Wamalwa and I had been partners in the Mateus Rosé venture, came to run a new camp at Bisanadi, thirty miles away on the other side of the river. It was a long way to go for a drink but it was good to have such a close friend nearby. Ben had been one of the first professional black hunters but the ban meant his triumph hadn't lasted for very long. Even today the safari business remains dominated by white Kenyans and expatriates, testament more to the racism of the clients than of the safari business itself. Visitors still want to be guided by Robert Redford in his Denys Finch Hatton role: black Kenyans just don't attract the rich clients the way white ones do so Ben's achievement had been significant. He was also worth every penny.

Former hunters always insist that their departure hastened the slaughter of the elephants and I don't suppose we'll ever know the truth. We were on the very front line and it was total war up there for a while. I can't see how a few professional hunters could have stood up to the mechanized killing outfits sent down from the north, like Geronimo trying to stop the buffalo killing in the US. And I still find it hard to believe that you have to legalize something's killing to protect it. It's the old apartheid defence and it just doesn't pass muster. Nevertheless, it must be said that as soon as game no longer had a value, people stopped investing in protecting it. On Galana, for example, the owners immediately squeezed funding to Ken Clarke's anti-poaching teams. The results were shattering and immediate. The ranch was overrun by poachers. On 2 August, I heard the scratchy voice of Ken's eighteen-year-old daughter Caroline on the radio. She was trying to get through to Nairobi Control but they couldn't hear her because of a bad 'skip'. She had to relay her news through me. 'Daddy has been killed,' she told me. The poor girl was in a terrible state, unable to call directly for help and stranded on Galana with her father's bullet-torn body.

It was one of the most frightful things I've ever had to do. We had only been with Ken – a big, happy, tough, kindly man – a few brief months before. He was one of the few, the new breed of rancher/wardens who would lead the way in the preservation of wildlife against well-armed gangs of poachers. Others after him turned a blind eye. But for now there were family to inform in Nairobi, the radio was crackling and fading, everyone was shouting and repeating back fragments of messages, and other people were trying to barge in as they couldn't hear anyone else on the frequency. It was awful. When it was all over and I'd told everyone I had been asked to, George and I had a silent drink to Ken and tried not to think of our own vulnerability.

It emerged that Ken had chased some poachers after he had come across a herd of slaughtered elephant on the ranch. One poacher had stayed behind and shot Ken in the stomach as he set off in pursuit. It was a terrible way for a brave man to die. Ken's death was yet another example of how the country was buckling under pressure from its northerly neighbour. The Northern Frontier District and the Ukambani region of Kenya were already destabilized by the poaching gangs and they were now threatening the rest of the country. The government had been trying to sweep the problem under the carpet but the problem was bigger than the carpet. Just a few days after Ken's death, Game Department pilot Wazir Ali's plane was hit by poachers in Tsavo, bordering Galana. Young rangers were being killed weekly – giving their lives to save the elephants. Vast swathes of the country were becoming inaccessible and the Somalis had long ago formed a bridgehead south of the accepted geographical Tana river dividing line. I still had to make supply trips to Garissa every three weeks or so and they were becoming increasingly hairy. It wasn't just us under threat: the army and police were always tearing about the place, trying to take the fight to the poachers but, with little support from Headquarters, they too were fighting a losing battle. Philip Kilonzo – the deputy head of police in Garissa – said that he was happy to provide me with an escort to Kora. 'But who would escort the escort back?' he asked, shortly before he was transferred.

Even with the threat of ambush, going to Garissa was always fun. I usually took Erigumsa along to help with any breakdowns or punctures on the way because the only thing that was certain about a trip to Garissa was that it would never be eventless. The road was so rough that bits always fell off the car, yet more so because we had to keep the speed up in order to get there and back in a day. As the months went by and the poachers became more daring, speed became even more crucial: a speeding car provides a harder target. Luckily there was almost no traffic: if you met someone, you didn't just wave, you stopped for a chat and a drink. Once I had a car full of people and was hurtling along the sandy track when I hit a rock and the radiator fell out of the Land Rover. It took all our ingenuity to get it back into working order. I tapped a frankincense tree for some of the thick gooey incense, then heated it on a spade and used it to plug the radiator's holes. Erigumsa braved the crocodiles to get some water from the river two miles away to refill the radiator and we made rope out of strips of bark to tie the thing back into the engine compartment. We were late into Garissa but we made it.

The first thing I would do on arrival in Garissa was to stop for a drink at Mathenge's Bar just before the bridge on the way into town. An old-style shebeen on the edge of the river, its toilets and short-time rooms were always falling into the muddy waters below as the torrent eroded the foundations. The bridge was a magnificent structure, always guarded by a collection of police and soldiers from the nearby camps. I knew almost all of them by name. The town was on the other side of the bridge, dwarfed by it – just three streets, a couple of mosques and a petrol station, all there because this was the only bridge for hundreds of miles. A frontier town indeed, and one in which I have always felt at home.

My first stop after the bar would be Fahim Bayusuf's house. A real wheeler-dealer, Fahim was a Kenyan Arab with fingers in many pies. From his small office behind the counter of his hardware shop, he would send minions in all directions, looking for parts for the cars, pipes, tools or anything else on my shopping list, which would then be delivered back to his shop. The Bayusufs now own one of the biggest trucking companies in East Africa. While we waited for things to arrive, Fahim's mother would feed me up in the knowledge that I would need a full stomach as a foundation for my day's drinking. I had many wonderful breakfasts there of tea, deep-fried doughnuts and whatever fruit was available before I started the day's meetings.

I found a typical shopping list of the period just the other day:

sugar
30.06 ammo
1 case tinned carrots
drill bits
sardines

1 snake-bite serum
1 tin Cape gooseberries
whisky
orange squash
corned beef

Ours was not a luxurious life!

After breakfast with the Bayusufs I would do the rounds of the tiny but throbbing town. I always visited the police and army messes, greeted Philip Kilonzo at the police station, and went to see if there was anything to learn at the Game Department office. Usually I called in at the police workshop to scrounge a part or two for the cars. There were many other small shops where I would receive a welcome as warm as that from Fahim's family but none looked after me so well as the Bayusufs. Every now and then I would nip into the bar by the bridge for a sharpener until all my errands were finished. I would often have to leave orders with Fahim for things to be collected at the next resupply. Amazingly they would appear before our return from camp, delivered by bus or brought up by a friend in a pickup.

The five-hour drive back to Kora was always a grind after a long day in Garissa, but as we got closer to home, the soporific effect of the beer would wear off and the occasional glimpses of the river become more familiar. For most of the way, the road follows the Tana but the thickness of the riverine forest hides it from view. Nothing, however, can hide the three soaring inselbergs that rise above the camp at Kora – Kora Rock, Christian's Rock and Kora Tit make an exciting target, particularly as you drive the final few miles. Approaching cars can be heard from miles away so the big chain-link gates used to swing open as we arrived home to be greeted by the hornbills, the ravens and the mongooses. George would have a cold drink ready for me, Hamisi the cook would be stirring something disgusting over the fire, and the lions would be pacing the fence, waiting for me to exit the little gate in front of the mess and greet them formally. It was always great to be home.

We would never have lasted so long without the help of our many friends and as ever it remained the unlikely people that helped us. The British Army, for example, were invaluable. The commander at the time was a Colonel Chris Lawrence, whom I had met one day while visiting some army friends at Kahawa barracks. He had been rather interested in what I was doing in their spare-parts store. Chris was in charge of all army training in Kenya and used to send up teams of men to overhaul our equipment and service the Land Rovers – great training for them and a wonderful gift to us. We showed them a good time and they got to see the lions and experience our life in the wilds by way of recompense, but it wasn't a fair deal. We were extraordinarily lucky. It made a huge difference to have proper Land Rover mechanics working on our equipment, particularly as all of it was well past its sell-by date.

Father Nicky Hennitty should have despised us as godless heathens but instead he went out of his way to help us long before he became the firm friend that he is today. Nicky occasionally arrived at camp with truckloads of adoring nuns, all of whom referred to him as 'The Man'. Amazed by my long hair, they called me 'Jesus Christ Superstar'. It was quite as bizarre as it sounds.

In the middle of 1977 George had to go to Nairobi for an operation, which meant I had to look after the lions on my own. Always a crushing responsibility, it was even harder now that we had four different groups. George was integral to what made Kora special, and when he wasn't there, the things that we enjoyed doing together soon became hard work. With George, walking the cubs was exciting and fun, but on my own, it was extremely stressful as I had to keep an eye on them at all times or I would be up all night searching for them with no one to watch my back.

George felt this responsibility much less than I did: they were his lions and he knew what was best for them. I had to decide what was best for them *and* anticipate what George would want for them. The stress was not from the animals themselves but from the worry of 'What if I lose one while he's away?' Suleiman and Sheba were still causing problems, and while George was away I had to keep them firmly under control. Growlie had come back with her cubs and taken an instant dislike to the newcomers; Jojo and Kaunda were terrified of them. When I wasn't there, George had to keep Suleiman and Sheba locked up for long periods. It took a lot of physical strength to manage them so I tried not to be away, except for the briefest of trips.

One such trip took place when George had returned from convalescing after his operation. I headed off to Nairobi for two days, warning him that he shouldn't let Suleiman and Sheba out of their holding cage. I had decided that the only solution to the problem was to set up a satellite camp where we could prepare the newcomers for release without disturbing the progress of the other groups. I had not thought it through properly, though, and needed to sell the idea to George before we did anything. For the time being, I told George as I left, he shouldn't let them out at all. He didn't listen.

The morning after I reached Nairobi, Lindsay received a call from Kampi ya Simba asking her to send the Flying Doctors: George had been mauled by a lion. Their chief pilot, Jim Heather-Hayes, offered to take me with him so it was just a few hours after the attack that I arrived back at camp. We found a badly shaken George sitting on his bed, looking all of his seventy-one years. He was covered in claw and bite marks and had lost a lot of blood.

'Why did you let them out?' I asked.

George just burst into tears. The shock of seeing him cry was much worse than seeing him hurt.

When I arrived back at Kampi ya Simba, having put George on the plane, I went to my normal seat. It was only when I looked at his empty chair that I saw he had left a letter for me on his typewriter. It explained in calm and measured detail what had happened. Ken Smith and a friend had been in camp the day before and George had let the lions out to show Ken how well the programme was working!

While I was fending off Sheba, Suleiman got behind me and jumped on my back, siezing hold of my neck in his jaws. I tried to whack him with my stick, but this made him angry and he started to growl, dig in his claws and close his jaws. Thought this was the end! could feel his teeth going in. Pulled out my revolver and fired two shots in the air. This had no effect. In sheer desperation, I reached over my shoulder and pulled the trigger. Immediately Suleiman let go, uttering a slight grunt. And ran off a few yards to where Sheba was sitting, a little above me. Thought it best to get out as quickly as possible, before I started to feel groggy. I was bleeding quite a lot. Got to the car and drove back to camp. Fortunately, Terence had just returned. Sheba started to follow me down the hill as I returned to the car, but then decided to return to Suleiman. I have no idea how badly Suleiman is hurt. He was sitting up when I left. The place where I left him is about twenty yards above the top end of the rock bar and slightly to the left going up. If you go to look for Suleiman and find him still there, it means he is badly injured, when it might be best to finish him off. If only slightly injured, I think he will come back to camp with Sheba. Without my revolver, Suleiman would have surely killed me.

Shocked, sore, weakened by blood loss and knowing there was infection and exquisite pain to come, George had sat and written to me, detailing exactly where I should go to put Suleiman out of his misery. As always his first concern was for the lions. Shortly after he had finished the letter, however, Suleiman and Sheba had come back to camp. George straightened his shoulders, got his head in gear and walked out from behind the wire. He managed to lure the lions back into their holding cage with some meat from the fridge. His extraordinary display of bravery allowed Suleiman and Sheba to live another day and encouraged me to address the problem.

The immediate situation was that we had two quite big lions prowling the holding cage, one of which was wounded. I sat and looked at them for a while, mustering the courage to go in there. They seemed calm enough but they had given us all a fright and I was a little nervous, to say the least. I knocked back a couple of stiff gins, grabbed a bucket of water and walked into the cage. The two lions greeted me as always and behaved as if nothing had happened. Suleiman even let me feel where the bullet had entered under the skin on his shoulders; just as with the one fired by Ken Clarke it seemed to have missed muscle and lodged in fat beneath the skin. I left it where it was.

George came back to camp a few weeks later, recovered but still weak. It was apparent to us both that we couldn't leave Suleiman and Sheba locked up in the holding cage and if we let them out they would continue to be attacked by the older groups. Oscar, Kora and Daniel tended to ignore them but Arusha and Growlie hated them and beat them up badly whenever they had the chance. We were loath to think what would happen if Blackantan, a new wild lion who was sleeping his way through the pride, came across either Sheba or Suleiman on their own. Eventually we built them a small holding cage five miles from Kampi ya Simba in the upper reaches of Giraffe Lugga. The other lions were not so threatened by them now they were away from the main camp and they immediately started to thrive. Suleiman, however, continued to be a concern.

Suleiman and Sheba were not my only anxiety. George had been away a great deal throughout the whole of 1977 and I had been left to cope alone with the ever-growing number of lions. Only a few of them were particularly difficult; the problem was that rearing one lion is a two-man job, and by this time we had four big groups to look after. Leakey and Freddie had crossed the Tana together in early 1976 but Arusha was still thriving and had just produced two cubs, which she showed to us when they still had blue eyes. Gigi had produced a litter with Blackantan, as had Growlie with Daniel. Kaunda and Jojo were becoming increasingly independent, and so were Suleiman and Sheba.

The stress of looking after all the lions, or maybe just being on my own, had turned me increasingly towards the bottle and I knew I'd been drinking too much. After I had made many transgressions, my girlfriend Lindsay had almost dumped me and I was seldom able to leave camp for fear that George wouldn't be able to manage. It was an unfounded and ill-aimed fear. It was me who was unable to cope, and in March 1978 matters came to a head. I had a raging row with Hamisi, our cook, who was vigorously and rightly defended by George. George and I had our first ever angry words. I stormed out of camp and went AWOL.

To this day I can't remember what I did but I know I went on a hyperactive safari all over Kenya – upcountry, the coast, the deserts. The photographer Peter Beard told me later that I spent two weeks with him in Tsavo. I have no memory of it at all. By the end of four months I was burning the candle at both ends and had nowhere left to go. I had no money, I had fallen out with half of my friends, I had nothing to do. And Lindsay had had enough of me. I was desperate to get back to Kora but too proud to ask. When Kitch Morson – one of George's oldest friends – came and saw me, bringing a note from George, I almost kissed him. I'll never know how it was all worked out but I'm sure there was some sort of intervention. Did George's friends think he needed help? Did George think *I* needed help? Or did everyone think we both needed help? Whatever happened, it was done so that neither of us lost face and could get back to doing what we loved most. Kitch said he had just been to Kora and was shocked at what a state the camp was in. The staff were demoralized, he said, the lions were too much for George and the cars were falling to pieces. George's note came as close to saying, 'Please come back,' as it ever would, and I needed no extra encouragement. I rounded up a couple of mechanics and headed for Kora immediately.

'Hello, Tony. Good to see you,' said George.

'Harrumph,' said Terence.

My absence was never mentioned and life continued as before. It was great to be home.

All the lions were a little surprised that I had been away but recognized me straight away and greeted me as before. There was sad news, though. Suleiman had been killed by a hippo while I had been away and Sheba had been left on her own. This situation, however, had righted itself: Kaunda had crossed the Tana and not been seen for some months, allowing Sheba and Jojo to become friends. We were concerned for Kaunda but relieved that things had worked out for Sheba. She had been so fond of her brother that when he had died she had led George to the spot, watched him bury Suleiman, then sat on the grave for days, refusing to leave him alone. Tricky bugger he may have been, but there must have been something about Suleiman to inspire such devotion from his sister.

I threw myself back into work. All the vehicles had been driven into the ground and needed major repair work – the Land Rover that we used to fetch water from the Tana could scarcely make it up the hill any more. The fridges had deteriorated and a monitor lizard had made its nest in my hut. I worked incredibly hard, cut back on my drinking and went for long walks with George and the lions. I was back to fitness within weeks and not long after that everything at Kampi ya Simba was working as it should.

The same could not be said of Kenya and its immediate environs.

In August, Jomo Kenyatta, Kenya's founding president, died in Mombasa. His death sparked a period of uncertainty that continued for some years and was felt particularly in front-line areas like Kora. There were still a few elephants left to kill in Kora at this point but they had become quite canny at avoiding humans so the Somalis had moved on to killing the human population: much easier. The nearest village, Asako, was under constant threat and any cars on the very few roads in the region were at great risk from the well-armed bandits. Every time I went to Garissa I was convinced I would be ambushed by *shifta* but strangely it never happened. It did, however, add a certain piquancy to the trips. Philip Kilonzo took our safety so seriously that he advised us to dig slit trenches in case we were attacked but, having done so, we kept falling into them after a couple of beers so filled them up again.

When the Somali problem was really hotting up we had an interesting visit from an old friend of George's. Mohamed Sigara was a journalist on Kenya's *Nation* newspaper, the son of a Somali chief who had worked with George for years. He was horrified by what was happening in the area and explained to us how the elder system, which had regulated Somali society for years, had now all but broken down. Population growth and war meant the young men no longer had mentors and, without them, were running riot. Big Men (warlords had yet to be named) in Somalia itself and in Kenyan Somalia were using the young men to terrorize the rest of society and become ever more powerful. Kenyan government policy was extremely anti-Somali and was helping to radicalize Kenyan Somalis, who saw none of the benefits and many hardships from being Kenyan. Mohamed was impressed by everything that we were doing and wrote some very favourable articles about us – but, more importantly, he also gave us a fascinating insight into how things were for his people. The administration was using the 'Somali menace' as a way to unite the country behind the new president, Daniel arap Moi, and many peaceful Kenyan Somalis were being discriminated against. Kenyan Somalis had completely different ID cards from other Kenyans; if they were found without them, they were treated as illegal aliens and deported to Somalia. This alienation fomented the rebellion that makes Kenya's Somali areas today such natural breeding grounds for Islamic extremism.

At the time extremism was starting to grow in Iran, in opposition to the Shah, and having an impact on our visitor numbers because it had caused a world shortage of aviation fuel. This was a relief as George's fame continued to grow and Kora was becoming something of a tourist attraction. The good and interesting visitors continued to make it through. Intrepid safari guide Richard Bonham used to fly in every now and then. And Joan and Alan Root spent a lot of time with us working on a documentary called *Two in the Bush*. Famous already for their spectacular wildlife films made for National Geographic and the BBC, they were now filming each other in order to create a 'making of' film. It was wonderful having them in camp and I learnt a huge amount from them. Alan helped me by letting me fly his plane and talking about aviation, but it was their knowledge of the bush and their patience that I was in awe of. They made a wonderful piece about the hornbills at Kora, which required them to spend months in a hide filming the male delivering food to the female which, like all hornbills, he had sealed into her nest with river mud. The final scene of the film was meant to be the male helping the female to chip her way out of the nest after incubation, then the pair flying off into the forest wing in wing. After months of meticulous filming they missed the moment yet hardly turned a hair.

I wished I had their patience in the search for Kaunda, who had now been missing for a good few months. You get to recognize lions' roars and Kaunda's was very distinctive; we had heard it a couple of times on our long hunts for him and we had heard reports of him from friends but we hadn't seen him for months. In October, however, Ben Ng'anga and Chris Matchett got in touch from Bisanadi Camp, up on the border of Meru National Park, with what sounded like a positive sighting. They had spotted a lion, wearing an old collar, near their landing strip that seemed to fit Kaunda's description. Since they had both seen Kaunda often, we thought it was worth a trip. I drove up the river to the bank opposite Bisanadi and made my way across by boat.

Chris offered to drive me towards the spot where they had seen the collared lion. Just as we were entering the park, he put the Land Rover into low ratio and took us through a steep river crossing. He stopped at the top and out of the bushes by the side of the road came a large and handsome lion. He banged his head on the driver's wing and loped round in front of the Land Rover. The tiny hairs sprang up all over my body – it was Leakey. No other lion in the world greeted Land Rovers in the mad fashion that had so endeared him to us. They saved their head-nudging for other lions and for people they loved. I hadn't seen Leakey for two years and here he was, the same lovable goof who had crossed the river with Freddie. My whole body was covered in goose bumps. Then came the soft call of another lion from the bushes, with a distinctive hiccup in the middle. It was Freddie. Freddie, my first lion. Freddie, my favourite. I reached for the handle. But then I stopped. I knew I shouldn't do it. Here were my boys in the wide-open spaces right next to Meru National Park, on Pete Jenkins's doorstep, with thousands of protected buffalo and antelope to mull over for lunch. They were strong, thriving, successful and free. I asked Chris to drive on, tears pouring down my cheeks. It was the hardest decision I had ever made.

We never found Kaunda on that trip but I did fly over him a few months later with Fritz Strahammer, of Wings for Progress. He was sitting on a game-park signpost cairn, looking out over the Meru plains. He seemed happy and healthy and wise and he looked up as if to say hello. I had the same feeling of pride I had experienced when I heard Freddie's roar. We had done it! Everyone had said it was impossible to reintroduce lions to the wild successfully but we had proved them wrong. Leakey, a traumatized orphanage lion, who couldn't even play when we'd first got him, Fred, a tough Somali, and Kaunda, another product of the orphanage. They were all doing well, following in Christian's footsteps: living, thriving proof that our lion programme worked.

Predictably, after such a wonderful surprise, everything was about to go horribly wrong. Rather more of a surprise was that Terence got attacked by a lion this time: he usually kept as far away from them as possible. It should never have happened but he was doing the one thing we all knew was extremely dangerous: he was crouching in the rubbish dump just by the gates of the camp in exactly the same place that both Stanley Murithii and I had been attacked. As he was kneeling on the ground trying to light a fire, a lion rushed from the bush and bit him in the face. It was Shade, one of Koretta's pride – he ran away as soon as Alan and Joan Root rushed out to help Terence. We should have shot Shade there and then but George was so angry with Terence for inviting the attack that we didn't. I regret it extremely: we think Shade went on to kill a Somali girl out herding goats. An innocent, she didn't deserve such a death.

The Roots disinfected Terence's wounds, gave him some painkillers and flew him immediately to Nairobi. '*Atakufa*, he will die,' said the camp staff, recalling when he had said the same of me. No, he wouldn't. He had a hole in his cheek and a rip in his eyelid but was otherwise unharmed. He had been extremely lucky that Alan and Joan were nearby – it was neither the first nor the last time that Al came to the rescue. Within a couple of weeks Terence was healed and back in camp.

Shortly after he returned Ken Smith came to close us down.

'No more lions,' we were told. John Mutinda had done his best for us but Daniel Sindiyo was in charge of the Game Department now and it was obvious that the pressure from Ken and others like him had become too intense. As long as we had kept quiet and avoided doing anything controversial everything had been fine, but Terence being mauled was too much – especially for his last surviving pal, Ken. The government stopped sending us lions and wanted us to close completely but we managed to convince them that we had to stay around to integrate the lions we already had. George advised, 'We keep going forward one step at a time.' We decided to carry on and stay very quiet. It was easier said than done. The world was coming to get us.

A couple of weeks after Terence was mauled the Somali poaching war moved into a new and terrifying phase. Almost all the elephant had been hunted out and the Kenyan Somali clans had been busy fighting each other over the few that remained, but the Ogaden War, between Ethiopia and Somalia, had ended in ignominious retreat for Somalia and suddenly a lot of well-armed Somalis were flooding across the border into northern Kenya. They weren't even poachers: they were bandits – well trained, ruthless and armed. On 19 January 1979 one of six gangs operating in our area attacked Bisanadi Camp, just thirty miles up the river from us. They killed two people, injured more, stole all the cars and looted the camp of everything of value. My friend Ben Ng'anga, who was managing the lodge, had to walk many miles to get help. The injured were eventually airlifted out in a Game Department helicopter.

The Bisanadi Camp attack marked a big escalation in the undeclared war and made things even more hazardous for us: Kampi ya Simba was the only other target of any value for hundreds of miles. When Wazir Ali flew into camp to tell us the news, I took the opportunity to hitch a ride to Garissa to find out what was going on there. We were buzzed by three F5 fighter jets on the way, an indication of how the incursions were beginning to worry the Kenyan authorities. Noor Abdi Ogle was at his desk (a great rarity – he led from the front) at the Anti-poaching Unit: he was horrified by the attack but told me that George, Terence and I didn't need to worry. It was one of those remarks you don't query too closely but I believed him and it proved the right decision.

Other government departments were not so sanguine. The police and General Service Unit told us they could no longer offer us protection and that we ought to move out of Kora; the Game Department temporarily based an Anti-poaching Unit team at Kampi ya Simba but they were soon withdrawn. I found it particularly frustrating as I had just been issued a new work permit as 'Assistant, Kora Game Reserve'. It looked as though the government was giving up on the game reserve before I could be of any assistance. George managed to allay my fears. As with the lions, he decreed that we should just keep our heads down and carry on taking little steps forward as quietly as possible. The government would forget about us and the Somalis would probably go away. For a while he was right.

The authorities had what they needed: a letter from George absolving them of responsibility if anything did happen to us. We settled back to carry on with our lives as we had before and the government was far too busy chasing *shifta* to bother about us. We spent long evenings by the campfire thinking about how to get round the 'no more lions' ruling. Astonishingly, it was Terence who came up with the leopards idea. We had often discussed it, but had let it slip until Terence raised it again. There wasn't much we could do without any leopards, but I figured if Joy could do it so could I. She had spent the last couple of years living at Shaba near Isiolo raising a leopard called Penny that she had been given as a cub. Kora is ideal leopard country but they had been shot out in the 1940s when leopardskin coats

were all the rage: in all our time there we saw no evidence of any
wild leopards.

It was a shame that we were living under such menacing conditions as it was a great time for the lions. The only big problem
we had was when Jojo got caught in a snare a few weeks after
Suleiman was killed. Her leg was badly cut and she was snarling
with rage and fear when we found her. George and I managed
to communicate with even completely wild lions on such a level
that we didn't often need to use drugs, even when they became
safer and more widely available, but as soon as I saw Jojo in the
snare I jumped in the car to fetch from the camp the tranquillizer
capture pistol Aart had given us. By the time I returned George
had calmed the agonized, angry, fully grown lioness and removed
the snare without sustaining a single scratch. It was like living
with Doctor Dolittle. His courage was rewarded when, soon
after, Jojo produced her first litter. She could easily have aborted
had we used drugs on her.

Arusha, Gigi and Growlie all had healthy families, and Sheba
was helping Jojo with her cubs, but our activities at Kora were
stagnating. We knew we weren't getting any more lions; it was
unlikely anyone would give us any leopards and, even if they did,
we were penniless. Joy was coining it for the Elsa Trust but she
regarded George's lion venture as an old man's vanity and refused
to give him any money from the proceeds of the books and films.
George was too much of a gentleman to complain.

We decided that George would stay with the lions while I went
to Europe and tried to set up some sort of fundraising operation.
I left for Nairobi feeling invigorated and ambitious, but Nairobi
itself was very strange. My great friend Pete Gilfillan had been
killed in a plane crash shortly after the attack on Bisanadi Camp
and the Long Bar had closed. Mike Wamalwa was still around
but I had never known Nairobi without Pete. It seemed back
then that a lot of people were getting killed all of a sudden; the

death rate has only accelerated since. My youth was running out.

PA had sent me a plane ticket to Sweden, the Marrians gave me a sofa to sleep on in London and Terry Fincher, who had just done a big piece about us for the *Sunday People*, gave me the proceeds of the syndication to live on. It was amazing to be back in Europe after so long, but it was pretty intimidating too. I was lost and didn't have a clue what was needed to set up a fundraising vehicle. I started to flounder and lose confidence in my mission. I saw AC/DC and The Who in concert and found it utterly bizarre after so many years in the bush – but the real shock was seeing how my friends had grown up. I had been having the time of my life and had done some fabulous things, but they weren't very tangible. Back in London, my friends were all married and successful, with children, cars, houses and bank accounts. I was in my mid-thirties and had absolutely nothing to show for it. I was entirely reliant on their generosity and it wasn't a feeling I liked. It was similar to when I had come back from Kenya with Ian Hughes at the end of the sixties. Ten years later I still had no paying job to go back to and no money in my pocket. I couldn't afford to buy a ticket home to Kenya and, more importantly, I couldn't face going back to George and telling him I had failed. We had harboured such hopes for my trip that to return empty-handed would be a desperate humiliation.

By the time I headed to Paris in October I was feeling pretty sorry for myself but also trapped. I just wanted to get home – but home triumphant, not home defeated. My last chance was discussing matters with my friend Henri Behar, who, I thought, might have some good advice. He didn't but he put me up and shoved me on to a *bateau-mouche* one cold morning for a tour up and down the Seine – a voyage that was to change my life. I was slightly drunk and bumped into a stocky man in shorts on the gangplank.

'*Pardon*,' we said simultaneously, in the same execrable schoolboy French.

I walked on, then looked back – it really was the same French. The man I had bumped into was Bob Marshall-Andrews who had busted me out of school in his dad's car in my last year at Mill Hill. We hugged like long-lost brothers. Gill, Bob's wife, and the children sat upstairs watching the sights as we lurked below deck, watching the slime-covered embankments go by and drinking the bar dry. We roamed the streets of Paris together. I played lions with their kids Tommy and Laura in a smart restaurant and we bit the diners' legs. Meanwhile Bob sorted out all my problems and, with Gill, has continued to do so ever since.

Bob had become an eminent barrister while I had been working with George but, amazingly, thought that what I had been doing was wonderful. He realized immediately that we needed a trust and said he would help set one up for us. As soon as we got back to England he started working through his address book and urged me to use mine. He set up a meeting at his and Gill's house in Richmond, with the lawyer Tim Razzall and Roger Deakin of Friends of the Earth. Tim agreed to write the trust deed and gain charitable status for us, and Roger put together a simple black-and-white brochure. Dr Keith Eltringham, the chair of applied biology at Cambridge University, and Major Bruce Kinloch, MC, the former head of National Parks in East Africa, agreed to join the board with Tony Slesinger and Ant Marrian. Suddenly we were respectable.

They were a brilliant board: they all understood what it was like in the field but had respectability in the eyes of the more sober world of charitable trusts. Keith was a kind, humorous and quietly spoken man, who was highly regarded in the academic world. If we ever received any negative criticism from the academics for our methods of working with lions, he would bang it on the head straight away. And such was the respect he enjoyed that he kept them off our backs for thirty years. Bruce always gave great guidance and was also highly respected in the wildlife world.

We set up the Trust in the nick of time because Terry's *Sunday People* story had been picked up by *Woman* magazine and a few others and we needed somewhere to direct well-wishers. I managed to spread myself between friends so no one actually killed me before I roared back to Kora, feeling very pleased with myself, the Trust deeds safely locked away in my bag. I had taken my time but I had managed to do the business and set up a really impressive trust. I had raised our profile in Britain and I was riding high. George was over the moon. We had a glorious New Year at Kora, sitting on the rocks, toasting the future and feeling really positive for the first time in a year.

The next day I set off to Mwingi for a resupply with a spring in my step. I returned more subdued: *shifta* had robbed the only shop in Asako and three people had been killed in a raid on Brother Mario's petrol station. When I returned to camp Terence's face told me immediately that this was not all: Joy had been killed by a lion in Shaba.

6. Assistant No More

It was agonizing. For the second time in a year I was watching my hero cry. And it was hard to be of real support to him when he knew how I felt about Joy. She had been an extraordinarily difficult woman – indeed, a recent study has shown that she may well have had Asperger's syndrome – and we had never got on. There was no way I could suddenly pretend otherwise. Nevertheless, I had always admired her. She and George together had transformed the way the world felt about conservation, about keeping animals in captivity and about looking after the environment. Even when she was at her most tricky her courage impressed me. We shared many of the same views but she had adopted them first, distilled them into a coherent argument and had stood by them against a largely hostile world.

When George and Joy met in 1942, Joy was already on her second husband, but he had seen past her racy image to the raw woman – a woman who could keep up with him on his travels, who could look after herself in the bush, walk as far as him, endure hardship like him and care as much as him. She was truly remarkable in that respect. Her whole life through, she went on long safaris alone, in remote and dangerous areas. And by alone I mean not just without other Europeans – as 'alone' was defined in those days – but also without the vast staff that people took on safari with them and which tended not to get mentioned in travellers' tales. Even when George and she were still living together, Joy spent months in the most Spartan camps while he was on patrol for the Game Department. And she had shown her commitment to animals again and again. She reintegrated Elsa the lioness, Penny the leopard and Pippa the cheetah and gave almost all the earnings from her books towards their welfare. It seemed ironic beyond measure that she should have been killed by a lion. And, indeed, it soon turned out not to be true. As more news began to filter through, it emerged that Joy had not been killed by the animals she had devoted her life to protecting. She had been murdered by her least favourite species: man.

At Kampi ya Simba George soon dried his tears, pulled himself together and came out of his hut. Racked by guilt that he had not been there to protect Joy, he knew that he must now go to Nairobi and make sure that, in death, her wishes were complied with. He left Terence and me at the camp to look after the lions and flew to town with our good friend and supporter Fritz Strahammer, who had kindly come to tell him the terrible news in person. A few months later George asked me to visit Shaba, where Joy had been killed, to make sure that the police investigation had reached the truth – never a foregone conclusion in the murky world of Kenyan police inquiries. George felt uneasy about several parts of the story and wanted to know as many of the facts as possible.

Joy's death, in 1980, was a personal tragedy for George but it was a public-relations disaster for Kenya. Then, as now, Kenya's two biggest sources of income were foreign aid and tourism. Kenya's is a small economy, fragile and subject to big shocks caused by the smallest of incidents. In such a context Joy's death was anything but a small incident. She was a poster girl for Kenyan tourism, her work with lions was known all over the world and her books had been multi-million-copy bestsellers. For Joy to be murdered in a national reserve was the last thing the new and fragile government of Daniel arap Moi needed.

It took me a whole day to get to Shaba, most of it driving in the wrong direction because there simply aren't any roads between the two. I first went to Isiolo, Shaba's nearest town, where I was lucky to find that an old police inspector friend from Garissa was involved in the investigation. He opened up immediately, told me the facts of the case, then added his own interpretation. Joy's body, he said, had been discovered by Peter Mawson, her South African assistant, who had gone out to search for her when she hadn't returned from her evening walk. He had picked up the body and driven it by a circuitous route to Isiolo where her death was certified and reported. Mawson told the police he thought she had been killed by a lion. Over the next few days her corpse was transferred to Nairobi for post-mortem examinations where it was immediately discovered that she had been killed with a sharp weapon rather than by a lion. This tallied with investigations at Shaba, where suspicion had fallen upon Mawson and a former staff member called Paul Ekai, who had disappeared. My friend had never thought Joy had been killed by a lion and found it hard to understand how anyone could believe it.

Paul Ekai was tracked down by the police and soon confessed to killing Joy with a short sword or *simi*. He said he had murdered her not because she had fired him for theft a few weeks earlier but because when she had paid him off she had bilked him out of fifty Kenyan shillings. It was a tragic and sordid end for a woman who had done so much for African wildlife, yet also a sadly predictable one: she had treated people badly – husbands, friends and staff alike. The authorities made rather a mess of the whole affair and it was two years, with much press speculation about Peter Mawson's involvement, before Ekai was convicted and jailed. By that time he had revoked his confession, but since he had previously led police to the murder weapon, it is generally assumed that the crime was a simple one and that Ekai had indeed committed it. I reported back to George that Paul Ekai had been correctly accused: I think it put his mind at rest.

Joy was cremated in Nairobi but she had requested that her ashes be scattered in Meru where she had lived with George and

Elsa. On 24 January Meru's warden, Peter Jenkins, flew into Kora to pick up George for the ceremony. Pete had thrown George and his lions out of the park ten years earlier, after Boy had bitten Pete's son in the arm. He was one of George's oldest friends but had fought a spirited campaign to have George banned from reintegrating lions anywhere in Kenya. They hadn't spoken for a decade.

That day I took George to the airstrip. Pete got out of his Cessna 180, took his pipe out of his mouth and said, 'Hello, George.'

George walked towards the plane, took his pipe out of his mouth and said, 'Hello, Pete.'

Pete said, 'Well, shall we go, then?'

George said, 'Yes, let's go.'

This time it was me who was crying.

When George got back, we didn't really talk about the funeral or the ceremony in Meru. He obviously wanted to get on and would talk when he felt he could. We went off tracking the lions together and spent a couple of days quietly catching up with our camp chores. On the second night back, George sat on a rickety chair at his tiny table outside the mess. Made from a piece of quarter-inch ply with local poles and half a dozen nails, it was always falling apart. He chuckled away to himself a few times and eventually I asked: 'George, what is it?'

'Oh, nothing really,' he said.

'Go on, tell me.'

So he told me this story.

'If anyone drove Pete Jenkins to distraction it was Joy,' said George. 'When we arrived in Meru Park the other day, Pete drove us all over to Pippa's burial site [Pippa was the cheetah Joy had brought up in Meru]. A few words were said and I scattered half of Joy's ashes over the grave. Then we all got back in the car and set off to Elsa's grave by the river. The road was overgrown and

Pete was very apologetic, explaining he had so little money to keep the roads up. It was very hot and we eventually found Elsa's burial mound by pushing through some overgrown bush. I opened the canister and threw the rest of Joy's ashes onto Elsa's grave. Just at that minute, a dust devil whipped up. It blew Joy's remains all over Pete. He leapt about like a marionette, dusting the ash off his jacket as if he was on fire. As usual, Joy had the final word.'

Joy had left a very little money to George in the form of a yearly income from one of her trusts. It added to his pension and the small amount we received through the Kora Trust that Bob Marshall-Andrews had helped me to set up. Even then it almost doubled the money we spent on Kora. We really needed it because Kenya's newly formed Wildlife Conservation and Management Department (WCMD) certainly wasn't spending any money on the reserve, and as the years went by matters only got worse. The Treasury took the money from game park receipts and gave little out to preserve the country's parks and reserves. Rangers and anti-poaching patrols sometimes went for months without payment and often had to buy their own ammunition. It's not surprising that a few swapped sides and became poachers.

Kora became increasingly busy. For a while a section of the Anti-poaching Unit was based close to Kampi ya Simba, but it received few supplies and no back-up so they seldom ventured out on patrol. They would often accompany us to the water point or come up to camp to ask us for food or fuel but we soon reached the opinion that we were more likely to be shot by them in error than we were by the *shifta* on purpose. In March we received news that we were too complacent: seventeen *shifta* had come to Asako and set an ambush ready to attack us when we next went for meat. However, they had got bored after two days and moved off. Increasingly the *shifta* were aiming at people rather than animals; they had killed most of the animals and, if the instructions of the new WCMD were anything to go by, they would soon be allowed to move further afield. In March, a command was issued to all rangers that they must under no circumstances risk their lives. This soon became known to the poachers, who now carried out their grisly work with impunity in the sure knowledge that their opponents were under orders not to intervene.

About this time, we were told once again that we were not to continue the lion project and must start to run it down – something it was doing pretty much of its own accord. It wasn't an order we could ignore. A few weeks earlier, Arusha and Growlie had left us and headed across the river upstream. Koretta and her new cubs were still around camp but we often didn't see them for days on end. Gigi and her cubs, Glowe and Growe, were doing well. Jojo and her brood were thriving. By this time we were monitoring twenty-two lions at Kora but the original entrants were fully reintegrated and the ones that had been born in the wild were coping very well indeed. Knowing that we would get no more lions from the authorities, we started to think seriously about leopards. Jack Barrah and others in authority had gently hinted to us that this was the way to go. The problem was that we didn't have any and we had been told firmly that we could work only with Kenyan animals. Leopards are notoriously hard to catch, and in those days if a farmer ever managed to do so, he would shoot it immediately. There were a few at the orphanage but most were too old and we were not in favour there following Terence's incident.

Towards the end of the year, I started building a camp for the fantasy leopard project at the foot of Komunyu Rock a few miles away from Kampi ya Simba, more to keep the project's momentum going than because we had any real aim in sight. George despised sloth and always advised, 'Keep going forward one step at a time.' A few Scots Guards were staying with us at the time as part of their training. They had a long association with George: Boy and Girl, the lions from the film of *Born Free*, had previously been their regimental mascots. The Guards did an amazing job, helping me to build a leopard cave and a big compound surrounding a climbing tree. Whenever we were in Nairobi we would hear rumours that we had been given permission to start working with leopards but the all-important piece of paper never appeared. We began to get quite depressed. This was the ideal time to be bringing in new lions – Arusha, Growlie and Kaunda had moved on and the younger lions were doing fine on their own, but they were lingering too close to home when they should have been seeking pastures new. An injection of new blood for a new project would divert our preoccupation with them and they would get the message that they should get on with their own lives.

I was spending a bit of time away from camp, working on fundraising for the future but sometimes having fun too. I had made a great new friend in Khalid Khashoggi, the son of Adnan, who was then one of the richest men in the world. Khalid used to fly into camp and whisk me off to ever more glamorous locations where we would behave very badly and have a great time. He was learning to fly and we would go off on flying trips with his long-suffering instructor Franz Lang. It wasn't all play, however. I spent a lot of time working on the Trust, which we had now set up in Kenya as well. One of my most noble contributions to the Trust was playing Tarzan for a Japanese TV company. Thirty years after I had first read the book, here I was, at last, playing the part. They came up to Kora and filmed me bounding bare-chested across the rocks in very tight shorts and bare feet, doing lots of rough-housing with the lions and swimming in the river with crocodiles. Then they took me off to Naivasha where I had to run around with zebra, waterbuck and giraffe on the grassy plains by the lake. They were all terrified of the bush but had no qualms about telling me to perform the most absurd feats, which had all been dreamt up in Tokyo and bore no relation to animal behaviour. They maintained a rigid adherence to the script throughout months of filming.

In the middle of the year we had to do some scenes down in Tsavo with Eleanor, an orphaned elephant. The night before the filming there was a huge party at Tsavo Headquarters to celebrate Bill Woodley's forty years as a warden. Bill was one of my heroes and quite a drinker himself, so the next morning I was feeling extremely hung-over when the film crew dragged me from my bed to make the best of the early-morning light. The director sent Eleanor and me off into a thicket from which I was meant to emerge appearing manly and action-packed. As is usual on a film set nothing happened for ages and we were left hanging around in the thicket. A big bull elephant followed us in and didn't like the look of me at all. Eleanor protected me from him with long swings of her enormous bottom while letting me shelter between her front legs. Discouraged, the bull elephant soon moved off and I was feeling so rough that I fell asleep, leaning against one of Eleanor's big wrinkled legs.

I awoke to the sound of very quiet shouting. 'Tarzan-san, Tarzan-san,' called the producers, trying to wake me up without annoying Eleanor, of whom they were in considerable awe. I woke, puffed out my chest, pulled in my stomach and bounded from the thicket, looking purposeful. I asked them afterwards if they had the footage of me sleeping between the legs of a fully grown elephant.

'No, Tarzan-san. Not in script,' they blithely replied.

Shortly after I returned to camp I celebrated my thirty-sixth birthday. It was a great day – one that I will never forget. We could hear Koretta mating with Blackantan near camp. Naja, one of Jojo's daughters, was nearby. George and I were mending a gate when a plane flew low over the camp and I rushed off to the airstrip, thinking it was Khalid come to say happy birthday.

Instead, out of the plane hopped Michel Jeanniot, an Air France pilot who had been visiting us for years. In his hand was a little wicker basket that I recognized from earlier visits. The gingham cloth that covered it was renowned for hiding the wonderful cheese and wine that Michel would bring from Paris in his Boeing 747.

'Tony. I 'ave a present for you,' he said, in his comedy French accent.

I hungrily opened the basket hoping for a baguette and some Brie. Inside was something much better: two six-week-old leopards that Michel had just smuggled from Paris via Réunion, Antananarivo, in Madagascar, and Nairobi. I was overjoyed, elated and utterly astonished. Forget permits, we'd work that out later. As my vicar friend Mike Harries says when he preaches his famous Tony Fitzjohn sermon: 'Tony is the kind of person who would rather ask for forgiveness than permission.'

It turned out this was the best policy.

The cubs were dehydrated and hungry after their long flight so George and I tried to feed them while Michel explained their origins. Michel, it emerged, had a friend called Jean-Louis who worked in a Paris bar. The bar's main claim to glory was that at one end it had two leopards in a glass cage and at the other two cheetahs. Jean-Louis had become much attached to the cats and had been appalled when the bar closed and the owner sold the valuable animals to a circus. No cat likes to be kept captive but leopards hate it most; from that day Jean-Louis devoted himself to acquiring their freedom. It took him years to save up but eventually he earned enough money to buy them.

He had taken them home and set them up in a large compound in his suburban garden, separating them whenever the female came on heat. It wasn't ideal but it was better than a circus. And he loved them. A romantic man, as soon as Michel had told him he knew a place where leopards and lions were rehabilitated by the famous George Adamson, Jean-Louis stopped separating the pair and the two angry little bundles George and I were trying to feed were the consequence.

Young as they were, they refused to drink milk from the teated whisky bottles George and I offered them. Tired out, we put the cubs down and as soon as we left them alone they started lapping hungrily at the bowl we had left in their box. It was our first lesson in the difference between leopards and lions: lions are gregarious, leopards solitary.

George was delighted with the leopards and with Michel's story. But we were worried: the authorities were not going to like the cubs' provenance.

'Oh, God, here we go again,' said George. But he was smiling broadly for the first time in ages. Kora was back in business.

We had done a lot of work on the leopard camp during the Scots Guards' visit but progress had tailed off somewhat while I was away playing Tarzan. We threw ourselves into getting everything up and running, and within three weeks the leopards and I were ready to move. Kampi ya Chui (Camp of the Leopards) was about six miles from Kampi ya Simba, in the lee of another big inselberg that soared out of the *commiphora* bush a few miles back from the river. The camp was tight up under the rock, which climbed two hundred feet above it and was shaded by huge *Acacia tortilis* trees. It was entirely fit for habitation – by leopards. All I had, however, was a small hut with no door and a camp bed with a mosquito net until months later when we had time to build something more permanent. Nonetheless, after the first visit by the lions, I decided to put a door on the hut. When I could, I slept outside under the stars as it was so much easier to hear sounds at night.

The camp had few amenities – it was a nine-mile walk to the river for a shower – but what it did have was independence. I loved working for George and continued to do so for years, but from day one at Kampi ya Chui I was in charge. The leopards were my project and I was assisting no one. With this freedom came great pressure. I was being given a chance and couldn't afford to fail. I immersed myself in the new challenge and, as when Freddie had first arrived, girlfriends and social life fell by the wayside.

The leopards loved the camp straight away. They shot into the artificial rock cave I had built for them and spent practically all their time in there while they adjusted to their new lives. Later they came and played in the tree that we had enclosed or on the swing we had made with an old tyre, but the cave was always their favourite spot. Unlike the lion compounds, the leopard compounds had to be fenced across the top as well as the sides. The chain-link was buried three feet into the ground and secured there with rocks before the earth was replaced and packed tight. This wasn't so much to stop the cubs escaping – although it did – as to stop predators getting in. As with lions, almost everything kills leopard cubs – from the usual suspects like lions and hyenas to more unlikely creatures, like snakes and baboons. Baboons are famous for their eyesight, waterbuck for their hearing, so they tend to live together, watching each other's backs and thriving on the symbiosis. In Kora this relationship had gone one step further – with the shooting of all the leopards in the 1940s, the baboons had multiplied in both numbers and effrontery to the point at which they constituted a heightened danger to the new arrivals. The ones that lived on the rocks above Kampi ya Chui were furious with the usurpers and were always looking for ways to get at them.

When I had first arrived at Kora, George had asked me what I'd like to do: be warden of the area or set up and run a leopard camp? 'The leopards,' I replied, and ten years later I had got it. The lions had been George's – except for Freddie – but the leopards were mine. It was exciting to have a project of my own.

Although much of the work we had done with lions was transferable to leopards, I often had to review our methods because the leopards were so solitary, shy and small. After a couple of weeks I started putting minced meat into their milk. Gradually I added chunks and eventually whole animals. I once stole a dik-dik from a martial eagle that had just killed it, and had no qualms about feeding the cubs roadkill or anything else I found. I wanted them to get used to wild animals rather than the domestic meat we bought in Asako for the lions. There was plenty around for them – leopards will eat anything, from lizards and birds to kudu and warthogs. The local elephants came to investigate the new camp, sniffing the poles and the mesh with their trunks, and after a month or two of great circumspection, Koretta and the other lions came for a look too.

I found that leopards were much more nocturnal than lions, which was handy because I had by no means given up on the lions. I spent most of my days with George, following our normal routines of looking for and walking with the lions, then returned to Kampi ya Chui where the leopards were just starting to wake up and play. Intrinsically cautious and untrusting, the leopards nonetheless allowed me into their lives, a privilege that came with huge responsibility. We called the male Attila, after PA and Agneta's surfing dog; the female we named Komunyu after the rocks above camp but we usually called her Squeaks because of her large compendium of strange noises. The leopards were at their most active between three a.m. and dawn so I didn't get much sleep. I had always drunk very little in the bush, making up for it when I was away, but with the arrival of the leopards I stopped drinking almost entirely: I didn't have time for a hangover.

It was fortunate that around the time I started living with the leopards a Nairobi doctor called Andrew Meyerhold started visiting Kora. He and Fritz Strahammer often came up for the weekend in separate planes, merely for the joy of flying and spending some time with George and the lions. Wonderful guests, they always brought fresh food and other supplies and Andrew was able to keep an eye on both Adamsons' health and, indeed, mine. George and Terence were getting old and often fell prey to infections brought in by the myriad visitors. Terence had suffered a stroke during one of his bouts of malaria and George was developing all sorts of strange allergies that eventually required him to sleep with an oxygen cylinder by his bed and cut down heavily on his pipe. Andrew's visits took a great weight off my shoulders and I'm sure the Flying Doctors were pleased too as Andrew spotted many of George and Terence's illnesses before they became emergencies.

Shortly after I had moved down to Kampi ya Chui, Bob and Gill Marshall-Andrews came out with their kids. It was wonderful to be able to show them my achievements. One day I went in with the leopards and got scratched on my hand. Laura, their nine-year-old daughter, who is now a highly qualified doctor, remembers to this day my coming out and washing my hands in Ajax cleaner. 'Best stuff for it,' I said. I had nothing else around.

We now had a leopard and lion programme going strong, and although we lived on the breadline, our achievements then were pretty impressive to an outsider. Jojo's daughter Naja had two new cubs, Koretta had hers and the leopards were thriving on their diet of milk powder, cod liver oil, minced meat, Farex and calcium lactate. It was good to show people who had spent so much of their own time setting up the Trust for us that we were genuinely doing something useful. In Kora, I was in my element. When they had seen me last I had been in theirs. Nevertheless, things were not running as smoothly as they might have been. The origin of our leopards was still a problem, although George had driven to Nairobi and written to Daniel Sindiyo, the new director of Wildlife, pleading to be allowed to keep the cubs.

The leopards were so different from the lions that it was hard to adjust from minute to minute. I had to be careful that I treated them appropriately and remembered which particular big cat's world I was living in. You have to watch your back with lions but they are much more friendly than leopards – they are always greeting each other and they greeted us but you can't force a greeting out of a leopard. Although they can inflict a great deal of damage, leopards are much smaller than lions. Leopards hide and never show themselves unless they have to, while lions only hide when they are hunting or protecting their cubs. Leopards still live right in the centre of Nairobi but the residents never see them. They only notice they're around when they return home to find their Labrador's eviscerated remains at the bottom of the garden – one of our leopards came to us when it was trapped, drinking out of a bath, on a new Nairobi housing estate. Lions are gregarious and relaxed in the open; leopards are nervous and solitary and hide in caves. They can also run up to the thinnest of branches in the tallest of trees.

I had learnt from George and the lions that it's no use trying to treat a wild animal as a pet. If you do, you take away their innate wildness, which is the exact opposite of what we were trying to do at Kora. You cannot impose yourself on a big cat. You have to attune yourself to working with it so you think and react as it would, behaving naturally and firmly without a hint of fear. They can smell pretence and panic from miles away. It's hard to learn *how* to do this; you just have to do it. Gradually you get better and better. George, even at the end of his life, was able to work with lions born in the wild and in captivity in a way that I don't think anyone will ever rival. They knew he was old and frail, yet they treated him with respect until the very end.

George and I survived with big cats for so long because we came instinctively to understand not just their behaviour, their flicking tails and their crouched shoulders, but something more than that. 'It' had to be felt. And over the years we felt 'it' more and more. The key was to embrace their wildness, not try to tame them. Sometimes that wildness would trigger something in them: lying down in front of the lions, for example, triggered a charge. Sometimes in play they wanted to get rougher with us but were stopped by our voices, which reminded them that we were just human beings. It wasn't us ordering them to stop as one would with a dog. It was them deciding to stop.

I, too, had what might be called 'a way' with lions and leopards. It came, I think, from total absorption and from the fact that they knew I would do anything for them. As with the lions, I offered the leopards my friendship; I spoke kindly to them and looked after them when they couldn't look after themselves. Initially they were deeply suspicious but gradually they let me do more for them, to the point at which I was able to fit them with radio collars and tend even the most painful of their wounds. I felt an extraordinary responsibility for them and threw myself into providing their care. And I would like to think they felt safe with George and me because they saw that we understood them and were sympathetic towards them.

By the end of 1981, the leopards were becoming well adjusted to life in Kora and would come for long walks in the bush. Squeaks was much more relaxed than Attila but both greeted me and came to my call. Walking with lions had been very different. Unless they are hunting, when they skulk almost as well as a leopard, lions walk down the middle of the road, heads held high, afraid of nothing. Leopards are always on their guard, slinking from cover to cover, quick to climb a tree at the slightest hint of trouble and quite impossible to see unless they want to be found. We were able to introduce a few of our close friends to the easier lions under very controlled circumstances but with the leopards I had to be very careful. They do not like and are wholly suspicious of people. In Squeaks's case, it was even worse. She adored

18. Coming in for the night: Freddie flying through, Arusha below him and Gigi outside, waiting for her turn

19. In the camp with Kaunda

20. With George and Kaunda down near the river

21. Jojo comes to Kora

22. Lindsay visits after the mauling

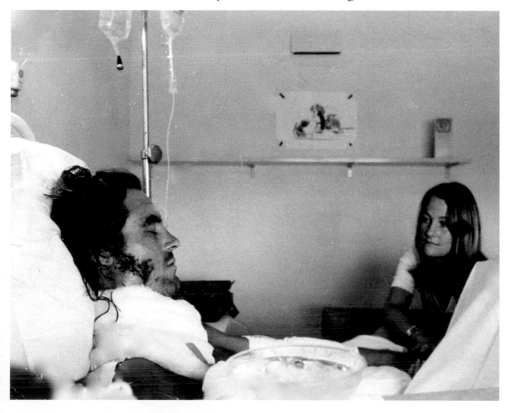

23. With Orma tribesmen, passing through Kora

24. Collecting water, Erigumsa in the river

25. Radio tracking in the early days

26. Kampi ya Chui after completion

27. With Attila. Leopards won't take a bottle at this stage

28. Attila and Squeaks explore the bush on their morning walk

29. Sharing a tree with Squeaks

30. Teatime with Squeaks

31. Palle released into the wild from his holding *boma* near the Tana

32. With Bugsy. No greater love …

33. Bugsy and Squeaks – the best of friends

me and was jealous of any women that came into camp. I had to keep my girlfriends well away from her or she would go for them with teeth and claws bared.

Dave Allen, an ace bush pilot, wildlife guide and former hunter, often used to fly in with his clients and we would always try to show them the lions; we could seldom let them interact with the leopards. These flying visits were always a treat as Dave never came empty-handed and his clients would often leave us a cheque to pay for some camel meat or fill up a car with fuel. On one of his visits Dave delivered a letter from the director of Wildlife. George passed it to me without a word. I feared the worst when I saw the National Parks rhino crest on the writing paper but I need not have worried. Jack Barrah had worked his magic and asking for forgiveness had worked: we could keep the leopards.

George and I were now living eight miles apart and the only way we could talk to each other was by driving to and fro. It was a crazy and potentially dangerous situation as security deteriorated. Howard Wood — a friend and communications expert — met me at Wilson airport one day where he had devised a VHF system for us that he later helped me install at Kora. It transformed our lives almost as much as the radio collars had done in the seventies. George and I could now talk from camp to camp and in between cars. We could communicate much better with the outside world through the Laikipia security network and even with Maalim Shora in Asako. He kept us abreast of *shifta* movements. Even better, on the long nights I spent at Kampi ya Chui I could imitate Tony Hancock and get in touch with people all over the world on a new HF set. I joined the Radio Society of Kenya and even started to learn Morse code. Little did I know that my growing interest in communications would provide a stick with which the authorities could beat me.

While I was down in Nairobi I witnessed a tragic moment when my great friend Bill Woodley's flying career came to an abrupt end in the harsh glare of Kenya's flying community. Bill was one of the best pilots I have ever flown with; he had a sureness yet delicacy of touch in the air that was admired by all. He had spent tens of thousands of hours on small planes, flying mountain-rescue and anti-poaching missions for the National Parks, and had helped me to learn how to fly. That day, we had lunch at Wilson airport's Aero Club with Cheryl Tiegs, the American model who was dating the photographer Peter Beard, both of us showing off in front of the world-famous vision of beauty. I watched as Bill and Cheryl walked across the apron to fly to Tsavo after lunch. Cheryl had the best legs I have ever seen. Only a fool would have left them unwatched. As they taxied out for take-off the plane veered to the left and started going round and round in circles. I ran out to help and dragged Cheryl from the plane as aircraft mechanic Alan Herd reached in and turned off the power. Bill had suffered an epileptic fit and lost consciousness. He never flew again.

There were good things about lack of communications: people would just appear from nowhere and whisk us off in their planes for the day. Whether it was Dave Allen flying us off for a quick swim at the lodge in Meru National Park or Alan Root offering lunch in Naivasha, I had a fixed policy of always saying yes to an adventure. In late July, Franz Lang flew me down to Malindi to join Khalid deep-sea fishing. I love surfing and swimming but deep-sea fishing is a rich man's sport I had never played. Khalid was richer than Croesus so we did it in style. We set off in a brand new game-fishing boat before dawn and, despite feeling a bit green about the gills, were starting to enjoy the beers as Khalid played his guitar and we waited for a marlin to strike. We had just arrived at the fishing grounds when a squawking voice came over the radio.

'Return to Malindi,' it advised us. 'There has been a coup in Kenya and the air force has taken over.'

Khalid was shattered. Adnan Khashoggi had given all his children their inheritances early and Khalid had spent a lot of his on Ol Pejeta, a 90,000-acre ranch. Fortunes were blown there on both useful and utterly pointless infrastructure. Mike Harries – the RevCop: so-called because he was chaplain general to the police for many years – had built a bridge there that was designed with the sole purpose of allowing Adnan to drive his low-clearance Mercedes from one side of the river to the other. It still bears a notice asking elephants to show due care and attention by only crossing one at a time. Khalid was terrified that his investment – which borders Kenya's main air-force base – was about to go up in smoke.

'Don't worry,' I said, with the nonchalance of one with nothing to lose. 'In three days it will all be over. In three months, people will be asking, 'What coup?' and in three years everything will be back to normal.'

I was right. Even by the time we got back to Malindi everything had calmed down. It was a bit quieter than usual but the police told us we were all welcome and everything was under control. It was the only time I have ever seen Khalid really rattled. Khalid was one of the richest people in the world in the eighties but now lives in a tiny apartment in New Jersey, completely adjusted to the change in his fortunes and as loyal a friend as ever. It must run in the blood. His mother, Soraya, was once famous for her riches yet now sells flowers to the people who used to laugh at her extravagance and lives in a small London flat with her son Hussein, who now goes by the name of Sean. How the great fall – the Khashoggis with more style than others, it seems.

When we eventually flew back to Kora a few days later we were full of the news. 'George, there's been a coup,' I said.

'Yes. I heard about that. I can't find Koretta.'

I felt much better after the break in Malindi. I had been working very hard, stretching my time between Kampi ya Chui and

George's camp and I was going to need all my energy for the next stage of the leopards' reintegration. At the beginning of September, after fourteen months of hard work, I fitted collars on to Attila and Squeaks, then released them. So far they had done very well but I was scared they might get themselves into trouble, which was why I had held back their release for so long. Only a few days earlier we had suffered a terrifying experience with a troop of baboons that had highlighted the dangers of life in the bush but also showed me how well the two young leopards could cope.

The three of us were walking on the rocks above camp when we were surrounded by about sixty baboons. Baboons are immensely strong, well capable of ripping off a grown man's arm, and have huge teeth that rival those of a lion. Furthermore, a full-grown baboon weighs more than a young leopard, particularly Squeaks who was very small indeed. The baboons screamed and bared their teeth at us, making quick lunges towards us and goading each other to attack. I was terrified – and so was Attila, who shot off into the nearest cave. Squeaks, however, looked disdainfully down her nose and carried on walking towards the baboons as if nothing was happening. I followed her lead, pulse pumping, sweat pouring off me as the big males barked and shook their fists. But they were not as brave as Squeaks and melted away when they realized they weren't going to get a rise out of her. I was so proud I thought my heart would burst.

Attila immediately started marking territory and disappearing on long safaris; Squeaks made the area around camp into her territory and was always dropping in to say hello. The radio collars that we had to modify for use on the small-headed leopards worked well when they were out in the open. The problem was that leopards are rarely out in the open. They favour thick bush or caves, which muffle radio signals. Unlike the lions, they were almost impossible to track from a vehicle and it became ever more apparent that we needed an aeroplane if the project was to continue successfully. Whenever friends flew in, I asked them to take me up with the radio-tracking equipment, allowing me to cover a huge area in a much shorter time. George continued to hate aircraft but I loved them and was always trying to get people to teach me the rudiments of flight.

Dave Allen – like Bill Woodley and Richard Bonham – was one of the many people who helped me learn to fly when he came to camp or, as often happened, whisked me off for a party. In 1983 Dave and I flew up to see our trustee-lawyer Anthony Gross marry Rowena Murray. It was a great wedding but, as so often happened, there was near disaster while I was away. Squeaks was badly mauled by a warthog that left a puncture wound in her thigh. She was waiting at camp when I got back and, despite the pain, allowed me to clean deep inside the wound with iodine and antibiotic powder. It was astonishing what she allowed me to do for her: it must have been stunningly painful and she could have bitten my hand off in a second. There was great news from Kampi ya Simba, though: George had managed to track down both Growe and Glowe, who had been missing for months. And Glowe had a new set of cubs.

The *shifta* and poaching wars were getting ever more intense as the days went by and the wildlife community was already losing faith in the newly formed WCMD. Ian Hughes had resigned from the old Game Department and given up his anti-poaching patrols a few years back. He felt that the government didn't give him the support it should – in fact, quite the opposite – and that he was being asked to risk the lives of his men for window dressing. This opinion was becoming ever more widely held as it grew increasingly apparent that some of Kenya's elite were more than involved in poaching: they were managing it.

Great men remained at the forefront of the anti-poaching effort but they received no support whatsoever. Ted Goss had recently flown into camp and taken me to see the powers that now prevailed in Garissa. We met the new police chief, then my friend Mohammed Aden at Anti-poaching and some of the provincial authorities. Most were brave men, fighting the growing insecurity with almost no assistance. Ted told me that the entire country was receiving only $6,000 a month for anti-poaching and I'd learnt a few weeks earlier that now game wardens had to fuel their own vehicles or give up patrolling. And poaching was only part of the problem: poachers were branching out into ambush and extortion. At the end of April they ambushed a WCMD truck full of armed rangers in the middle of Kora. They very nearly killed a good man called Sergeant Longoji and would have succeeded if I had been unable to get hold of the Flying Doctors. As usual, the Flying Doctors braved the insecurity and bad weather and saved another life. We were reminded again that George, Terence and I would have died years earlier without their courage and commitment.

Catastrophic as most of the news from the WCMD was, there were occasional rays of sunshine, like when the authorities told us they had plenty of leopards at the orphanage and we could have as many as we liked. There was a problem, though: they were all female, old and unsuitable for reintroduction. Squeaks really needed a partner. Without one she couldn't move on to the next stage of her reintegration: mating. We had always said with the lions that they needed to be able to hunt, carve out a territory and mate with wild animals before we had succeeded at reintegrating them. Attila had gone a long way from Kampi ya Chui, and although we had reports of him occasionally or picked up the signal from his collar, we didn't know whether he had found a mate. With Squeaks, I knew. There were no mates around. She kept coming into season and throwing herself at me in the absence of a better option. This was scary stuff as she would work herself up into a frenzy, throw herself around, jump all over me and scratch me with her teeth and claws out. Flattering though it was, I had to be careful — leopard claws are notorious for passing on infections. Squeaks was also intensely jealous of anyone who came to camp so we had to spend a lot of time reinforcing the cages and building tunnels to protect our visitors.

My two main helpers were Mohammed Maro and Ali Tukuna, known as Ali Oil Can. Both from Asako village, they knew the area well and were hard workers without whom I would have had great difficulty juggling everything. Two other people helped me too — Patrick 'Bunter' Corbally-Stourton, a tubby little Catholic on his year off who took everything I threw at him, and Pete Silvester. Pete is one of the world's best guides and used to stay with me between safaris, helping to rebuild the cars, erect huts and do all the work that Terence did at Kampi ya Simba when he was in better health. A brilliant businessman, far-sighted conservationist and top-end safari operator, Pete is now one of our trustees and remains a great friend. Patrick, like so many others in this story, died in a plane crash a few years ago.

Observers seldom appreciate the amount of work required to look after animals. The boring behind-the-scenes work far outweighs the exciting stuff you see on the National Geographic TV channel. Throughout this period, I usually spent five days a week maintaining the vehicles at both camps, fixing the huts and building new holding cages. The other two days would be spent on administration, writing letters to donors or doing supply runs. Only at night and in the early mornings would I get down to the exciting work with leopards and lions, work that always amazed my friends.

It was sad that when my father, Leslie, came out to visit Squeaks was on one of her rare walkabouts but it was great to see him in Africa, which he hadn't visited since he'd fought across it in the Second World War. I was proud to be able to show him what I had achieved. As ever, we didn't talk much but it was great to spend some time with him after so many years. My mother couldn't come and died soon after Dad returned home, but I hope that he was able to convey some of the wonder of my life in Kora to her. I know he understood what we had never been able to put into words to each other: I had found a home in this harsh corner of Africa with two taciturn old men and an ever-growing group of wild animals and in doing so I had come to appreciate what Leslie and Hilda had done for me. They had provided me with a loving home I could abandon, and got me into a good school, but that was only part of a much wider background that had formed me and allowed me to achieve what I have today. At Mum's funeral in Cockfosters later that year, I sat in church with Dad, Margaret and the Hat Brigade, wondering at how my life had changed. I wish I had been able to show Kora to them both but at least I showed it to Dad and I know he 'got it' because, years later, my sister told me so. The choir was as bad as ever.

The work never slowed when guests were around and it was purely a matter of luck how much time we would be able to spend with them – when Dad was around we went on a short safari, looking for Squeaks. Sometimes people would turn up when we scarcely had time to speak to them. Palle and Caroline Rune were in camp when we were suddenly given a male leopard by the orphanage. We were thrown into an insane round of compound building and reinforcement. He was huge, with enormous teeth, and although it was hoped he would mate with Squeaks and let my sorely scarred thighs recover from her endless attentions, he needed to acclimatize before we could bring the two together. Palle and Caroline saw so little of me that I named the newcomer Palle as a peace-offering. Another was named Khalid because he came from Ol Pejeta, Khalid's ranch at the foot of Mount Kenya. Up at Kampi ya Simba, Koretta and Naja had five more cubs between them but they were sadly poisoned by illegal grazers before we could even think of names for them.

Squeaks, too, was poisoned but by a snake rather than a Somali herder. She very nearly died. Oil Can and I found her in a cave near camp in a catatonic state and she growled at us to tell us to stay away. Twelve hours later she limped into camp in the evening with a most terrible wound on her right foreleg. All the skin and flesh had been eaten away as if it had been dipped in acid. I could see her bone. It was such a horrifying sight that I locked her in a compound, jumped in the car and drove through the night to Palle's farm in Thika. He gave me some cortisone and penicillin and I drove straight back to administer it, arriving at lunchtime. George was very worried when I returned, warning me that she was no better and in terrible pain.

Jock Rutherford had come back with me to help out at Kampi ya Chui. He was a godsend, a retired farmer who had followed myriad different careers, including one as a giraffaroo when he had lassoed Rothschild's giraffe on horseback for Rick Anderson's family, the Leslie-Melvilles, who had set up a sanctuary for them in Nairobi. He had also worked with Joy in her final years at Shaba and because of this knew a lot about leopards. Jock seconded Palle's course of medicine, as did the vet, Dieter Rottcher, when at last we got hold of him on the radio.

I went into Squeaks's compound with a great deal of trepidation. She was almost out of her mind with pain and the monstrous hole on her leg was getting worse as the flesh dissolved away. I gave her two huge injections and hoped for the best. She allowed me to do it but she wasn't happy and when I poked around in the wound to see if her nerves had been destroyed I soon discovered that they hadn't. As quick as a cobra she had my whole hand in her mouth, her teeth just about to rip and tear before she realized her mistake and let me go with a growl. I held out little hope for her leg but, amazingly, the injections worked. Gradually the flesh regained its hold on her shin bone and was covered once more by skin. In time she made a full recovery.

The insecurity never stopped because we were busy or one of the cats was missing or sick; the illegal grazing and perimeter poisoning was becoming institutionalized. The WCMD was falling to pieces and didn't even try to stop the poachers, and the police no longer did anything to deter illegal grazing. It was obvious that they had been told from above to turn a blind eye. Indeed, the grazers, when questioned, always claimed that they had permission to graze from one of the local MPs; before Ted Goss eventually gave up and resigned, he told us stories of tanker trucks full of ivory being allowed to pass through checkpoints because the owners knew the right people. The country was becoming ever more lawless and there was little anyone could do to change it. We hated the destruction the Somalis did to Kenya with their stock but they were poorly provided for and, at times, it was hard not to sympathize with them. In early 1984 there was a massacre at the Wagalla airstrip near Wajir, the dry northern area where Freddie the lion had come from. To this day no one knows the full details or what the provocation was but it is thought that more than a thousand Kenyan Somalis were shot by the security forces there and in surrounding *manyattas*.

Simultaneous with the political unrest, a drought combined with an invasion of army-worms that ate all the crops still standing. In Ethiopia, where the weather was much more severe, the drought became the Live Aid famine. We didn't have it so badly because there were good rains in the middle of the year but it was with relief and trepidation that I set off for Minnesota in the summer. Two visitors who had come to Kora over the years had got together to help me earn my flying licence. Larry Freels paid for my tuition, Bryan Moon paid for my accommodation and the company he worked for, Northwest Airlines, did the tickets. As I swotted under the summer thunderstorms of the Great Plains, I knew Squeaks was in the best of hands: Jock and George between them would keep everything safe and Jock knew exactly what to do with the new arrivals – two more illegally imported French leopard cubs from Michel Jeanniot! I would deal with that problem when I returned from America, refreshed and, I hoped, equipped with the wings I longed for and knew were essential to keeping our project alive.

America was a shock and initially very frightening. I had spent the last eighteen years living in the bush and was now in the most developed nation on earth. As I was learning how to fly a tiny plane around the Great Lakes, NASA's astronauts had recently mastered the Space Shuttle. Even so, these were the days before global positioning systems made flying easy and everything had to be done with maps and compasses. I was very glad that there were water towers all over the Midwest on which kindly local authorities had written the names of their towns for the benefit of passing pilots. I will always be grateful for having done my flying exams properly in the States. When I returned to Kenya and did my Kenyan exams, I was fully aware of my own limitations – an important bit of self-knowledge for any pilot.

Bryan and his son Chris had spent much of the summer putting together a music-video-style presentation with slides for the Trust. Chris was in the music business – he had discovered the rock star Prince – and in those early days of MTV, it was a great boon for us to have such a snappy fundraising tool. They tested me out on some of their friends in LA and elsewhere and I was able to hone my skills as a fundraiser. A lot of people took me and our work seriously but many others didn't. I was going to have to focus my mind and articulate my case if we were to persuade donors to part with their money to finance our dreams for African wildlife.

I headed back to Kora via England where I had yet more terrifying challenges to face. Learning to speak in public had been almost as hair-raising as learning to fly, but nothing could have prepared me for *Blue Peter*, a television programme on which I had been raised as a child. It was a national institution. To be asked to appear on it live was, frankly, terrifying. After weeks of waiting I managed not to fluff too many of my lines.

It had been a strange time to be away. Kenya had become ever more dangerous but it wasn't alone. The IRA had bombed the Tory Party conference while I was in England and had very nearly succeeded in killing Margaret Thatcher. A month after my return Indira Gandhi was gunned down by her own bodyguards. In comparison to the outside world of Reagan's Star Wars and Andropov's death in the Kremlin, Kora seemed quite tame. It was full of illegal stock, some game rangers had just been caught with a load of ivory, and we heard poachers shooting on my first night back. It was great to be home.

Jock had done a wonderful job in looking after the animals but there was a huge backlog of maintenance. The cars all needed servicing and fixing and the Bedford truck I had picked up at an auction had a host of problems. Mohammed Soba, one of the local MPs, visited soon after I returned and we talked about building a tourist lodge in Kora. An architect he brought with him had lots of exciting ideas, including one for building a bridge across the Tana, but sadly the lodge never took off. It might have forced the government to invest some manpower in protecting the area. The bridge was properly surveyed by an engineering team but was costed at a minimum of $200,000. Neither the government nor the Trust had that kind of money so that idea, too, was mothballed.

With a knack she had shown all her life, Squeaks had come back the day after I returned and jumped straight into my arms. Her leg had healed astonishingly well and you could hardly see where the gaping hole had been. Jock said she'd been away for ten days most recently but had been out for twenty-eight before that. It was great that she moved around so much but it was a problem that she was so attached to me. It wasn't safe to have a jealous and fully grown leopard around any other people.

The two new cubs had been named Chaka and Kazi. Collared and reintegrated, they had been eventually let go but they still came back to my call if I was in the right area. Palle, Khalid and Adnan were also doing well. The leopard programme was really coming into its own. On many days, friendly pilot permitting, we could pick up bleeps from five different animals on the radio. They were surviving! Their return to the wild was always fast compared to the lions'. Maybe I had been over-cautious in keeping them back for more months than was necessary but now they were out there thriving and doing their thing. I was truly proud of how the leopard programme had done so well against all the acquired wisdom and published theses.

All was well at Kampi ya Simba too. On Christmas Eve 1984 Koretta, Naja and four new cubs turned up to say happy Christmas to George. He called me on the radio and over I went. We celebrated long into the night. Koretta had another litter in the middle of the year, but for me 1985 was all about leopards and flying. I was determined to make the most of having learnt to fly so, despite all the work I had to do on the vehicles, the lions and leopards, I kept swotting for my exams so that I could convert my American flying licence into a Kenyan one. Everybody has to do it but I had just faced my first exams for twenty years and doing it all again immediately was hard.

I was able to throw myself at the leopards because of two wonderful coincidences. George and Terence were now showing their age – but we were in luck: a wonderful intensive-care nurse from Germany called Elke came and stayed at Kampi ya Simba where she kept a close eye on the ailing old men. And, more importantly, George had an operation on his eyes in Austria that almost completely restored his sight – he had been going blind for years and, although his health was bad, the restoration of his sight knocked years off him overnight.

My dad came and stayed again at the start of the year and was able to meet Squeaks this time. We went on a safari to Mbalambala thirty-five miles away to try to find Chaka, whose radio signal had been picked up there. We didn't find him but someone in Asako said they had seen a leopard with two cubs a few days earlier. This was true reintegration! I was thrilled – and so glad that Dad had come to Kora when the leopard project was going so well. We were inundated with leopards in the months to come, all from Dr Chaudry at the Nairobi orphanage – therefore with the coveted WCMD seal of approval. Two females and a male were named Amina, Fatima and Ngoto. I had to build a new compound down at the river to house them all but our main problem was keeping Squeaks out. Her passion for me showed no signs of relenting and she would break into camp whenever she had the chance, scaring the life out of Mohammed and Oil Can and causing an ever-growing danger. Funny as it was, it was also unsafe and she seemed capable of penetrating almost anything I built to keep her out. It was particularly frustrating because her reintegration had otherwise been a great success. She had her own territory and she killed for herself, but she wouldn't mate however hard I pimped for her. She shunned Palle, Adnan, Khalid and now Ngoto in favour of her abiding love for me.

The only other male in which she showed any interest was, of all things, a lion. One of my ex-girlfriends found Bugsy near the water-holes in the Komunyu *lugga*, about a mile from camp, lying next to the dead body of his sister. The young male was tiny, three or four weeks old, and extremely sick. I grabbed him as he tried to run off and took him back to Kampi ya Chui. George came down with feeding bottles and we decided that it was better for me to look after Bugsy (properly named Lucifer) as I was better equipped than he was. Kampi ya Simba was crowded with too many people and had so many lions coming and going that George would have had to handle Bugsy on top of all that without me as back-up. Neither George nor I could work out who

Bugsy's parents were and we found no trace of them where the cubs were found. We were not at all sure he would survive but, fantastically, Dave Allen brought in a vet called Jenny Price who gave him a drip for blood plasma and did a blood test. She treated him with Vitamin B12, antibiotics and glucose, then sent us medication for hookworm when she got back to Nairobi. Without her, Bugsy would surely have died.

We were terrified that Squeaks would kill the cub the next time she managed to break into the compound but, astonishingly, when they met, they touched noses through the fence and Squeaks was extremely gentle. Leopards hate lions but from the moment Squeaks met Bugsy she was utterly fascinated. With no fence between them, they played together for hours and became the best of friends.

All the other leopards we released back into Kora set off on totally independent lives and made their homes in the ideal leopard country around us. Squeaks, however, defied all fashion. First she fell in love with me, then with a sickly lion cub that any other leopard would have killed. So extraordinary was this relationship that a Japanese TV crew soon wanted to come out and film it. The show was being presented by a famous actress called Tomoko who was absolutely tiny and had a squeaky little voice. She had had a big fright when she was out with George: one of the young lions had jumped onto her back and scratched her – but nothing could have prepared her for what happened at Kampi ya Chui. We had finished all the filming for the day and were inside the cage having supper when Squeaks broke through the electric wire and jumped down on to the wooden charcoal water cooler. I threw myself towards her but was nowhere near fast enough. She shot past me, turned 90 degrees in mid-air and buried her teeth in Tomoko's neck. It was horrifying – fast, vicious and deadly.

I managed to force my hands into Squeaks's mouth, open it and get her off Tomoko. I threw her into a cage, then treated

Tomoko's neck but it bled slowly all night until the Flying Doctors came in the morning. I felt absolutely terrible. But not as bad as Tomoko. I thought that with the electric wires in place we were secure. I was wrong and it was entirely my fault. Amazingly, Tomoko flew back a few days later with a fractured and punctured neck to finish filming – but the attack did my position no good at all.

Six weeks later, I received the expected letter from the director of Wildlife. The Leopard Rehabilitation Project must close down forthwith: it was of no conservation importance.

7. The End of the Game

I didn't have long to feel sorry for myself. Shortly after I received the letter that closed the leopard camp, I had another bout of malaria and went to Jens and Tutti Hessel's house up in the high, cold country to recuperate. Jens was a wonderful pilot who did all the bi-plane flying for *Out of Africa* and helped me when I was trying to increase my knowledge of flying and keep my hours up. The Hessels always had me to stay when I was recovering from my various illnesses. It was Jens therefore who came into my room on 5 April 1986 and gave me the bad news. Terence had died at Kampi ya Simba.

I was utterly devastated – and shocked that his death affected me so much. Terence and I had lived together for nigh on two decades, vying for George's affections in our completely different ways. We got on each other's nerves – but you don't live with someone for that long without growing fond of them. Andrew Meyerhold flew in to pronounce Terence dead of a thrombosis so that he could be buried on Boy's *lugga* next to Supercub, the only lion he had ever been fond of. When I got back to camp a few days later the new priest from Kyuso came in to do another little ceremony as we planted the tree given in Terence's memory by the chief of Asako.

I'm so glad that Terence wasn't alive to see Kora unravel, the roads he had hacked from the bush used as camel and cattle paths. He was eccentric, cantankerous and downright irritating but he was a grand old man and I missed him when he was gone. George missed him terribly. Terence's death hit him very hard and he became ever more fragile. The cataract operation that had so transformed his life was not enough to face down the indignities of old age and the loss of his brother. Every few months now there would be some new health problem – asthma, malaria or another fall – and there was nothing anyone could do to fend off time. Maybe he would have been in better physical health if he had lived his life a little slower and a lot closer to a hospital but his spiritual wellbeing would have suffered. Indeed, I now think leaving Kora would have killed him. Just like Terence, he insisted on staying there and I believe he was right. That's not to say it was a good place to be in the late 1980s. Indeed, at times it was hellish.

Not least of the hellishness was the sheer number of people in camp. We had always been so isolated and George was such a gentleman that when visitors did come he welcomed them at Kampi ya Simba as if he were David Niven in the bush. Towards the end, however, we got more visitors than anyone had ever bargained for and it was always the most useless ones who hung around for months. The good ones came bearing gifts, took one look at the hangers-on and left.

Some of the visitors also caused terrible problems with the staff. George and Terence had always run a very tight ship with clear lines between management and staff, a tight ship that had lost its bearings a little as they became more ill. The brothers had been born in colonial India and behaved all their lives pretty much as the colonial officers they had been. That's not to say that they weren't good to and close to their staff but in a totally different way from how we are today. However, the endless visitors, the death of Terence, and George's increasing frailty blurred the line between the workers and the management. Another big problem was that some of the guests slept with the camp staff, then left, leaving all sorts of problems in their wake. Without Terence in charge, Erigumsa took over the road crews and did a brilliant job, but some of the other staff resented his new position. Erigumsa didn't have Terence's vision and inbuilt GPS, but he had all of his extraordinary energy. Other staff members leant on George for money and many of them took time off without permission or invented Muslim holidays that they hoodwinked George into accepting. He was getting forgetful and this was often used against him.

I didn't know about much of this until later when George asked for my help to kick people out of camp and get things under control. I didn't do this very well: I either didn't go far enough or went over the top, shouting at the hangers-on and telling them to leave, before heading back to Kampi ya Chui. George had a habit of using me as the Bad Guy so he could play the lovely old man with beard and pipe. It didn't come easy to him to be rough with people. He tired of many of the visitors as much as I did and was desperate to have the camp back to the way it had once been – peaceful, quiet and concentrating on the lions. The lions were unsettled by all the visitors and Doc Meyerhold felt, too, that they were putting a strain on the Old Man. He insisted that George get in a manager to run the camp and stop welcoming every waif and stray that came his way. The manager couldn't be me as I had been told pretty clearly by the authorities that I was no longer welcome in Kora. Dougie Collins, an old colonial DC who was living in Lamu, volunteered to come and help. He did a good job of getting the camp back into shape but I still had to do all the maintenance, help George with the lions and keep track of the leopards while taking down my camp and proving to the WCMD that I was on my way out.

Alan Root, Richard Bonham and many other friends kept telling me I should move to Tanzania and offered to assist me. It was clear to everyone except me that I was no longer welcome in Kenya's wildlife parks and reserves. The Tanzanians, they told me, were desperate for all the help they could get. At last I accepted their offers to help and set off for Tanzania, with a fresh scar on my stomach where a duodenal ulcer had just been removed and a letter in my pocket from Alan Root recommending me to Fred Lwezaula, Tanzania's director of Wildlife, an old-fashioned gentleman who knew exactly what was going on in Kenya and acknowledged that Tanzania had similar problems. We had a long meeting during which he pulled out a map of all Tanzania's parks and reserves and told me I could go anywhere I liked. Still blind to the fact that Kora for me was over, I hesitated and said I needed time to think about it.

'You have all the time you want,' said Fred.

I don't know what Alan wrote in his actual letter to Fred, but the version he gave to me was a little too honest.

In your job I am sure you sometimes think 'Where can I find a completely useless gin-sodden hooligan who, for no pay, is prepared to ruin a decent bit of country by racing around yelling, breaking up cars and running over animals?' Well, here he is. If you know of an opening for such a man you would be doing the world a favour by sticking Tony into it.

Back in Kora after another bout of malaria, I started walking Bugsy on his own. At the beginning Squeaks stayed out of the way, and I remembered what fun it had been walking with George and the lions – they're so much easier than leopards. It was great to be out with George again too, just like the old days. The bizarre relationship between Squeaks the leopard and Bugsy the lion continued to grow. Lions and leopards are not meant to get on, yet they were the best of friends. Bugsy was now absolutely huge but Squeaks went off for walks with him all over the place and seemed to look after him whether I was there or not. I was a bemused observer, never bringing them together or pushing them apart. It was extraordinary to watch.

Squeaks and Bugsy were wandering around the immediate area together with a complete absence of fear. I was worried they would be poisoned by the Somalis as the Komunyu water-holes were so close, but there was nothing I could do about it except keep my ears and eyes open. I couldn't lock them up. Squeaks lived completely without my assistance now and Bugsy came and went as he pleased, although he never went too far and still came home at night. After a while even he knew where and what to stay away from.

I set off for the UK and the States with my girlfriend Kim Ellis to let our trustees know what was going on at Kora and of our plans for Tanzania. They were disheartened by the news from Kora but excited about Tanzania, warning only that we would have to change the name of the Trust if we were to expand our operations. They recommended it be named after George rather than Kora.

When I returned, Koretta and her cubs had moved off to Asako where they were raiding stock from our last remaining allies in the area. Once more Kora was full of Somali herders and we were worried again that we would lose the lions to poisoning. Coopertox, a cattle dip, was used against them and has been a huge contributor to their current endangered status. There was also another issue. During the 1982 coup President Moi was saved by our old friend from Garissa, Mahmoud Mohammed, the Kenyan-Somali head of the army. The rumour brigade said that the Somalis taking over Kora and many other reserves were there with the nod of the president as payback for the Somali community. We never got to the bottom of this but it was apparent that the wildlife authorities, the police and the army were forced to sit by until the entire region had been reduced to barren bush. It takes decades if not longer for fragile land to recover from such intense burning and overgrazing. After the camels came the goats, which ripped out all the roots and reduced everything to desert. And every day there were more. From the rocks at Kampi ya Simba we could see the fires burning. We would bump into armed Somalis whenever we went to collect water and, even though there was so little game left, we would still hear the poachers at night.

I continued to be torn in several directions, but it wasn't all doom and gloom. George had been given some money for appearing in a Japanese advertisement and I had received enormous help from Pete Brandon, an old friend in England. This allowed George and me to buy two desperately needed new Land Rovers. Even more amazing was the anonymous donation we received. I had recently set up international trusts to help fund Kora and Mkomazi when I had visited the UK, US and Canada. Now money from the Canadian Trust was earmarked for a plane and two years' running costs. The plane was exactly what we needed for Kora; it was brilliant for tracking the animals and it turned our project into a much more formidable operation – we were able to react to emergencies in real time rather than Kora time. I had just passed my Kenya Air Law exams so I was suddenly airborne. However, I was completely broke. I had a good second-hand Land Rover in Kora but when I flew the plane to Nairobi I had to scrounge a bed and hitchhike from the airport! It was a mad situation, which continues to this day. The Trust pays us nothing but I have an aeroplane, cars, fuel and housing provided. It can be quite amusing when, despite all the trappings that facilitate our work, people realize this.

Our local MP, Mohammed Soba, continued to try to help us but he was up against an immovable object. It was apparent that the power brokers in the area wanted all Europeans to go but they drew the line at George, content to wait for him to die. They were scared of him talking to the press – but they were not going to give up until I had gone. On top of this I had a melancholy trip to Lamu to see PA, who was dying of cancer. Lamu was a glorious place, a peaceful little desert island with wonderful people, beautiful architecture and paradise beaches. It was completely divorced from the Kenya that was being destroyed on the mainland. Seeing PA again reminded me of all the fabulous times we had enjoyed together in the sixties and seventies, the Blue Marlin Hotel in Malindi, the Long Bar, and PA and Agneta's restaurant in Nairobi. Everyone seemed to be dying and my life was a mess. I was drinking too much again, and the one thing I had invested myself in – Kora – was a disaster, bursting with domestic stock, buzzing with flies and stinking of death.

George could see the end coming too. We would go on walks together when he could get away from the visitors, down to Terence's grave to water the tree that the chief had given us. It was not like him to be sentimental but there was something special about the walks we took then that reminded us of the early days. There were no new lions coming into Kora and, of course, no new leopards.

In 1986 Kora was extraordinarily beautiful. The rains came early so there was a carpet of wildflowers along the banks of the *luggas*, tiny resurrection flowers iced the tops of the inselbergs and the 'sex smell' of *mswaki* and henna pervaded the riverine forest. Everything suddenly seemed better. The rains were keeping the visitors at bay and had dispersed the Somali stock now that grazing was more easily available across the river. In the bubble of Kora, I had a newish plane, a newish car, and the Old Man was fitter and happier. For a short time it was like the old days.

Then came the Ngomeni bus attack. Just forty miles away, fifteen people were massacred on a bus by *shifta*. They went further than they had done before, cutting off three men's testicles and stuffing them into their mouths. Retribution from the police was swift and terrible. They charged into Somali areas, beating up random Somalis and dragging them off to jail. Local people stoned one Somali to death. A few weeks later six cattle buyers were ambushed and killed at Kinna. The country was eating itself as fast as the cancer that was eating away my great hippie friend PA.

I had to go to London again to see the trustees about changing the Trust names and to report on our progress, but just before I left something happened that would change my life for ever. A girl from London called Lucy Mellotte arrived in Kora, razor sharp, drop-dead beautiful and scarily young. I was smitten from the first moment I saw her. However, Kim was still around; we hadn't been getting on well for ages but we had been together for a while and she had contributed a great deal to our lives at Kora and on the trips to Tanzania. Her parents had helped with the American Trust and she had worked hard in Kora, taking photographs, writing newsletters and trying to keep me out of trouble. But gratitude can't heal a broken relationship. I headed for London, worrying about what I should do, but I knew in my heart I wanted to be with Lucy.

I returned to more drip-feed disaster. George was in hospital again and our beloved Kenya was in a truly pitiful condition. It was the repetitiveness that was so draining: the same mistakes were made over and over again. It was hard to believe even then that Kenya's death throes could be so prolonged. Government appointments and jobs in the police and civil service were being bought and sold like doormen's positions at luxury hotels. Under Jomo Kenyatta corruption had been rife but under his successor Daniel arap Moi it had become institutionalized: citizenship cost $3,000; vehicle inspection cost $10; the police charged 'customers' for the privilege of recording a crime. The country was falling apart. Businesses, like security companies, rubbish removers and generator suppliers, made money from citizens who had to pay for what was no longer provided by the state.

In the summer of 1987 the harassment campaign against us moved up another notch. I had been identified as George's heir and 'they' wanted to abolish the monarchy. The campaign was managed by a senior cop in Hola, the district town two hundred miles down the Tana. To this day, I don't know who was pulling his strings but it was apparent from the very beginning that he had backing from on high. President Moi himself had told the owners of the nearby farm Galana that they had to leave because it was politically impossible for Europeans to own that much land, however fairly they had acquired it. The European researchers had been turfed out of Wenji months ago and people proselytizing in Garissa too. I should have seen it coming but I was busy with the leopards, maintaining the camps and trying to protect George from visitors. My role had slowly evolved into one of keeping everything safe and working, and making the decisions that needed to be made – a role I still play today. Back then, I lost sight of the wider picture and didn't realize we were the only ones left until it was too late.

I was regularly ordered to drive the eight hours through bandit country to Hola to show my documents and permits to the police. In August 1987, on one particularly unpleasant occasion, I was charged with the fantastic crime of dealing in wild animals and running a tourist camp without a permit. If it hadn't been such a nightmare it would have been laughable: my entire life was devoted to the conservation of animals and I lived in a snake-infested cage with a leopard that wouldn't even let my girlfriend near me, let alone a tourist. I had no option but to plead guilty and pay the two-hundred-dollar fine. To do otherwise would have meant staying in prison for a month awaiting trial and then more months of deferred court cases. Even I wasn't that bloody-minded.

I felt as if everyone except George wanted me out of Kora – even my old allies, the police. After seventeen years in Kora, protecting it from herders, poachers, then bandits, I had been defeated by a shadowy enemy I still cannot identify. Everyone I spoke to had a theory about who wanted control of the area – cattle barons from Somalia, Somali citizens of Kenya, Rift Valley politicians. At that time there were so many people lining up at the trough that it was impossible to differentiate one from another, particularly when the end result was the same.

On 2 September Ted Goss flew up in his donated helicopter and explained to George again that I had to go. Ted had been warden of Meru for many years but had now assumed a consultancy role whereby he was the free airborne conduit to and from the director of the Wildlife Department. Ted said he had had no official word but unofficially had been told that Hola Council wanted no *mzungu*s (foreigners) left in Kora; they would wait for George to die but the rest had to go. That way they would be able to do what they wanted with the reserve. The department, he said, was still hoping to protect the reserve and, indeed, raise its status to that of a national park. He insisted that I had to prepare to leave immediately or things would get even nastier. Ted was a good man whom I understand much better now but we clashed at times as I felt he failed to stick up for or support George as much as he should have done. Maybe I was asking too much, but he was a Kora trustee and I thought he should have represented us to government; too often it was the other way around.

That afternoon we started dismantling Kampi ya Chui as Bugsy and Squeaks looked on. They seemed perturbed as we started taking down the cement-covered hessian walls, packing up the holding compounds that I had built with the help of the Scots Guards and dismantling the swing that the younger leopards had so enjoyed playing on. The baboons on the rocks above us stared down triumphantly from their roosting place, their snouts crinkling to display their yellow teeth. I felt like shooting the whole lot of them.

Later I drove to Poacher's Rock where the old radio-repeater had been positioned until we were forced to pull it down. Shora's radio in Asako had also been confiscated so we could no longer hear and be warned about ambushes and trouble. I climbed to the top of the rock: there was no rain and no animals. It wasn't until then that it hit me I was really going to have to leave. We had always ignored setbacks in the past and hoped for the best, but this was something I couldn't dodge. Lyndon B. Johnson said of Vietnam that he felt 'like a hitchhiker on a Texas highway in a hail storm. I can't run, I can't hide and I can't make it stop.' I knew what he meant. I was heavy-hearted and desperately sad. And, as realization dawned, I became increasingly scared. I didn't want to go to Tanzania and I didn't want to leave the Old Man. What was I going to do?

The only option was to try to put all the bad things to one side and get on. Kora remained bursting with domestic stock throughout the rest of the year; there was nothing we could do about it and nothing the government would do about it. I spent a lot of time travelling up and down to Nairobi, trying to find help for George with the few authorities that were still willing to do anything, but in the climate of the time everybody's hands were tied. Even Richard Leakey's brother, Phil, who was assistant minister for tourism and wildlife, admitted there was nothing he could do. As he had known George for years I felt he was telling the truth. Phil had even lent a car to Ace and John when they had first brought Christian out and I'm sure he would have helped George if he could.

The police from Hola were taking no chances that I might renege on my decision to leave and kept the pressure on continuously. Over the next two months we had many visits from various people coming to see our firearms licences, radio licences and work permits. Given that we were five hours' drive from the nearest police station, this was attention of the most dedicated sort. In the way that things happen in Kenya, these visits usually ended with the police officers asking if they could have some petrol so they could get back to town. Oh, how I missed the days of Philip Kilonzo in Garissa, but we had lost touch after his transfer to Nairobi and I'd stupidly let slip my relations with his successors.

There was so much domestic stock around that we were terrified one of the lions or leopards would cause an incident. Thousands of cattle were being grazed in the immediate environs of the two camps. In October George went to see Perez Olindo at the WCMD and begged him to enforce the law by pushing out the stock. Perez promised George that as long as he was director not one Somali would be allowed in Kora. A few days later Ted Goss flew in and said that the Somalis would be pushed out with helicopters. The entire thing was madness: everyone knew that nothing was going to happen but Ted and Perez were obliged to say the opposite. Soon after, the researchers in the old Royal Geographical Society camp left, having completed what they had come to do, and we were definitively the last *mzungu*s left on the Tana. We couldn't concentrate on our work at all. It was just a matter of hanging on for as long as possible, helping George plan for his future. As long as they were after me with such energy, I figured it meant that George would be left alone. But I wasn't as sure as I made out.

On 19 October, Bugsy walked calmly out of Kampi ya Chui and was never seen again. And two days later we found his oldest friend, Squeaks, poisoned on the rocks above George's camp. We were sure that Bugsy had been poisoned too, and never heard another bleep from his collar, dead or alive. I had thought I couldn't get any lower. Squeaks and I had been together for five years since she and Attila had come from France. Together we had proven that there was life after captivity for leopards and that they could be reintegrated. Unlike all the other leopards we released, we were able to watch her growing up because she had chosen to make Kampi ya Chui the centre of her territory but she had been completely independent and capable of surviving with no help from me. Nothing, though, could save her from the *shifta* who were destroying Kora.

The poaching now was countrywide, mechanized and organized, but no one would do anything about it. The only person standing up and making a noise about the way the country was going was Richard Leakey, the rambunctious head of the East African Wildlife Society and head of the National Museums. He took great personal risks to rage against what was happening to his beloved nation but only the West was listening. And they weren't doing anything.

George was in hospital over Christmas while those of us in Kora tried to hold back the hordes of Somali grazers by our presence alone. The daily sound of camel bells tonking drove us mad. All the inselbergs had armed young men posted on them, watching our every move. Four days after George returned came the next insane twist in the saga. Ted Goss flew into camp with a letter saying that four sub-adult lions and a lioness were ready for collection at the Nairobi orphanage. When could George come and pick them up? George was eighty-two years old, and the reserve where he worked was overrun with domestic stock. Yet the same department that had closed him down four years earlier when Terence had been chewed up now wanted him to start up the lion project again. But this time alone. He was to be allowed one assistant who had to be an indigenous Kenyan chosen not by the WCMD based on an ability to work with wildlife but by Hola Council – on who knew what basis?

At the end of January, I headed down to Tanzania to have another look around. In a strange twist of fate, just as Kenya was destroying itself Tanzania was emerging from decades of isolation and doing exactly the opposite. They were desperate for help from wherever they could get it. Fred Lwezaula renewed his offer of the run of the parks and reserves. Engulfed in a haze of self-pity and rage, with alcohol taking an ever-stronger grip on me, I couldn't see past the slings and arrows to realize my outrageous good fortune. I was forty-four and had nothing – everything I had been working on for the last eighteen years had been destroyed – but now I was being offered a chance to drag my life back from the brink of disaster. I'm ashamed to say that it took me a while to react. Nonetheless, by the time I left in the middle of February, I was pretty sure that Mkomazi was the place for me. The 1,350 square miles of national game reserve was completely undeveloped but had huge potential. It bordered Tsavo in my beloved Kenya and was somewhere I could submerge myself in hard work. I headed back to Kenya with the beginning of a spring in my step, keen to discuss the idea with George and beseech him to come with me.

When I arrived back in Kora there were three wounded Somalis at Kampi ya Chui. I managed to get them evacuated and taken to hospital by the Flying Doctors, but George was harder to move. Kora was not like it used to be. Many of the old staff had left and their replacements were not what I would have wished. Faithful Hamisi was still there, cooking up his foul brews, but most of the other staff were new. George was being looked after by a young girl called Doddie Edmonds, of whom he was very fond. Over the past few years she had come to Kora and nursed him through many of his asthma and allergy attacks, which were occurring with increasing frequency. I flew him to Nairobi to see Doc Meyerhold, but he insisted on going back to Kora before being medivaced out again in early March.

George was very concerned about leaving Doddie on her own and about his firearms licence. He had left his guns in camp, an offence that could have led to his licence being withdrawn. He asked Ted Goss to put some rangers into the camp to look after Doddie, then asked me to go up and sort everything out. First I went to the Firearms Bureau, explained that George was in hospital and got their permission to move his weapons to them in Nairobi. I picked up some air-crew friends – James Young, a senior captain on Boeing 747s, and Sally Trendell, a purser – and flew them up for the night. Thank God I did or I don't think I would have survived the visit.

Soon after we arrived at Kampi ya Simba we decided to take George's broken-down station wagon to Kampi ya Chui as my friends wanted to see where I had lived. The Land Rover had been playing up for a few weeks and Doddie had been unable to start it so I thought I'd see what I could do. I put my pistol in the central compartment and got the car started. Two rangers – whom I had known for years and who had been stationed at the camp – came out and tried to stop me, telling me the car was theirs. I thought they were joking and replied in a humorous fashion. One of their colleagues came out from behind George's hut and head-butted me in the face. Bare-chested, he stank of alcohol, which we later discovered had been stolen from George. He head-butted me again, punched and kicked me, while his friends put a few boots in as well. I was soon falling in and out of consciousness, amazed at and confused by what was going on. So surprised and stunned was I that I never put up any real defence.

They tied me up with a length of rope and threw me into the back of the pickup where I sat as they argued with James and Doddie, who insisted that they would follow wherever the rangers went. Eventually they drove me to Asako, followed by James and Doddie in the car. Poor Sally, a Surrey-born air stewardess who was just looking for a nice afternoon out in the bush, was left in camp with the very worst of George's staff – they had sat back and watched as I was beaten up. Tied up in a pickup on roads as rough as Kora's is no way to travel. You can't protect yourself as you're rolled against the wheel arches, tail-gate and the boots of your captors. As I lay there, I could hear the three rangers deciding that – much as they would like to – they couldn't kill me for trying to escape because there were too many witnesses. I was very relieved that James had stood up to them and followed me to Asako or they might have carried through their plan.

In Asako, I was taken to the rangers station, which I had helped to build with the money given to us by Prince Bernhard of the Netherlands. We then returned the thirty miles to Kampi ya Simba for the night. The next day the rangers took George's vehicle and drove me to Hola. On the way they told me they would kill George if I didn't leave Kora quickly. The boss wasn't in the Hola police station when we arrived so they took me to see his deputy and said they wanted to charge me with trespass. 'Don't be ridiculous,' said the officer commanding the station. 'He is still Mr Adamson's assistant and lives in Kora. How can he be trespassing?' I was relieved by this but perturbed when, as soon as he was out of the way, I was put into a cell and left to stew. Hola is seldom less than 40 degrees centigrade so 'stew' is really the only word for it. Hola prison is no 'cooler'. There was no access to a land-line and cell-phones hadn't been invented so I had asked Doddie to get through a radio call to Nairobi the night before. By mid-afternoon it was clear that she had been stopped from doing so. I was getting pretty desperate. It was with great relief that I heard, along the corridor, the patrician tones of Anthony Gross, hotshot lawyer, pilot, polo player, Kora trustee and great friend to this day. Immaculately suited in finest Savile Row, he sliced through the bureaucracy and had me bailed within a few minutes. We headed off to a nearby guesthouse, Ant rubbing his hands with glee at the prospect of defending me for trespassing on the place where I had lived for eighteen years. We rejoiced too soon: after an hour someone returned and promptly raised the charge to 'threatening to shoot a ranger'. I was now in very deep trouble: get the wrong judge and I faced ten years.

The case was 'mentioned' in court the next morning and I was released on bail, but this was by no means the end of the affair. Thenceforth Ant and I had to return to Hola every month for the case to be mentioned and adjourned again. The WCMD were plainly embarrassed by the whole thing and wanted their rangers to drop the charges but the process had already begun. My reputation didn't

34. 'The Old Man'

35. George with his last pride

36. On recce to Mkomazi, 1988

37. Fringe-eared oryx in the Supabowl, Mkomazi

38. Early days at Mkomazi. Making the first road in

39. With Fred Ayo by a baobab tree at our first workshop

40. Fred and Jumanne Mkuta building our house at Mkomazi

41. With Hezekiah Mungure in Mkomazi

42. Elisaria Nnko steers the project

43. Godlizen Mlaki and Fred Ayo in the new workshop, Mkomazi

44. Costa Mlay with Lucy and Mukka

45. Our wedding at the foot of the rapids, Kora, 1997. Elisaria took the photo

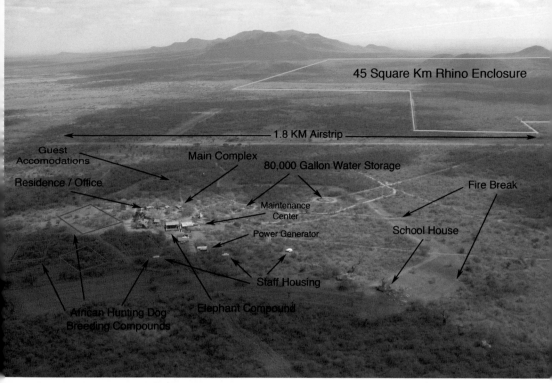

45 Square Km Rhino Enclosure

1.8 KM Airstrip

Guest
Accomodations

Main Complex

80,000 Gallon Water Storage

Residence / Office

Fire Break

Maintenance
Center

School House

Power Generator

Staff Housing

African Hunting Dog
Breeding Compounds

Elephant Compound

46. Mkomazi takes shape

47. Elisaria checks on our first litter of
wild dogs born deep underground

48. Coming up for dinner

49. Wild dogs in the *boma* devour their carcass

50. Aart Visee (*right*) and Sangito Lema taking blood samples from the wild dogs for DNA analysis

51. Kisiwani Secondary School built by the Trust. They couldn't even wait for the contractors to finish

52. The first group of four rhinos from South Africa land at Mkomazi during the El Niño rains

53. The rhinos arrive: Brigadier General (retd.) Hashim Mbita shaking hands with Pete Morkel while the South African ambassador looks on, Charles Dobie wearing sunglasses in the background; Rose Lugembe and I embrace, Lucy behind me

54. Lucy and Badger

55. Badger gets his teeth fixed – Pete Morkel centre right

help. Ted Goss had been misinformed by his rangers, who had said that I had been waving a gun around and deserved everything I got. I was lucky on two fronts: there had been three independent witnesses to the assault – Doddie, Sally and James – and I had a great many more influential friends than I had realized.

For the time being I had to continue moving out of Kampi ya Chui without being allowed to go there. Eventually, a few weeks later, Kim drove up with a friend in our old lorry to collect as many of my possessions as she could but several had disappeared or were held back by the rangers, who wouldn't allow her to take them. She had a long chat with Doddie, who had been having a terrible time at Kampi ya Simba. The rangers had stolen George's booze and one young man had been causing all sorts of trouble with the staff. George had given him a break but, with the Old Man in hospital, he had been stirring up Terence's largely unemployed road crew and the camp staff, who didn't have enough to do. It was pretty overstaffed for a small, simple camp: George only needed a cook, a driver and a couple of guys to get water and firewood. I felt very guilty at not being there: it was my job to sort that kind of thing out, raise morale and weed out the chancers.

Throughout the rest of the year, George was in and out of hospital, and I was in and out of Kora, just nipping in to check that George was OK but never allowed to stay overnight. Indeed, I wasn't meant to be there at all. The politics of the time were completely insane; Kenya had suddenly become a menacing and scary place. One of the few really good guys was Stephen Kalonzo Musyoka, the young MP in Ukambani and Deputy Speaker of Parliament. He called me into his office after he'd heard how things were going from the district officer for Kyuso, David Amdany. He soon came in on my side, as did many others, but other, more powerful, factions were at work. My old friend Noor Abdi Ogle from the Anti-poaching Unit, with whom I had spent a lot of time in the bush, had recently become an MP and was soon to be an assistant minister. He told me that it was best that I was out of Kora as they were going to get me.

I said, 'Who? The Somalis?'

'No, the other lot,' he replied.

In September, a young girl was murdered in the Masai Mara. Her death and its subsequent cover-up were indicative of everything that was going on at that time. I had met her a couple of months earlier as she was renting my friend Doug Morey's guest cottage in Nairobi. A pretty twenty-eight-year-old, Julie Ward was having the time of her life, travelling round Kenya and indulging her love of animals. She came into contact with the wrong people and paid a terrible price.

As soon as she went missing, her father John begged the authorities to search for her. When they failed to do so, he flew from England and organized a search himself. She had last been seen in the Masai Mara Game Reserve and her car was found almost immediately the search began. Soon after, some charred body parts were discovered nearby. The government's chief pathologist reported that Julie had been killed by lions.

Lions with matches and sharp knives? queried the Scotland Yard pathologist employed by John Ward. This was just the beginning of a twenty-year search for justice that has yet to bear fruit. John Ward has spent almost his entire fortune pushing the Kenyan government to prosecute people shown to have lied under oath. There have been inquiries, court cases and killings, none of which have even touched upon the true perpetrator of the crime. The entire sorry situation has been a grotesque parody of justice.

Julie's death threw the government into paroxysms. Pretty blonde tourists being murdered and dumped in game parks was about the only thing that could hurt them; it was simply not good for tourism in this beautiful and friendly country. Two other tourists had been murdered in Meru National Park, which was now overrun with poachers and would soon be closed to the public. Even the British Foreign Office – famed for its quiet and utterly ineffective diplomacy in Kenya – was starting to impose a tiny bit of pressure on the corrupt government of the time. The authorities tied themselves in knots, ordering inquiries, charging fall guys and disappearing witnesses in a desperate bid to cloud the issue.

My little problem was tiny compared to Julie's murder but I think her death shows how things were at the time. Everyone was very frightened indeed and didn't dare to stand up for people even when they knew something was wrong. And there was something wrong with the whole country. My friend Philip Kilonzo got caught up in all this. While my head had been buried in the sands of Kora, Philip had been forging ahead and had recently become commissioner of police. He was pulled in all sorts of different directions and even then you could see how it was hurting him. As soon as Deputy Speaker Musyoka told him about my problem in Hola, Philip called me in and asked my side of the story. 'You'd never threaten to shoot someone, Tony,' he said. 'You'd do it if necessary but you wouldn't talk about it.'

It was great to have a pal in the police who thought he knew me. Philip pulled the files just as the charges were dropped. Ant Gross had already won the case but judgement had not been forthcoming. This was great for me but it's not the way things are meant to happen in a democracy and it left a sour taste in my mouth. Philip had been so straight when he was in Garissa but I know he must have been involved in some very murky goings-on as police commissioner.

At the end of 1988 Philip came good for us. He said that if George insisted on staying in Kora and I couldn't be there to look after him, he would station a team from the General Service Unit in the reserve to keep an eye on the Old Man. The GSU are equally feared and admired. The elite paramilitary wing of the army and the police, they have been trained by the Israelis to 'deal with situations affecting internal security throughout the Republic [of Kenya]'. They are very good at their jobs and can be used as a force for good or bad. At this time it was mostly bad, but the ones who were looking after George were great and, double standards be damned, I honour Philip for sending them.

They remained in Kora for ten months and completely transformed the situation in the reserve. For years now Kora had been overrun with *shifta*, poachers and grazers. There were no rhino and hardly any elephant left by the end of the eighties. Merely by being there the GSU forced a *shifta* retreat. The *shifta* knew that they were up against stiff competition and went off in search of easier pickings. Sadly they moved into Meru and reduced that once wonderful park to a killing field that was not reopened until the late nineties. It was a lull just when we needed it.

The presence of the GSU allowed me to get on with my new project: the by now unavoidable move to Tanzania. Knowing that George was safe, if not exactly happy, I was able to head to the States to do some fundraising. In the midst of all the horror – with me in court and George in hospital – I had nevertheless been able to go to Tanzania and work out a rough agreement with the authorities. They had identified rehabilitating Mkomazi Game Reserve as a 'national priority project'. I agreed that I would do it for them if they pushed all the cattle out that had been grazing there for the past ten years. What I said then and keep reminding them now was: 'I'll back you up as long as you cover me.'

A couple of months earlier we had finally changed the name of the Trust to the George Adamson Wildlife Preservation Trust so that we could raise money for wider projects – not just for Kora – and we were going to need a lot of money to transform Mkomazi. It was 1,350 square miles of bush that needed roads, airstrips, fences and everything in between. I had a wonderful time in the States, away from the deadening pressures of being in Kenya or Tanzania, but fundraising, even when it's going well, is the least favourite part of my life. I find the whole experience extraordinarily uncomfortable.

When I got back to Kenya, I headed up to Kora as soon as I could. At first view, George was in much better shape. He had four lion cubs to look after that Ian Craig, of Lewa Downs, had flown in to him, thinking that I was still there. George was walking with them every day, but he was getting very old and he couldn't deal with them as he used to. He was controlling them by will-power alone. It worked on full-grown lions – but on the people who had invaded Kampi ya Simba it had no effect at all. They – many of them young girls, whom George loved having around – were going to get their ego trip in the sunshine with the Lion Man of Kora if it was the last thing they did, competing with young guys who were angling for George's attention. A similar thing happened to Wilfred Thesiger at the same time, but he was a difficult old sod so it was never quite so bad for him. It was impossible to get away from them and George had taken to spending long hours in his hut going over 'important mail' or sneaking out for walks on his own during siesta time when no one was about. In my final days I managed to get most of the staff under control – sending some on leave to Asako, getting rid of others and letting people know that George was not alone. On my last day George and I went for a walk down to the river. He said there were too many people around. Could I do something about it? He was really upset, but I hardened myself and said, 'George, I'm always the bad guy. Can you do it this time?'

He never did, of course. He was too much of a gentleman.

On 20 August 1989, I was driving from Tanzania to Kora to tell George about all the exciting developments at Mkomazi when Kim, who was in America, managed to call me at a guesthouse where I had been delayed by torrential rain. George had been murdered.

His death made me rail with rage and fury. And it came coupled with terrible guilt. If I had been there, I told myself, it wouldn't have happened: the Old Man would still be alive. I was boiling with anger for getting myself into so much hot water in Kenya that I'd had to abandon him. I still find the guilt painful to bear and often ponder the ifs and the wherefores. It was only a few months ago that I was able to talk through what had happened with Ibrahim Mursa, a Kora ranger and one of the first people to reach George after his death. It had been too painful to do so before. And I now know that one of his alleged murderers, who was found not guilty in the ensuing court case, still lives locally. I am sure that our paths cross occasionally.

The facts were less clear at the time but various people, including myself, George's biographer Adrian House, the police and myriad journalists, have looked into the circumstances of George's death. The catalyst, it seems, was that after ten months of peace, the GSU pulled out of Kora on 13 August: the poaching war in Meru and bandit attacks in Bura and Garsen had been hotting up and they were needed as reinforcements on the other side of the river. Philip could no longer justify leaving a unit of men based in Kampi ya Simba.

It's hard to do such a thing quietly; the poachers and thieves came back almost immediately. Meanwhile at Kampi ya Simba, George had managed to get rid of all his guests except for Inge Ledertheil, a German who spoke virtually no English but had found her way to Kora through sheer force of will. There were about ten staff members at camp, mostly old-timers with whom George had worked for years, as well as some of my staff from the now abandoned Kampi ya Chui.

At lunchtime on 20 August, everyone was just beginning to think of their siestas as the heat bludgeoned them into inactivity. I can vividly imagine George's expression as an expected but uninvited aircraft buzzed the camp, a signal that the occupants wanted collecting from the airstrip. Inge volunteered to go and set off in one of the Land Rovers with Osman Bitacha, a jack-of-all-trades and long-term employee.

Ten minutes later George and the others left in camp heard shooting from the direction of the airstrip. Inge and Bitacha had been ambushed on the way to collect the visitors. Gathering up a motley collection of weapons, George set off to the rescue with Mohammed Maro, Keya Solola, Ongesa Dikayu and Hassan Godana. Meanwhile Inge and Bitacha were dragged from the car and asked for money and valuables. Bitacha protested when the *shifta* started to rough up Inge and was clubbed to the floor with a crowbar for his trouble. Their leader then deliberately and methodically broke Bitacha's thigh with the heavy metal bar before returning his attentions to Inge.

As George hurtled down the road towards the ambush, he saw Inge being dragged into the bush screaming and crying and Bitacha lying on the ground, his bleeding leg bent at a perverse angle. Inge was clearly pleading for her life. George didn't hesitate to save it. He pulled out his pistol and accelerated. Mohammed and Hassan jumped out as they careered towards the ambush but Keya and Ongesa stayed put. All three died as the five *shifta* let loose a firestorm on the Land Rover, then ran away as fast as they could. George went out blazing, his old service pistol in his hand, like a charging lion, outnumbered, outgunned and, finally, out of luck. He was a courageous man who knew what he was driving into. Ibrahim said he had never seen bodies shot to bits like that.

Stranded on Mount Meru in heavy rain I was horrified by the tales of a bloodbath that were coming through to me. Communications being what they were, it wasn't until seven on the evening that George had died that the outside world came to hear about his death. Kora Assistant Warden Mwaura had been alerted by Moti and Deru, who had walked to Asako to report the carnage. He rushed to Kampi ya Simba and treated the wounded. But he had never used the radio before and couldn't call for help. At last, at call-up time, he managed to butt into the evening security check and informed Jane McKeand of the deaths on the Laikipia radio network. She reached Richard Leakey, the new director of Wildlife. And so the rumour mill started.

As with Joy's and Julie Ward's deaths, this was not the kind of news that the government wanted flashed around the world but it was too big a story to suppress. Five tourists had been killed that year and the tourist industry – overextended by the extraordinary success of *Out of Africa* – had been brought abruptly to its knees. As usual the authorities made matters worse with the cover-up of what had actually happened. To his eternal credit, Richard Leakey followed a policy of telling the truth and trying to catch the bad guys. He succeeded. Two were killed in a shoot-out and one stood trial but got off because it was his word against Bitacha's. Two more were never apprehended.

I can remember little of the drive up from Arusha, much of it spent crying and beating the steering-wheel with self-loathing and anger. And where was I going? What was I going to do now? Of course I wanted to go to George's funeral – I'd already missed Ongesa and Keya's – but what would I do after that? Kora would remain closed to me. And what was it without George? A patch of grey scrub full of *shifta* and illegal grazers. So absorbed in my misery was I that I put aside Mkomazi and the exciting work George and I had discussed doing there. I was only doing Mkomazi because I couldn't live in Kora; and without George, my very *raison d'être*, what was the point of doing Mkomazi at all? It would just be hard work with no George to approve of it.

Nairobi was grim and grey – typical August weather and one of many reasons I have never lived there – when I eventually made it up through the flooding the next morning. One of the first people I came across was John Lee, Nairobi's premier undertaker, known as the Elvis of Death in homage to his remarkable jewellery and quiff.

'I've got George in the freezer,' he said. 'Do you want to take a look at him?'

I really couldn't. Even at eighty-three the Old Man was one of the most vital people I had ever known. To see him on a slab, naked, his jaw and chest shot away, his legs in pieces, without his teeth in, stripped of the straight-backed dignity he had always displayed – I just couldn't do it. But I did want to pay my respects and events were conspiring to stop me doing so. The whole event was being stage-managed by Joy's Elsa Trust to which George had left all of his money at my instigation. Most of his friends wanted to bury George in a quiet funeral next to Boy at Kora where he had told me he wanted to be buried, but another party said he had wanted to be buried by Terence and Supercub. It really didn't matter where he was buried – both sites are just as beautiful and he would have loved either. But it would have been nice if his friends had not been muscled out of the ceremony by the press, the assembled ranks of hangers-on and the Game Department rangers who had never been there when he needed them but turned up *en masse* to guard the funeral when it was too late. The Elsa people wouldn't let me speak but they did say I could be an usher! How could they have got it so wrong? His many friends knew their place: without all the crowds they wouldn't have needed any ushers.

I asked Doug Morey to come with me to the funeral. He's a brilliant pilot and I didn't feel very confident about flying through all the weather round Nairobi. We were almost the last to arrive. I had never seen Kora so crowded. There were cars everywhere, while aeroplanes and helicopters covered the little strip that Terence had hacked out of the bush. George would have hated it. It was all so *not George*: he loathed fuss. His body was flown in by an army Puma helicopter and escorted to the grave by a rangers guard of honour. Then a priest nobody knew murmured some pointless words over the coffin. He would have preferred to be buried by his friends and talked about by someone he'd known. Surely we knew enough priests?

At the time I hated the whole funeral and thought some of the guests were jumping on the bandwagon but, looking back, I'm glad that George's importance was recognized. Richard Leakey had just taken over as head of the newly formed Kenya Wildlife Service. He did a great job and used the funeral as a platform to make a whole new stand for wildlife protection. What better place to announce his retaliation against the poachers than at George's funeral? Would he ever be able to sort it out? we asked ourselves. Richard had only just been appointed to his new job when George was killed but we soon found out that we should never underestimate Richard Leakey.

At George's funeral Richard drew a line in the sand of Kora, a line that was seen by the *shifta*, by the wider Kenyan public and, indeed, by the world at large. He used the enormous press interest to get backing for his anti-poaching shoot-to-kill policy; he used it to push for extra funding from the World Bank and others. His genius, however, was in manipulating Moi, the self-styled professor of politics who had appointed him. Within the next two years Richard not only had Kora gazetted as a national park but also policed as one. More importantly, with the great Costa Mlay, Fred Lwezaula's replacement in Tanzania, he turned the war back on the poachers. In 1990 he even got Moi to burn the country's stockpile of ivory in a spectacular stunt that led directly to the world ban on trading in it. I didn't have Richard's vision at the time, but I know now that he paid a fitting tribute to the Old Man, which I have tried to emulate in Mkomazi. No one remembers what Kenya was like in 1988 before Richard took over. Wildlife was finished and conservation had reached its nadir. It truly was the end of the game. Richard managed to bring it back from the brink, an achievement that should never be forgotten.

I cleared out as soon as I could after the funeral, Jack Barrah's words ringing in my ears: 'If you'd been here, Tony, this would never have happened.' He meant the words kindly, as a curse on those who had thrown me out, but they hurt. I couldn't bear to stay there among all the strangers, as isolated as the inselbergs that look down on George's grave and will do so for ever more. I would, doubtless, have got drunk and ugly. Instead I flew back to Nairobi with Doug, leaving Kampi ya Simba in the care of Dougie Collins. It would be a long time before I returned.

In the days after the funeral, I felt not as if a chapter in my life was closing but as if the entire book had ended. I didn't know what to do. I didn't want to go to Mkomazi. I just wanted everything back to the way it was before; before the government started destroying the country; before the *shifta* came; as it had been in the beginning, those golden days with George, Christian, Lisa, Kora, Leakey and Freddie. But I had to go, and there were things to do before I left. I went to see poor Bitacha, who was still in hospital recovering from the hideous wound the *shifta* had inflicted upon his thigh. He was being looked after by the Elsa Trust, thank heaven, for I had very little to give him.

My last meeting was with Philip Kilonzo, the police commissioner. He burst out crying as soon as I arrived in his office. 'I'm so sorry,' he said. 'I should never have pulled out the GSU.' But he had been forced to do so. Nothing had happened in Kora for months and he had been obliged to move his crack team elsewhere. I understood that. Everybody did. He was a good man, Philip. But he knew too many secrets. He paid the price for it – poisoned in his own bar.

It was a good time to be leaving Kenya and going to a country that wasn't destroying itself. The Old Man was dead. I missed him then and I miss him now. I got into my plane and flew into the future, desperate to drown myself in hard work and rid myself of the feeling that I had failed the Old Man.

8. Back to the Future

Tanzania and Kenya are very different countries today; in 1989 the contrast was yet starker. While Kenya rushed forward and modernized after winning its independence from Britain in 1963, Tanzania had already veered off at a tangent that brought about an economic emergency. Post-independence Kenya embraced capitalism and profit with a zeal rivalled rarely in history. Its southern neighbour on the other hand took a different route. The government adopted socialism with a fervour, which established a strong national identity but brought the country to its knees economically within just twenty years of independence.

Much of this was down to Tanzania's founding president, a small, unassuming teacher with very big ideas. Known as Mwalimu ('teacher' in Kiswahili), Julius Nyerere was a brilliant academic. The only thing we had in common was Mateus Rosé, his favourite tipple. Nyerere created a political philosophy that is often described as African socialism. *Ujamaa*, familyhood, involved millions of peasants being shunted around the country so that they could all work together to help each other and their country to grow. Part of the philosophy involved principled stands – against Britain for supporting white minority rule in Rhodesia, South Africa for actually having white minority rule and Idi Amin's Uganda, which Nyerere courageously invaded because no one else would. *Ujamaa* was a philosophy based on the best of intentions but it beggared Tanzania, transforming it from the biggest agricultural exporter on the continent to its biggest importer in just a few years. It caused an insane bureaucracy to be built up to administer the state's interference in every part of people's lives. But despite the failures of his economic policy Nyerere was hugely admired as a man of principle who stood up for what he believed in. Unlike his neighbouring East African leaders, Nyerere did not loot his country: he devoted his life to trying to make it better and it is a tragedy that so many of his strategies ended in failure. Like so many others, I respected him greatly. On his death in 1999 he was mourned across the globe.

When I moved to Tanzania, ten years before he died, Nyerere had already resigned the presidency but his influence lived on in every part of Tanzanian life. The country was being helped back on to its feet by the World Bank and the IMF (who were no good at running a country) and the result was shortages of everything. It was hard – often impossible – to get tyres, fuel, spare parts or even sugar. To print or photocopy anything involved a two-day round trip from Mkomazi. In short, Tanzania was the perfect place for me to bury and reinvent myself after the events of the past few years; it even had beer shortages.

I felt like a heel and a failure when I got there but I had realized that Mkomazi was my last chance at redemption. I was forty-five years old and had little to show for it – no house, no car, no kids, and my relationship with my girlfriend was an ever-present nightmare. Astonishingly, there were people in the world who thought there was more to me than the evidence suggested, people who had seen the things I had managed to do with leopards and lions in Kora, how I had kept it going there for as long as I could. They were willing to help give me another chance with the new project in Mkomazi that George and I had discussed for so long.

Mkomazi, like Tanzania itself back then, was something of a disaster area. Established in 1951, it covered 1,350 square miles and, to its north-east, bordered Tsavo National Park in Kenya. I knew the *miombo* and *commiphora* woodland that characterized the reserve from all the time I had spent in Tsavo. I recognized the wildlife, the trees and shrubs and the birdlife, and I could see that the reserve had the potential to come back from the brink. Mkomazi's first warden, David Anstey, had been lucky in the early days of the reserve: he had been lent a bulldozer and a grader by the Ministry of Works. He had cut a road from south to north, then put in a single road circuit around the north-western end of the reserve, but he could do little else. He built no access tracks to poaching and elephant areas as there were not many poachers and plenty of elephant. He levelled a couple of airstrips and dug some wells. David also worked closely with the wildlife authorities in Kenya to make sure that migration routes were kept open and animals received protection on both sides of the border. He noted in his records that 'There are too many wild dogs'; when I arrived there were none. I knew that if he'd been able to do all that work in the fifties, I could do all that was required for the nineties and bring back the African wild dogs too.

In the seventies and eighties, a persistent lack of funds had forced Tanzania to allow most of its national parks and reserves to wither away. Nomadic herders were allowed to graze in them, professional hunters to kill in them and informal miners to dig holes in them. President Nyerere had exhorted his citizens in his *Little Green Book* to help themselves from the land if times were bad. Times weren't bad, however, they were terrible, and the reserves had paid the price for keeping the people alive and the lawless wealthy. It was in sad and stark contrast to his wonderful Arusha Declaration when he had stated that Tanzania's wildlife was a world natural resource and Tanzanians were its guardians. Mkomazi had been extensively burnt and overgrazed and poaching was rife. Almost all the elephant had been slaughtered, with numbers down from four thousand to just eleven individuals. Peter Beard had shot an amazing photograph of Mkomazi's elephants just fifteen years earlier for his book *End of the Game*. Taken from a couple of hundred feet while flying with Bill

Woodley, there wasn't enough room in the frame to photograph one herd.

Large, robust elephant populations are the surest indication of the health of a game park. If it's dangerous or there's nothing to eat, they stay away. I looked on that photograph as a challenge and still hope that one day I can re-create it. Elephants were not the only animals to have suffered in Mkomazi: from a high of at least five hundred, maybe even a thousand into the seventies, there were now no rhino left at all; that, too, was a challenge. Lions had been bashed, as had leopard and wild dog. Those that hadn't been shot by 'sport' hunters had been exterminated by poisoning, legal and otherwise. High-wire snaring had killed an enormous number of giraffe.

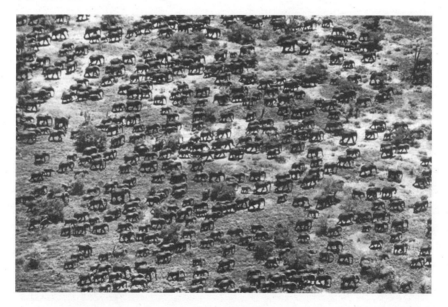

Just driving around the reserve was an eye-opener. Wildlife ran away as soon as they saw or heard a car coming, old elephant carcasses lay everywhere and we stumbled regularly over wire snares. At Kisima, a thick bush area in the central part of the northern section of the reserve, there were the neatly laid out powdery lower jaws of more than two hundred elephants and a

few dozen rhino that had been killed in the late sixties on a cull-
ing operation for 'scientific research'. One day we came across
the fresh carcass of a giraffe that had been strangled, its ten-foot-
long throat cut by one of the high snares. A wide swathe of grass
around the body had been flattened by the threshing of its enormous limbs. The knowledge that giraffe do not struggle for long
and just give up and die was of little consolation. When snaring
was deliberately aimed at the country's national emblem, we
knew we had our work cut out.

But there were good signs, too. Leopards were fairly prevalent,
if virtually never spotted; lions were seen along the Kenya border,
and in the north-west oryx and gerenuk had seemed to avoid
much of the slaughter. Lesser kudu and impala were everywhere,
along with a very reduced buffalo population.

Although Mkomazi was a mess, it was still wildly beautiful.
Just like Kora it could take a savage beating yet retain a fierce
beauty that squeezed at my heart. It was a tough and brutal place
– proper wilderness. Before George had died I was in two minds
about whether to go there. I kept on hoping that Kora would
somehow come good. If not, would I go to the Selous Game
Reserve in southern Tanzania? Would I try somewhere even
further south and just hide away? Would I go to Tanzania at all?
Now that George was dead, I knew I had to take on Mkomazi.
I wanted to keep his memory alive and ensure that not all he had
hoped for and believed in would be blown away in a hail of bullets
on a sandy track in northern Kenya. There were going to be no
more chances. I must take his vision south and restore this long-
suffering landscape to what it had once been.

For the first few days after I got back from George's funeral I
just wandered around the reserve wondering where to start. I
camped in the cab of my Land Rover because my tent had
perished; the car was laden down with spare fuel from Kenya
inside and building materials on the roof. I looked out at the vast

wilderness and just gasped. Then I pulled myself together and thought about what George would do. Of course I knew already: George would put his head down and keep going, one step at a time. It was the way he had approached everything and the way I eventually approached Mkomazi. I had learnt a huge amount from George and also from Terence, whose skill at putting in roads and cutting airstrips I had always laughed at while I was doing the glamour jobs of climbing trees with the leopards and walking with lions.

An enormous feeling of gratitude overtook me for the chance that Fred and Tanzania had given me. But it was daunting. I had to manage the whole project now, be in charge and give off an air of confidence that I didn't feel but which others could follow. I was no longer anyone's 'assistant'. I felt anything but confident inside but I portrayed myself as sure that we would achieve our goals and set about convincing everyone else that I was right. I was aided in all this by a wonderful man called Hezekiah Mungure, who was the Wildlife Division project manager assigned to Mkomazi, the African socialist equivalent of a Kenyan park warden.

Mungure's stature far overshadowed his actual size. He threw his personality like an actor throws his voice. An evangelist preacher, he spoke beautifully, in a lovely old-fashioned manner, in both Swahili and English, and commanded respect from all who knew him. Mungure was utterly convinced both that Mkomazi must be restored and of the legality of what we were doing, an important point when we came up against vested interests as we had at Kora. The reserve had been cleared of illegal grazers in Operation Uhai the year before. This combined operation of the Wildlife Division, the National Parks, the army, police and People's Army (who normally paraded with wooden guns) had arrested years of neglect, lack of management and a breakdown in law and order, but there was great resentment of it from our neighbours. It was part of Mungure's job to keep the illegal grazers out. He managed this by convincing others he was right; he didn't have the political backing, money or equipment to do it any other way.

Mungure had been associated with Mkomazi for almost ten years when I got there, and loved it as much as I loved Kora; he had been permanently assigned a few months earlier when the government announced that the restoration of the reserve was a national priority. This sounded good but actually didn't mean much. However important a project it was, there was absolutely no money to turn policy into practice. This was where I came in. The wildlife authorities were aware that I personally was absolutely penniless but they could see past that to the fact that the George Adamson Wildlife Preservation Trust could attract the sort of money and help they needed. They knew that I had rehabilitated lions and protected Kora against hordes of poachers and bandits and they didn't see why I couldn't do the same in Mkomazi. And if I failed, who cared?

I did.

The Marshall-Andrewses came out around this time to see me and Mungure and meet Costa Mlay, the new director of Wildlife. They were horrified to find legal sport-hunting parties based in the north-west of Mkomazi but operating all over the reserve. Apart from the ethics of it, they couldn't believe the look of them – 'Safari jackets, sleeves cut off, gaudy lion-tooth necklaces and menacing-looking gun-bearers perched up on the back of the vehicles. Giraffe meat in the freezer . . .'

When we had set up the international trusts, my old school and rugby friend Alan Toulson had joined the UK Trust and with the other trustees had personally guaranteed a bank loan to buy a tractor and trailer for me to start with in Mkomazi, an amazing show of faith that gave me a wonderful kick-start. In the USA Ali MacGraw and Antony Rufus Isaacs worked their contacts books to get us some financial backing to pay wages and running costs. Larry Freels, who had helped me learn to fly, set up a fundraiser in San Francisco. Peter Morton let us do another in his Los Angeles restaurant. In Canada the Mackenzies, who had visited Kora and had facilitated the anonymous donation of our plane, were working double tides to set up a fundraiser there. It was humbling how many people worked so hard for us and, indeed, continue to do so. They all supported the move to Tanzania but we needed the Tanzanian end to be working too.

Tanzania could have taught the Byzantines a thing or two about bureaucracy. And combined with African socialism there were some very odd outcomes. I spoke Kenyan Swahili fluently; in Tanzania, however, I was all at sea. *Bwana* – 'mister' or 'sir' in Kenyan Swahili – is used for everyone in Tanzania. African socialism, it seemed, transcended even sex. My Kenyan friend Charles Dobie, who had been working in Dar es Salaam for years, persuaded me that I couldn't live as I had done at Kora – failing to ask for permission and then asking for forgiveness later. In Tanzania, he explained, you have to have permits and licences for everything or one small problem can bring your whole project crashing down. 'Just get all the proper paperwork in place,' he insisted. And he was so right.

Charles set up a fabulous Tanzanian trust that could stand up for us in the corridors of power, as Anthony Gross and Palle Rune had done for us in Kenya. He put together a team of highly respected people who were prepared to believe in us and help move the project forward against a natural bureaucratic inclination to say 'no' to everything. They were led by Solomon Liani, Tanzania's ex-inspector general of police. Cautious and solid, with warm eyes that missed nothing, his presence provided us with great protection against the system but there was much more to him than that: he made sure we got the job done too and pushed us when we needed it. Solomon knew where all the bodies

were buried and was respected from State House to the smallest
shebeen in the back-streets of Arusha. He was a wonderful chairman, friend and guide, whom we miss to this day.

With such dependable backing, Mungure and I could start
doing the business in Mkomazi. For a start there was no longer
a road into the reserve: it was just a line on an old map. Mungure
brought in a gang of men to work with us and we started hacking out a road and an airstrip. It was now quite impossible to find
most of the roads that David Anstey had built, so quickly had
the bush reclaimed the land. In all our searching – and even with
the help of the man who had first cut it – we have never managed
to find the original airstrip at Kisima where Costa Mlay had asked
us to site our camp. Slashing through bush and cutting roads is
good, cathartic work. Utterly exhausting in temperatures seldom
below 30 degrees centigrade we went to sleep shattered every
night. Terence had taught me how to use the ridges and the natural contours of the land to make life a little easier but, even so,
this was back-breaking work.

In his ten years working on Mkomazi, Mungure had already
made many mistakes and was happy to admit to them. He saved
me from repeating them when I came on the scene. He warned
me off employing people who lived too close to the reserve: they
were always sneaking home. He warned me off people with
labour-intensive harvests who had to spend six months at home
helping out. He saved me from people who found Mkomazi too
hot and others who found it too cold. And he steered me towards
people from the lowland section of the tribe that lives around
Mount Meru. Had I done this alone, I would have been accused
of racism and favouritism but this was Mungure, a man of trust
and honour, picking men for me. A brilliant judge of character,
he was dead right. From the gang he brought in to start work on
the airstrip on 10 October 1989, Elisaria Nnko emerged, a natural
leader who demanded respect from all who worked with him. A

day labourer then, he's our operations manager today. Mkomazi would fall apart without him.

The camp at Kisima looks out over shimmering plains towards the Kenyan border. *Commiphora* and acacia-clad hills rise out of the savannah, like wrinkles on a well-used tablecloth, and behind us the Pare Mountains. On a clear day you can see Mount Kilimanjaro and Mount Meru from the hill behind the camp where we eventually put up our radio mast but when we started there weren't that many clear days: always there was smoke in the air from the incessant burning of illegal charcoal makers and grazers. There was little money to waste on fuel so we walked everywhere – a light march down to the airstrip in the morning to warm us up for a day's hacking at the bush. I lived off cabbage, garlic and cigarettes, and slept in the car.

As Mungure, Elisaria and I laboured together in the baking sun, we saw other talents show themselves among the men with whom we were working. One, called Fred Ayo, was a brilliant fixer and innovator who could mend anything. Over the years we have ripped apart Land Rovers and put them back together again, devised water-filtration systems and set up radio networks together. As everything we bought or were given got more complicated, so we became more skilled and knowledgeable. And as I concentrated more on management, Fred began to overtake me. Now he can coax an extra couple of months out of the hydraulics seals on a JCB and is one of the best aircraft mechanics I know. When the plane has to go for its statutory airworthiness tests every three months, Fred always checks it when the mechanics have finished and finds things they have missed, forgotten to put back or broken. He is now Mkomazi's workshop manager, in charge of ten four-wheel-drive trucks, three big tractors and trailers, slashers, harrows and scrapers. He has two water-tankers, three large and four small generators, a Caterpillar 12G grader, a JCB 3CX digger, three quad bikes, three motorbikes, eight pedal bikes and a pogo stick.

Another of the early arrivals was Semu Pallangyo, who combines the build of a weightlifter with a humorous and gentle nature. He can be just as stroppy and stubborn as I can. All my guys work incredibly hard for very basic pay, but Semu has boundless energy and can do twenty-hour days, week after week, when things need to be done. Semu is now our rhino sanctuary manager, with some of the rarest animals in the world under his control. People always go on about how privileged they are to work with such great people but imagine how lucky I was to find those three in my earliest days at Mkomazi, all suggested by Hezekiah Mungure, a born-again Christian who brought the same energy to restoring Mkomazi that he did to his preaching. Privileged doesn't even begin to describe it. I was blessed.

That's not to say it wasn't a complete nightmare trying to amass any solid achievements. Just glance at the figures again and compare it with looking after a garden. Mkomazi is 1,350 square miles and we were weeding it by hand! When I landed the plane on that hand-slashed runway for the first time in January 1990, we all felt a huge sense of achievement. Okay, so I trimmed a few branches on my way in but we had hacked an airstrip through clinging scrub and rough terrain and we now had an aircraft on the reserve. None of the guys working there had ever had a boss with an aircraft before; as well as being an invaluable tool, it gave us legitimacy and something to be proud of.

Others, too, were proud of Mkomazi. The reserve was part of the curriculum of the officer field-training centre at Mweka College of African Wildlife Management. The college had been founded by our trustee Major Bruce Kinloch at the end of the colonial era. All Tanzania's wardens knew Mkomazi well and had seen it being destroyed. They really wanted it to recover, as did the government, which continually stressed that our work was a project of national importance. Not everyone was helping, though. The local MP wanted access to the land for his constituents, and the way things happen in Tanzania often worked against us. Every ten days or so, I would have to drop everything and go to Same (pronounced *Sar-may*), which was our nearest town, Arusha, Moshi or Dar es Salaam to see the district commissioner, the regional commissioner or the district or regional this or that, to sign something in triplicate for my work permit and gun licences or get another letter to ensure our charitable status. It took years to sort out the legality of our presence in Tanzania and it took days to do anything.

Just making a phone call involved a six- or eight-hour round trip to Same. *If* the phone was working there was always a queue and *someone* listening in. The charges were astronomical. There was a telex machine in Arusha we could use but that was even further away – a whole day's journey. Keeping in touch was so hard that I became ever more cut off as I concentrated on George's mantra: just keep going forward, one small step at a time. Tanzania had no good-quality tyres – essential when driving in the bush on thorns and sharp rocks – and finding spare parts for our ancient Bedford was nigh on impossible. Fred became brilliant at designing and making spares from mismatched vehicles, wood or bits of metal that he hammered out on an old engine block anvil. The money to keep us going took a month at least to be transferred from America to the one tiny bank in Same, and as soon as it arrived the whole town knew about it. This was dangerous as well as expensive. In those days people were routinely murdered for a month's camp wages.

Tanzania is a huge place and close to the equator so it appears much smaller on a Mercator projection map than it actually is. Dar es Salaam was then a two-day drive from Kisima, compared to today's six and a half hours. Getting there used a lot of fuel so I often had to go by bus. The city has seen something of a transformation recently but it remains a hard place to do business. Well-designed Swahili houses with thick cooling walls and shady courtyards do exist but are jealously guarded by their residents. Back then government offices were either crumbling Communist-era East German-built blocks or tumbledown colonial mazes with ceiling fans but no electricity and huge piles of dusty files, gently rotting into each other in the humidity. Every now and then these buildings go up in flames when the records stored within become too embarrassing and need to be got rid of. On the Indian Ocean, Dar es Salaam has always been a hot and sticky place where everyone seems to move in slow motion.

Most of the officials I dealt with were charming and extremely helpful but there was no getting away from the fact that to do anything you needed an awful lot of forms stamped: I spent about 60 per cent of my time on administration. Later on, the Friends of Mkomazi in the US sent us a container of equipment, including VHF radios, tyres, tool kits, spare parts, generators and a quad bike – all essential kit that could have speeded up everything that we were doing. It took us an entire year to import it, by which time some of it was rotten and rusty and bits were missing.

All of our Trusts were astonishingly patient in this period: in Los Angeles or London, it must have been hard to imagine Tanzanian bureaucracy. And it wasn't as if we were achieving much. Game reserves need infrastructure long before you can do anything with animals. We needed to build more airstrips, security outposts, access roads, anti-poaching tracks, water systems and communications before we could realize our dreams of reintroducing wild dogs and rhinos. Security outposts are notoriously hard to sell to donors but you can whack stickers on them, saying who paid for them.

From this combination of Orwellian bureaucracy and pioneering hard labour, I flew to Canada where Marjoe Gortner had organized a fundraiser for us at Chateau Lake Louise in conjunction with the Nature Conservancy of Canada. High in the Rockies, on the path of the trans-Pacific railroad, it is one of the most beautiful places I have ever been. It was a huge culture shock to be there, which only diminished when I was taken on a helicopter ride by the warden of the national park. He had so many problems that were similar to mine: instead of elephants he had bighorn sheep; instead of no fences, he had fences in the wrong place; instead of villages and cattle camps he had a town in the middle of his park. And we both had a problem with mining, both legal and illegal.

I was on something of a high when I arrived in London for George's memorial service. It was great to see all our old friends and to tell them what I was doing to keep George's memory alive, but the most useful thing I did on that trip was go down to Dorset to meet David Anstey, Mkomazi's first warden. It had taken a visit by a mutual friend to track David down, but after years of listening to George and watching things unravel in Kora, I had learnt not to go flying in feet first if there was any wise counsel to be had elsewhere. David told me all about how things used to work and he was extraordinarily helpful when a later land-use compensation case reared its million-dollar head. He steered the government in the right direction and was the witness that exposed the dishonesty of the plaintiffs' case.

After all the glamour of the last few weeks, going back to Tanzania was extraordinary. The cattle had come back into Mkomazi and, with them, millions and millions of flies. Snare lines were going in all over the place and I had to get right back down to work to support Mungure in his battle to keep the reserve free of cattle and injured animals. His rangers were not all as honest as he would have wished and he had almost no money for patrolling. When the Trust's tax exemption certificate at last came through, I was suddenly allowed to do all sorts of things we had been waiting for and, most important of all, picked up the tractor that the UK Trust had donated. It took me three weeks of bad beer in Tanga to get it through Customs but I love that machine and it still works like a dream today. My old Kenyan friend Fred Decker, who was building a road near Same, helped us out with a bulldozer and we put in three airstrips in less time than it had taken to cut a third of the first by hand. We lent him the tractor in return and he gave us so much good advice that I don't know what I would have done without him.

By the end of 1990 we had made some genuine if slow headway. We had built the runway and assembled a hangar down on the plains; we had cut out some rough tracks to Same; and elsewhere, Mungure and his men were patrolling and we had put in a few more emergency airstrips. At Kisima I had started to build a one-room house for myself, and we had put up a mess tent to replace George's old fly sheet, my one inheritance from the executors of the Old Man's estate. Many months later I was given his remaining firearms, but was really annoyed to find that the .470 double I had always carried in dangerous situations had been flogged to a hunter in Tanzania. George would have been furious.

When I went off to do more fundraising at the end of the year, I handed over the keys to Elisaria in the certain knowledge that the operation at Mkomazi was in good hands. Twenty-one years later I have the same confidence whenever I go away. We're both a little older and wiser but the essential trusting relationship we developed in that first year remains the same.

I didn't realize for quite how long I had handed over the keys. It all started well with another amazing three-day event that Marjoe Gortner had organized, in Banff this time. Named after Mary *and* Joseph, Marjoe had the most incredible address book and a real belief in our project. He had been a child evangelist, spreading the Lord's word across the Midwest from the age of four. He excelled at selling our dream and made us believe in ourselves as much as he made others believe with him. Even with my limited experience of arts and the media I was mighty impressed. Ali MacGraw came up from California for the four-day event and Antony Rufus Isaacs made sure that everyone put their hands in their pockets for the greater good of the Trust. I was introduced by Scott Glenn and sat next to Clint Eastwood, who had just finished filming *White Hunter, Black Heart*.

However, other plans were afoot. When drunk I had been rude and aggressive to a number of people over the years, so it was no wonder that the US Trust discussed my needs at length and, unbeknown to me, booked me into Hazelden, the home of AA. I went straight from the high of fundraising dinners to baring my soul in Minnesota.

Other friends had talked to me about what they felt was a problem and I knew already that I couldn't carry on as I was. I was causing and feeling too much pain and my life was becoming blurred. Two great friends of mine were collapsing under the self-inflicted burden of alcoholism and I didn't want to go there too. I would spend long weeks out in the bush with nothing to drink, then go completely crazy when I got near a bar. Friends told me later that it was a case of 'Light the blue touchpaper and retire'. I was like a volatile, damp firework and no one could predict which way I would go. As one old friend has often said: 'You were lucky you were such a hyperactive drunk or you would never have got anything done.'

I did get a lot done in my drinking days but some of it was pretty destructive. In Nairobi Palle Rune had been forced to knock me out and hide me under a car to save me from a bunch of ravening Kenya cowboys when I threw pavlova down someone's dress. I had managed to offend one of our best benefactors by insulting a close friend of his. I was not a charming drunk, though always apologetic in the morning. The US Trust were nervous when they told me about their plans for me but I was ready and grateful. They convinced me that life would be much easier without the constant need to say I was sorry. And Ali MacGraw knew what she was talking about. She had made a lot of money saying, 'Love means never having to say you're sorry,' and had joined the Programme a few years earlier. My rescuers were helped by the fact that I was still feeling guilty as hell about George's death. On reflection I don't feel so guilty. Had I not been as hard and tough as I was at sticking up for what I believed in, we would have been steamrollered years before and a soft, easy target. But back then the guilt was acute.

It should have been much harder but my whole being was begging to give up drinking by the time I got to Hazelden. It was one of the most important turning points in my life. I pretended that I was doing it to keep the Trusts and sponsors happy, but after just a few days I wasn't even convincing myself. It was hard, especially the talking about feelings and apologizing all over the place, but it was astonishing how good people were to me there and when I got out. I can't remember how many people said to me, 'We're just so glad you're better, Fitz,' but there must have been hundreds.

Do they teach Americans how to be gentle with recovering drunks or are they just good, decent people? Whatever it was, I'm incredibly grateful – and it worked. Bryan, Cicely and Chris Moon helped me through the post-rehab decompression and soon after I concentrated hard on getting my instrument rating on a Cessna out of Van Nuys airport in California. Compared to the flying in Tanzania, where you can't find anyone to talk to on the radio for days at a time, it was like learning to drive at Hyde Park Corner. I came into Orange County one day with a DC9 on my nose and an Airbus on my tail. The radio controller told me to look on my starboard wing and there was a Mach 3 Blackbird spy plane speeding by overhead. It's not like that in the bush.

The flying gave me something to work at other than the AA meetings and the constant talking about my feelings. Everything was about facing your feelings rather than hiding them. I used to dread it.

'I had eggs and bacon for breakfast.'

'Well, how do you feel about that?'

I was resentful about having to 'share' and used to try and say what made me look better in the eyes of the group. That didn't work for long because they saw right through me. So I gave in and shared and it felt great, it felt right, and I found relief and hope. I wasn't so misunderstood and special after all. I was just like them and it was all about one thing: don't drink any more. Take the drink out of the equation and the rest was just a few basic rules.

My other big problem was my love life. I was OK in the animal world but that wasn't the case with human relationships. Now I had to face the world sober, like everyone else. And I was falling in love with Lucy. After nearly twenty years of living with two men who never talked about anything, it was incredibly hard to be honest with myself and with others. I had to learn how to operate without a drink inside me. So many friends helped me there, both in and out of the Programme, in the States and in Kenya, where I went for meetings on my return. I don't know what I would have done without them.

When I got back to Mkomazi four months later, they didn't know what had hit them. I was a reformed drunk and had nothing but AA meetings and work to occupy my mind. Their other boss was Mungure and he was on a mission from God. We must have been quite a combination to work for. Mungure had built up a wonderful team over the past two years and there were always new people coming forward: Zacharia Nasari, Sangito Lema, Erasto Enoch, Sifaeli Pallangyo and Isack Nasari had all come into their own while I had been away. We worked them into the ground and they lapped it up, all of us learning, making mistakes, solving them and moving on – nothing dramatic, nothing sexy, but at last we were making progress.

And when I was feeling the pressure I went to Nairobi for a Meeting, with a capital *M*. When I'd told them in LA that it was a long way – four hundred miles and in another country – to drive for a Meeting, I was met with withering stares and asked how far I had been willing to drive for a drink. Meetings were also a good way of keeping up with my meetings, lower-case *m*, with Steve Kalonzo Musyoka and Kenya Wildlife Service about what was going on at Kora.

At Mkomazi we had unswerving support from Costa Mlay, the director of Wildlife, but we were still having trouble with stock coming in and the continual senseless burning. Sometimes it was just like being at Kora – except that now we had our own aircraft and a nod from authority to operate. Fred and I used to push the cows back over the borders of the reserve, like collies with a flock of sheep. Our new plane, raised at another Morton's event, was a Cessna 206 with a STOL kit on. It was even called DOG – *Five Hotel Delta Oscar Golf* – and it's been a faithful companion to this very day. Our herding operations led to some great co-operation with Steve Gichangi, the new warden of Tsavo. One day after I had chased another load of stock across the border into Kenya, he flew straight into our camp at Kisima and said: 'Okay, Tony, you win. Let's talk.'

This was seditious language. Politically, Kenya and Tanzania were at daggers drawn, but the Tanzanians – aware that Mkomazi had two hundred miles of international boundary – trusted me to behave and keep them informed of illegal activity. It was a grey area for Steve to be in Tanzania at all but it was also insane for us not to be co-operating. So we did. And when the powers that be found out about it, we were working together so successfully that they turned a Nelsonian gaze upon the whole affair and ended up not just supporting it but allowing us a small over-the-border fly zone.

Building up the infrastructure, cutting firebreaks and getting patrols out into the northern part of the reserve was not very glamorous, but towards the end of 1992, we started noticing a gratifying increase in wild animals. In the wet season we now had more than four hundred elephants, lions were coming into the Maore area and leopard numbers were rising. At last we were able to start making plans, not just for the restoration of the park but also for its restocking. We had three big ideas – one elephant, four rhinos and as many wild dogs as we could get. Costa gave us the go-ahead on the dogs and the rhinos, but sadly he was soon to be replaced.

Joan Root had taught me all about wild dog when she had visited us in Kora and she had even convinced George that they were worth a Kora-like programme to help save them. Distressed by their hunting methods, which involve the relentless hounding of their prey, few in the wildlife world had been keen to do anything about their plight but Joan told us about their highly social and unusual pack structure and the threats they faced up to so bravely. They were also a great favourite of Brian Jackman, one of our UK trustees and a wonderful environmental writer and journalist. He wrote our first brochure and has always managed to keep us in the forefront of publicized wildlife programmes, which in turn stands us in good stead with Tanzanian environmental journalists. Wild dogs, also known as African hunting dogs, used to roam all over the continent but they have been hunted and poisoned almost to the point of extinction. They are also very susceptible to domestic animal diseases. Incredibly efficient hunters, they travel over vast areas in packs from three or four up to thirty or forty. In *Out of Africa* Karen Blixen said she once saw more than five hundred in one pack.

Mkomazi is great wild-dog country but by the early 1990s there were almost none left there. We started to make plans for bringing some in from the Masai steppe where they were hunted, poisoned and otherwise persecuted by farmers and herders alike. There, I could race around in the bush, not worrying about the poachers or bumping into people with whom I was competing for land. I travelled to South Africa and Namibia to learn more about working with the dogs and attended a Specialist Group meeting about them in nearby Arusha. After that I started building the *bomas* below our camp, where some of their offspring still live pre-release.

We needed to make a big noise to safeguard Mkomazi's new-found status, but wild dogs just weren't loud enough. We decided the best way to raise our profile would be to set up a rhino sanctuary. There was a desperate need for one. Kenya had many, but Tanzania didn't have one and the total population was under three dozen, down from well over ten thousand a few short years before. I had discussed the idea with Costa but although his successor, Muhiddin Ndolanga, gave us the go-ahead as well, we never had as good a relationship with him. In addition, Mungure had been pulled out of Mkomazi and sent on a nine-month microlight-flying course in the Selous. Given that we didn't have a microlight and you could learn to fly the Space Shuttle in nine months this was a waste of time and it impinged heavily on our work at Mkomazi. With Mungure away, I had to spend as much time as possible in camp rather than negotiating about rhinos and wild dog in Dar es Salaam. I kept my nose down and worked hard. Just like George.

As the year unravelled, so too did my relationship with Kim. We were going nowhere and in the course of the year we called it a day. I was now on my own. There was an enormous amount of work to do and a lot of flying, but I felt freer and happier.

For months I lived on the hill at Kisima. I didn't see many people but those who turned up seemed impressed by the work we were doing. Bob Marshall-Andrews had come up with the idea of the 'Friends of Mkomazi' and had gone around hitting up all my old mates to sponsor the running costs of the reserve with small monthly covenanted donations. In August seven came out to see us and were much inspired by the work being done with their money and tractor. They were particularly pleased with our road-grading method. Rather than buying an expensive grader – which I must admit I would have liked – we dragged a giant acacia tree behind the tractor on two chains. Mighty slow but it had almost the same effect in smoothing the roads and evening out the bumps.

Nigel de Winser, who had spent a lot of time in Kora over the years, was now expeditions director of the Royal Geographical Society. He was keen to set up an expedition to Mkomazi. I had managed to get Fred Lwezaula to write him a letter of welcome a few years earlier but there was now a new sheriff in town. With the support of our friend Erasmus Tarimo at the Wildlife Division, he made quick progress with the new administration and it seemed that an expedition, to be called the Mkomazi Ecological Research Programme (MERP), would be on the cards as soon as he could get it organized. It was reassuring that Erasmus was so helpful. The one time he had visited us an irate Masai poacher had chucked a spear at him. It flew right between him and Mungure without harming either man.

Mungure and I worked together on many things but while I was busy trying to get the infrastructure up to scratch, he was often out demarcating the boundaries of the reserve and keeping poachers and smugglers at bay. His rangers had the unrewarding task of anti-stock and anti-poaching patrols – hard, thankless work, it's dangerous and dirty with none of the glamour you see on *Big Cat Diary*. Rangers are paid peanuts to risk their lives daily. And if it's not heartbreaking you're not doing it properly: many of the people who are poaching and grazing are incredibly poor and pitiable and often related to the rangers charged with catching them. They are employed by big cattle barons who are very hard to prosecute. I flew at least five times a week, backing up Mungure in the field, watching out for trouble from the air, and we started building security outposts at strategic points way out in the reserve. One of the biggest problems we faced was smuggling, which was greatly encouraged by the differences between Kenya and Tanzania. Everyday basics just weren't available in Tanzania when on the other side of the border they were abundant.

Despite our inadequate resources we had to punch above our weight when smugglers tried to use the reserve as a shortcut. Sometimes it took great courage from people being paid a pittance to put their lives on the line for the love of their country.

One Sunday morning I was flying with Zacharia on the look-out for stock and snare lines when we saw a convoy of three big lorries about to come into Mkomazi from Tsavo in Kenya. They saw the aircraft and turned round, but when I doubled back later, huge clouds of dust gave them away on the main bush road to Kamakota. I called up everyone's locations on the radio. Zuberi Rajabu was driving the truck on the way into Kamakota from the boundary but he only had two rangers with him, armed with one gun with a bent barrel and no ammunition.

'Stop at the narrowest part of the road,' I told him, 'and when the lorries stop, tell them they're surrounded.'

Bravely he did just that, ignoring their threats, as I buzzed very low overhead in the plane. An agonizing twenty minutes later, Mungure came hobbling over the horizon in the little Suzuki the Trust had donated to him. He had three flat tyres but was loaded with rangers, casual labourers, people from the villages and various others he had managed to pick up. He took the lorries off to a remote track, let the air out of the tyres and offloaded the beer. Underneath the beer were hidden car spares, clothing, soap powder and food, all smuggled in from Kenya. To this day at the Namanga and Holili borders I hear Customs officers tell each other, 'That's the man who caught the White Star Smugglers,' and I have to go over the whole story again.

Early in 1993 my father suffered a stroke as he was walking to the shops. He managed to give my sister Margaret's name and address to the ambulance but never recovered so it wasn't long after that we all congregated once more in the church where I had been dragged as a child and where my mother's life had been commemorated ten years earlier. The crematorium was pure Hammer House of Horror, but I was able to console myself with the knowledge that my dad and I had at last seen the point of each other. 'You always were a difficult one,' he had said, when we had been together in Kora, 'but I must say it's stood you in very good stead.'

I went back to Tanzania and celebrated his life in the bright sunshine of Africa. Then I had to go back on the road. While Mungure continued his hard work in the field I was obliged to get on with the relentless graft of fundraising. I had learnt how to operate sober and I had mastered how to give a slide show, but how was I going to behave at the latest temptation to be waved in front of me? My crazy preacher friend Marjoe in LA had set me up with probably the best gig in the world for a single man: judge of a beauty pageant to crown Miss Hawaiian Tropic 1993. I had visions of Jacuzzis full of champagne and luscious beauties rubbing me down in hot oil. And what did I do on the way? Stop off in London and fall irrevocably in love with Lucy Mellotte, the girl who had come to Kora in 1989.

Despite my poor planning, the Hawaiian Tropic event made a fortune for the US Trust. It also produced an excellent joke. One of my fellow judges was Roberto Canessa, who had been in the Uruguayan rugby team that had crashed in the Andes and inspired the book and film *Alive!* Some of the survivors had snacked on the three-quarter line while waiting to be rescued. The first thing Roberto said to me was 'Tony, everyone I meet asks me what it is like to eat someone. Now finally I can ask you this – what is it like to be eaten?' He later complained that it was very unfair that he was ever asked, as he was one of the people who walked to fetch help. He did add, though, that since two of them were medical students they'd known where to find the best cuts.

I returned to Mkomazi with Lucy on my arm and a smile on my face. It was a while before I persuaded her to stay for ever but she still seems to be here and I still seem to be smiling. Lucy changed my world, brought chaos into order. She was as excited about Mkomazi as I was, though she must have found it very different and quite frightening at first. I knew I'd found my partner for life.

Lucy's presence in Mkomazi was a much-needed breath of fresh air. She made friends not just with all the camp staff, who adore her, but also with the control freaks, revenue collectors and bully-boys in various government departments who come to spoil, rather than create. Lucy handles everyone in exactly the same way, with genuine charm and interest, and they go away smiling, instead of with me in handcuffs.

Lucy handles all the office work and allows me to concentrate on being a good field manager and animal man, though she's catching up on that front too. She has braved the horrors of a house full of snakes, a bank account with no money in it, my rather prickly and difficult nature and long absences when I am off fundraising. I usually prefer to be flippant but Lucy really has made all the difference to my life and to our work here. I have been blessed with an incredible wife, friend and partner.

There was a lot of work to catch up on in the reserve. One of our biggest problems was water. Despite the fact that our camp was called Kisima ('water-well' in Kiswahili) we never seemed to have enough of it. We brought in a drill that managed to find water at Zange, the main gate. We had all sorts of grandiose plans to pump it to the local village but the government wanted us to pay for the privilege so it never happened. We did, however, do a lot of work with people in the surrounding area. I had learnt at Kora that there was absolutely no point in doing things for animals and conservation if the people who live around you don't know what you're doing or understand why you're doing it. We made sure from the beginning that we kept people informed of our plans and when we could afford it further down the line, we made sure that they benefited as much as possible.

Mkomazi Game Reserve Football Club was one of the many vehicles for making friends with our neighbours and by 1993 it was powering its way up Division Three. The people who really made a difference, however, were Harrie and Truus Simons, two Catholic pastoral workers who had been living and working in nearby Kisiwani for six years. They had started women's groups there, worked on long-term development projects for the Masai and set up dispensaries and physiotherapy units for disabled children. They were the exact opposite of my kind of people but an inspiration to all who met them, including me. Mungure was equally impressed so we started to work very closely with them and brought them on board as Mkomazi's educational outreach programme co-ordinators.

Sometimes it was hard to believe, during all the maintenance, politics and planning, that our work had anything to do with animals. But I had got the message from Charles Dobie: Tanzania was different. It was essential to do all the groundwork before we introduced any new animals. We had done a lot of work and now I thought we could be a bit more ambitious. The lion, elephant and buffalo populations were building up nicely due *generally* to the ban on ivory and the strengthening of conservation worldwide and *specifically* because of the sterling work done by Mungure and some of his rangers. But we worried that without Mungure the rangers could just as easily go over to the dark side as they had in so many other places. More elephant would come if the habitat was safe, but for the time being we had just clocked a thousand in the wet season and Fred Decker had helped us put in a compound for one more called Nina, who was being kept in a zoo in Arusha. We had promised her we would bust her out.

We had done some serious work on the wild-dog *boma*s and Aart Visee had come in to look at them and design a veterinary plan. The wild dogs were going to need some help to proliferate.

As soon as they started breeding on the Masai steppe we would be tipped off by our friend, Richard Kipuyo Loisiki, a concerned Masai elder who is also a senior Tanzanian government official. We could then start moving some of the dogs we collected to holding and breeding *boma*s in Kisima. We were going to have to go further afield, however, to find some rhinos because after years of poaching there were only about twenty left in the country.

My old friend Rob Brett, who had lived in Tsavo studying naked mole rats (interesting but as hideous as they sound), before becoming a world expert on rhinos, had told me a few months earlier about a group of black rhino living in South Africa's Addo National Park. The correct sub-species for northern Tanzania, they were for sale at an artificially created South African market price. We went down to South Africa to meet Anthony Hall-Martin, the head of Scientific Services in the national parks, who agreed to sell us four for US$45,000 a pop. This went down in the books as a donation to their rhino breeding programme and an acknowledgement for their having kept the species alive since they were moved there in the 1960s from Kibwezi in Kenya. That was the easy part. To buy rhinos, you don't just need money you need somewhere safe to put them and the support of the wildlife authorities. The last was easy. I flew down to Dar es Salaam and persuaded the new director of Wildlife, Muhiddin Ndolanga, to come and have a look at what we were doing. His staff begged him not to as he had meetings to attend but he did, and he left impressed. He had studied our plans for the future, seen what we had achieved so far and even met Harrie and Truus to discuss our education outreach programmes.

'Get the rhino sanctuary going,' he told me, as I dropped him back in Dar.

We took him at his word.

The first thing we needed was money. The rhinos were expensive enough to buy but building them somewhere to live was going to cost a mint of cash. We figured that we would need at least three-quarters of a million dollars, more than the Trusts had invested in Mkomazi over the previous five years. Laura Utley and Moritz Borman headed up the funding effort in the USA and Friends of Serengeti, Switzerland, and Robert Suermondt in Holland came in with huge donations to make it a reality. Without them, it just wouldn't have happened.

They were not alone. Over the years thousands of people have helped. Moritz has been an incredibly able and generous chairman of the USA Trust and, with fellow director Lee Baxter, has helped school our kids. Moritz's tiny office helped put on the Morton's events and also two fun fundraisers when, supported by the City of Beverly Hills and Tiffany's, we closed Via Rodeo and had a street party. Ali MacGraw has always been popular, ever loyal and supportive, and Jeff Stein and Georgianna Regnier became long-serving treasurers and kept us legal. Later on a very canny entertainment lawyer called Tom Garvin lent his considerable talents and generosity to the Trust. Laura Utley supported us in New York, and Peter Morton gave us his restaurant whenever we needed it. Antony Rufus Isaacs sold Mkomazi with fabulous enthusiasm and Larry Freels hosted our first-ever event in San Francisco. We had our good years and our low years but all of them have stayed with us and continue to help as we tend towards more institutional funding; we are hugely indebted to them.

While our long-suffering trustees hustled, I got on with the work. At first we had no cash so it was very slow. But it soon began to snowball as more and more people came on board. One of the first was Ian Craig, who had created the Lewa Downs rhino sanctuary in northern Kenya, and flew down in his Super Cub at his own expense to help me site and plan ours. He and Rob Brett advised us on all aspects of rhino conservation and told us what to expect. Mungure, Elisaria and I put the vision into action by walking the proposed boundary through thick bush on the ground. I had never realized how much space rhino needed: we ended up with a 32-kilometre line round a 45-square-kilometre sanctuary. Friends of Serengeti lent us a bulldozer to cut the fence line and Noremco lent us their grader. I loved those big yellow toys and they saved us so much time – I hadn't forgotten how long it had taken us to cut airstrips and tracks by hand.

We still had a long way to go. The rhino community is very particular about where their rhinos go so we needed to show them that Mkomazi was a worthwhile destination. I have a healthy disrespect for academics but sometimes they can come in very handy. Pete Morkel – top vet – and Mike Knight, one of the very few scientists that I listened to, came in and surveyed our proposed sanctuary to the highest standards. They wrote a scientific and environmental assessment that they then presented to an African Rhino Specialist Group Conference in Mombasa a few months later. Lucy, Elisaria and I had been unable to wangle an invitation or find the money to register at this gripping event so we hung around the hotel drinking lots of coffee while the boffins argued in plenary. Our proposal was grudgingly accepted, which they felt gave us the green light to start fencing the sanctuary. Little did they know that I was going ahead anyway.

Even everyday fencing is pricey but the kind of fencing that keeps elephants and people out and rhinos in is stratospherically costly. It also had to be electrified. We were many miles from the nearest power supply so Fred Ayo and I had to extend our stock of arcane knowledge to include power generation. The answer turned out to be solar and a lot simpler than we'd thought. And, many more miles from Mkomazi, it required our trustees and friends to dream up ever more effective fundraisers.

On 15 June 1994 Pete Silvester, Lucy and I met to discuss developing tourism in Mkomazi. We were always looking for new ways to attract money to the reserve and responsible tourism is one of the best. Pete agreed that he would bring his clients across the border and we would site a camp for them. The very next day we had an appalling shock. We discovered that someone in the Tanzanian government had sold off Mkomazi to a hunting company at an auction in Las Vegas. All the money our trustees had raised, all the work we had put into conserving the area had been wasted. We had been building up the numbers of lions, elephant and all sorts of game. We were investing in the most endangered species of all. Now a bunch of 'sport' hunters were going to come in and shoot the wildlife we had done so much to attract. It was heartbreaking but we weren't going to take it lying down.

9. Hunting High and Low

It was unspeakably hard not to give up when the hunters moved in next door to the research camp but I owed it to the team we had built up not to give in. Thirteen hundred and fifty square miles of Africa sounds like a lot of space but it's nowhere near big enough when it contains people who are trying to destroy everything you're doing. One of the many tragedies of the decision to allow 'sport' hunting within the reserve was that Mkomazi was beginning to bloom: the bush was recovering and the wildlife was making a comeback. It was as if we had stocked it especially for the hunters. There were lions everywhere and even the leopards were slowly becoming less cautious. In late June 1994 Lucy and Elisaria were driving home one night when they saw a cat walking across the road in front of them.

'That's a big small cat,' said Lucy, who was learning Kiswahili at the time.

'No. That's a small big cat,' corrected Elisaria, pointing to the mother leopard and her other cub, sitting just off the road.

We had been prepared for all sorts of problems at Mkomazi but it hadn't even occurred to us that it would be given over to professional 'sport' hunters. In Kenya, hunting had been outlawed many years earlier, and even in the worst days there, game reserves had been for preserving game rather than for hunting. One of the many bizarre things about the Tanzanian system is that the same ministry is responsible for all wildlife, whether for killing or conservation purposes. The minister was and, indeed, is perfectly entitled to sell the hunting rights to a game reserve on behalf of the government. It is, however, generally frowned upon to sell the rights to one of your relations so this is what we tried to highlight when discussing matters with the press and our trustees.

By the time the hunting started in July, we had done a bit of research and it was clear that this was going to be a long and wearing battle. The hunting lobby is extremely well funded and they do a good job persuading people of hunting's merits. Rich men – they're always rich men – pay a fortune to come and kill lions, leopards and buffalo. The argument goes that this money is then ploughed back into the local economy and everyone ends up happy: wildlife is given a value. I don't agree with killing for sport. Full stop. But there are a good few professional hunters whom I still respect. The one who fronted the operation in Mkomazi was not among them. Whether deserved or not, he was unpopular with hunters whose opinion I valued even if I disagreed with what they did for a living. Nowadays the hunting business isn't up to much, however powerful the hunters may be. The fact that the hunting rights to Tanzanian game reserves are auctioned in places like Las Vegas gives a good idea of the way the industry is run. It's a seedy, murky business.

When the scandal hit the newspapers, the press called upon the director of Wildlife and the minister to resign. In vain. Our local environmental journalist friends came up with good honest stuff against the lies and innuendo of the dirty-tricks brigade. The battles started with a vicious campaign to get rid of Mungure. Hezekiah Mungure is a good and honest man – one of the great wildlife conservationists of our time – and he did a great job at Mkomazi. As I said previously, you're not doing your job properly as a warden unless you're making enemies and Mungure did a very good job. The local MP and the cattle barons hated him because he stopped them grazing in the reserve, and the worst of the visiting scientists didn't like him because they had to operate in the reserve according to Mungure's rules. The men who respected him would have died for him – but what were they against ministers and millionaires? We had our own ministers and millionaires onside but, sadly, not even they could save Mungure. He was transferred to Dar es Salaam a few weeks into the crisis and was never able to return.

Faced with the nullification of our last few years' work, I really didn't feel much like showing any leadership but it was one of those times when I could feel George telling me to pull myself together and come to terms with reality. So we had to take on the hunters.

The key thing – as ever – was to keep the momentum going. We must always be seen to be making progress, however slow. Lucy did a wonderful job of keeping Elisaria's spirits up, and together we somehow kept everyone else on message. Our road-building team were hacking a route up to the top of the tallest hill in the rhino sanctuary so that we could put in a radio repeater network, the poles for the fencing were slowly arriving and the trustees continued to work hard on our behalf.

A pair of young Englishmen had started a charity called Save the Rhino International a few years earlier and had taken a shine to us. Brilliant fundraisers, they had roped in Douglas Adams of *Hitchhiker's Guide to the Galaxy* fame to climb Kilimanjaro with them. With Elisaria they walked from sea level to the top of the mountain wearing an indescribably smelly rubber rhino suit, designed by Gerald Scarfe. They gave us much of the proceeds from their climb. Save the Rhino has continued to fund us to this day and is now one of the most professional and respected wild-life charities in the world. They were a ray of sunshine in a grim year. That year, too, Sir Anthony Bamford gave us a JCB, an incredibly expensive bit of kit that was a godsend. Tusk Trust and the Elsa Trust gave us the money to transport it into the country. It was great that people still believed in us, particularly the Elsa Trust to which George had left most of his money – but there was a problem. Quite rightly, our Trusts were wary of funding a rhino sanctuary in Mkomazi when there was hunting going on. We needed to get rid of the hunters before we could translocate any rhinos.

Tsavo warden Steve Gichangi started exerting pressure through the Kenya Wildlife Service but, given the animosity between Kenya and Tanzania, this probably didn't help. Kenya was still suffering under Daniel arap Moi's jackboot while Tanzania was about to hold its first multi-party elections. Other supporters were more influential: Costa Mlay, now working in the Serengeti, pushed from his side, while Charles Dobie and Solomon Liani worked to influence players in Dar's stifling corridors of power. The key mover in ousting the hunters was a little-known MP called Philip Marmo. He was tasked by Parliament to set up a probe committee to look into hunting across the country, a job he fulfilled with aplomb. Lucy tracked him down in Arusha and briefed him about what was going on at Mkomazi. He invited us to make a legal submission to the committee, an opportunity at which we leapt. Written by Bob Marshall-Andrews, one of Britain's finest QCs, and with input from top lawyer and trustee Al Toulson, it was impressive beyond measure and encouraged the committee to visit Mkomazi and see the situation on the ground.

Every two weeks or so throughout 1994, either Lucy or I had to go to Dar es Salaam or Arusha to stave off another crisis. Much of the press had been bought off by our enemies and there was a concerted campaign against Mkomazi in which we were accused of using the park for illegal mining, smuggling and spying. Again! How anyone could think I was a spy really does beggar belief. Aren't spies meant to be discreet? The Civil Aviation Authority withdrew my flying licence and I had to go to absurd lengths to pretend that we had brought in another pilot so that we could keep doing checks on the poachers and the hunters. It was soul-destroying to watch what was going on: in just a few months they had shot nearly all of the lions that had started to come back in numbers to Mkomazi and a lot of the resident leopards. One lion they left close to the road at Maore to taunt us. Skinned and looking like an obscene jelly-baby, its paws and head had been cut off for the lucrative market in tasteless souvenirs.

In April 1995 Parliament upheld most of the findings of the Marmo Committee and ruled that all sport hunting should be banned in Mkomazi from the end of the hunting season. We were undeniably relieved but we had also become extremely wary. We decided that the Trusts' investments had to be safe-guarded by entering into a formal agreement with the Tanzanian government. Such an experience must never be repeated. The hunters got in their last despicable word when on one of the last days of the hunting season they came back to Mkomazi, drove straight through Headquarters and shot the last two lions at Maore.

That wasn't the end of it, though. We had irritated some very powerful people and, worse, we had taken money out of their pockets. The weapon with which they chose to beat us was Mungure's replacement project manager, Swai. He made accusations that were laughable but that didn't make them any less harmful or painful. Insanely he would devote his days to obstruct-ing us, then demand that the Trust pay his rangers and lend him cars. He persuaded the new director of Wildlife to ban our friends Harrie and Truus from Mkomazi and suspend all work on the rhino sanctuary.

It was something of a relief that we had another project on which we could concentrate. Bureaucrats in the Wildlife Depart-ment had closed down the rhino sanctuary, they had withdrawn my flying licence and done their utmost to squeeze us out so that a few officials could make some money out of big-game hunting but they had forgotten to close down the less glamorous wild-dog programme. We had been working on the wild dogs since we had first arrived in Mkomazi and the authorities had given us all the necessary permissions and paperwork years ago. Giles Thornton – a young adventurer on a motorbike who had worked with Alan Root in Zaïre – had got in touch and asked for a job. We had been a bit chary in the prevalent climate because we couldn't afford to put a foot wrong but he came highly recommended by Al and by Dave Stirling of Save the Rhino International; he promised to curb his enthusiasm. After a few months' working at Mkomazi, getting everything ready in the *bomas* with Sangito Lema, who would head up the dog programme, we sent him off to the Masai steppe to find us some dogs.

Giles spent months building holding compounds on a friend's farm on the Masai steppe, pinning down wild-dog dens and encouraging the Masai who lived there to leave them alone. Wildly dyslexic and not very good at maths, Giles got the exchange rate wrong and paid the Masai vast sums not to poison the dogs in their dens, as was their usual practice. He managed to rescue three litters, then put them in sacks and roared across the countryside on his bike to get them into the holding pens as fast as possible. Richard Kipuyo Loisiki, in his government capacity, gave him all the help he could. It was dirty, exciting labour that required great sensitivity in working with people, and different skills for working with the dogs. It was sad to see the parents come back to the dens to look for their pups, but they moved off after a couple of days and started breeding again almost immediately. Their pups would go on to live in the safety of the Tsavo/Mkomazi ecosystem rather than the unprotected Masai steppe and we hoped that our drastic intervention would soon start to increase their numbers from the almost untenable level of below three thousand worldwide, most of which were in South Africa.

I went to check on the pups and stay with Richard Kipuyo Loisiki, who had been such a help in tracking them down. Richard was having all sorts of trouble with anthropologists wanting to study 'his people'. He was particularly irritated by Henry Fosbrooke, one of the original conservators of the Ngorongoro Conservation Area, who was encouraging the Masai around Mkomazi to claim the area as their own. 'They justify their time in Tanzania by telling us to go back to our old ways. Quite a few Masai want to go forward with the rest of Tanzania,' he said. We rambled on about Fosbrooke and agreed that it would be fun to see what he made of Julius Leperez, a mutual friend and Kenya Wildlife Service pilot, who was the first Masai to go supersonic.

Semu Pallangyo, Sangito and Giles were having difficulty keeping all the dogs fed; they were so continually ravenous that Giles called them 'land-based piranha'. Nonetheless they managed, and on 3 September, they flew into Mkomazi with three boxes of pups. We let them loose in the *boma*s that had been waiting for them for so long. They greeted each other with delighted squeaks and twitters, like little birds, then settled down to eat an entire cow. With that one translocation, we brought back wild dog to Mkomazi. And soon wild dog that lived many miles away came up to the fence to greet the new arrivals.

It was with some glee that I sat down to write a letter to the director of Wildlife informing him of our success: 'Dear Mr Mbano, You will be delighted to hear . . . about the project you forgot to close down.'

It was just one of many official letters that we had to write that year. A daunting task at the best of times, it was made considerably easier when Bob Marshall-Andrews came out to stay for a while and helped us reply to the really intimidating ones. A great many people were using their high office to scare us and with Bob around – he saw through all their games – we suddenly weren't scared any more. There's nothing like a QC for writing a letter or seeing through the crap.

Erasmus Tarimo and he put together a memorandum of understanding between the Ministry of Natural Resources and

Tourism and the Trust. It detailed the money we had invested in Mkomazi, what our plans were for the future and the responsibilities of both parties under the agreement. We made it known throughout the government that there would be no further investment in Mkomazi unless the agreement was signed. It worked. On 21 September our chairman, Solomon Liani, and the permanent secretary in the Ministry of Natural Resources and Tourism signed the new agreement and we were able to get on with our lives again. Living in limbo had been unpleasant enough for Lucy and me but it had been terrifying for the Tanzanians working with us. This was their government, which was being manipulated by powerful individuals. They had known that what was being done was wrong but they had also felt that standing against it was a little bit like treason. To be working once more under a proper agreement was more than a relief for them: it was essential to their wellbeing.

Of course, there was much more trouble to come – we had irked powerful individuals and stirred up many hornets' nests but at least now we had an agreement on which we could build. I put down another deposit on the fencing contract and started importing 10,000 rhino-proof fence posts. We were back in business. And it looked like Tanzania was turning over a new leaf too. The first multi-party elections had taken place that year and Benjamin Mkapa had been elected president. A former journalist, he was a new broom and would lead Tanzania further into the modern era. There was a new permanent secretary at the ministry too. Rose Lugembe had a clear and direct approach to government, a welcome change from the obfuscation and shadowy power plays that we had experienced earlier. From the time of her appointment to the present day, the Trust has been partners with the ministry rather than the sparring partners of earlier times. By the end of the year Liani had even had my flying licence restored.

Lucy and I went to England that Christmas with a new spring in our steps. We had fought back disaster and now it was time to dance for the piper. I addressed the Royal Geographical Society at a fundraising evening organized by Tusk Trust. It was the first time that I had spoken to such an august body and I was frankly terrified but it was great to see so many of our supporters turning out for us after such a hellish year. Ali MacGraw introduced me, with Charlie Mayhew of Tusk. Save the Rhino's Dave Stirling was there, as was Nigel de Winser, the RGS's deputy director, who had stuck with us since the earliest days at Kora. Prince Michael of Kent walked in at the last minute to add to my nervousness. His appearance capped off a right royal year: we had entertained the Duke of Kent and Princes Claus and Willem Alexander of the Netherlands during some of its worst days.

By the time we got home I was feeling pretty pleased with myself because we had some good news up our sleeves: Lucy was pregnant. I was going to have my first child while my contemporaries were sending their youngest kids to spend their gap years with me. Late development was going to be fun.

There was progress in the reserve too. At last we could do some work with animals. The dogs were a fascinating and immediately gratifying project. With funding from the Ray Rowe Foundation and the Duffields, they looked to be doing really well. Aart Visee flew out from Holland to check on them and give them their jabs. We had been preparing the translocation for years so he had a detailed plan for all of their veterinary needs. Wild dog have been hunted as vermin all over Africa but their susceptibility to disease has brought them to the edge of extinction. They are particularly vulnerable to canine distemper and rabies from domestic dogs, so we also vaccinated them against leptospirosis and parvovirus; each one had a microchip inserted under its skin. From his earliest spectacularly sideburned days at Kora with Arusha the lion to his full-bearded present, Aart has been a constant support – a home-town vet who talks solid sense and spends less time in the field than he would like. As always, we were incredibly lucky to have him as a friend. He even spoke to Robert Suermondt in Holland, who was fascinated by the rhino project and gave it a massive financial kick-start.

Important as the dogs were, they lacked the glamour of rhinos. We knew that we had to throw more energy into the rhino project as it was already apparent that more storm clouds were gathering. There was a court case in the offing between the Masai and the government about land use in the reserve. And Mungure's replacement, Swai, had been so humiliated at being told to be nice to us again that we knew we had more trouble coming there. We raced ahead, planting the fence posts and building smaller holding compounds for the rhinos when they arrived. As with everything we do at Mkomazi, we tried to keep things as simple as possible because if anything breaks it delays all sorts of other things while we wait for spare parts and complicated machinery to be replaced. We thus made the holding *boma*s out of fence posts held together with more fence posts – no fancy electrics or hinges that could break under the pressure of a charging two-ton rhino. The result wasn't very pretty – indeed it looks like the Alamo – but we knew it would work and it still does.

We were lent a grader, which, in conjunction with the new JCB, meant we could move mountains – so we did. Now that there are so few of them left, rhinos are a big draw for poachers: we needed to ensure the very best security, which meant putting in a network of roads for our security vehicles. Just over the border in Tsavo, things were so bad that every rhino had its own armed ranger to protect it.

Anthony Hall Martin – who could have cancelled the sale of the rhinos if he had any concerns – came up from South Africa and was pleased with our new-found support in government circles.

In late 1995, I had flown up to Kora at the request of Stephen

Kalonzo Musyoka. Now Kenya's foreign minister, Steve was a serious player. Amazingly, he wanted me to come back to Kora, which, although it now had the status of a national park, was still suffering as if it were unprotected county council land. At his request I had had a look around. He and the new Kenya Wildlife Service director David Western wanted to revive our idea of putting a bridge across the Tana between Meru National Park and Kora. A major infrastructure project, this would make a huge difference to both parks and, crossing near Adamson's Falls, would be an impressive monument to the Old Man. I gave them the old bridge plans we had had drawn up years ago.

Before I met up with Steve and David Western again, I went back to Asako, the small village near Kampi ya Simba. I was horrified by what I found there. In just the past couple of years sixty-six people had been murdered in the areas surrounding the village. Erigumsa, who had helped save my life when I got chewed up by Shyman, had been killed by the *shifta*. Asako was under siege. I felt it was very important that the Trust devoted some time and money to the area that had been George's home for so many years rather than spending it all in Mkomazi. I had some great support in this from Prince Bernhard of the Netherlands, but the real power behind our work in Asako was Anne Spoerry of the Flying Doctors.

Anne was a remarkable woman who had qualified as a doctor in France before the Second World War. An important resistance leader, she was captured by the Germans, tortured and imprisoned in Ravensbrück concentration camp, whence she emerged emaciated but unbowed in 1945. She moved to Kenya and became one of the country's most valued Flying Doctors. In her small Piper Cherokee – call sign Zulu Tango – she used to fly anywhere at any time. She prolonged the lives of many thousands – George, Terence and myself among them – and she was the first person to whom I looked when I realized that Asako needed help.

Together we came up with a plan to provide a basic dispensary, regular clinics and clean water for the people there. Too far from an international border and very hard to get to, Asako is one of those places that always falls through the cracks: the closest they get to international aid is watching the vapour trails of UN planes, flying to more glamorous places like Somalia and Sudan. Anne changed that and brought a modicum of comfort to the people of Asako on which we have tried to build over the years.

We had not dropped the ball in Mkomazi but in May we did take our eye off it when our first child – Alexander, always known as Mukka – was born in London. We stayed at John and Mel Rendall's house in Gertrude Street, which is next to the trades-men's entrance of the Chelsea and Westminster Hospital and round the corner from where John had lived with Christian the lion. We were expecting a girl but, after forty-eight hours for poor Lu, we had Mukka. Lucy managed to look radiant through-out. I was thrilled beyond belief – and we would soon catch up with some girls. I'd never expected to have kids, given my way of life, but here was Lucy giving birth to someone who would be a pal of mine, I hoped, until I died. It was a very odd feeling. Would I make all the same mistakes that I felt my parents had? Would I be a good dad? What did I think I was doing starting to breed when I had no salary, lived on government land in the middle of Africa in a very insecure position? But the thrill of seeing that little boy put all my fears to bed. I knew that Lucy and I would manage somehow. And we have.

At much the same time as our life was so enhanced we also had a great loss. Solomon Liani, our redoubtable Trust chairman, died. He had done so much to protect us from the rogues, and his presence on the Tanzanian Trust had scared off many of the sharks. A great man, he was immediately and sorely missed. As something of a homage to him, I went to Washington and shot my mouth off about hunting and the trade in animal products at a congressional sub-committee. Permanent secretary Rose Lugembe had told me I could describe myself as an adviser to the Tanzanian government, a great honour and an extraordinary contrast with the previous year when we had almost been deported. I had been invited to give evidence to the committee a few months earlier, which I had done in writing, but I had been astonished to find out that they also wanted me to appear in person. It was exactly like it is on the television and I felt a bit like Oliver North, who had done so much for world peace a few years earlier. Like him, I came out fighting.

I went into lurid detail about the corruption, the payoffs, the blind eyes that are turned and the terrible damage that 'sport' hunting brings in its wake. I told the committee how wildlife tourism in a small economy is often the only foreign-exchange earner of any importance and how it was performing surprising CPR on the moribund Tanzanian economy. I explained how 'sport' hunting and wildlife conservation just do not go together; how most tourists are revolted by big-game hunters and put off visiting the countries that encourage them. I used Kenya as an example where, as soon as hunting finished, the photographic safari replaced and eclipsed it. The powerful hunting lobby, who were hoping to use the congressional sub-committee meeting as a test run for their proposal to downlist elephants to Appendix II at the next CITES conference, was furious but the US Fish and Wildlife Service loved it and soon increased their interest in Mkomazi. Giving evidence had been terrifying, if a great privilege, but it had also been an opportunity to raise our profile in all sorts of useful places.

There was still plenty of work to be done on the ground, however, and we kept at it as a stream of visitors came through Mkomazi to help us out. Aart came again to check on the dogs' progress. They were thriving and we had great hopes that we could soon start mixing them up and getting them to breed. We brought in rhino and dog experts to ensure that we were doing the right thing and our UK Trust chairman, Keith Eltringham, came to monitor our progress and to talk to the wildlife authorities. One of our key concerns was getting some sort of tourism under way in the reserve. Rhino sanctuaries and large wildlife reserves don't bring in any earnings unless tourists pay to come and look at them. Pete Silvester, who had helped me so much at Kora, now had a thriving safari business, based in Kenya but operating across the continent. He put together a management plan for a safari camp but Project Manager Swai put paid to the whole idea because he wanted hunting and all its attendant kickbacks. It was *his* last attempt to destroy us but it was by no means *the* last attempt.

We had thought Swai was awful, out for himself and willing to pervert any law or regulation to suit his own selfish aims, but his successor defied belief. Paul Marenga was bent entirely upon destruction. A headquarters apparatchik, he had almost no experience in the field. But this had nothing to do with the field: it was to do with power. He was much happier with an unfunded, decaying reserve in which he could do as little or as much as he liked than a rich and thriving reserve containing anyone who did not work for him. His first 'success' was to oversee the winding up of the MERP scientific programme. He had no use for the teams of scientists who had been coming out from the Royal Geographical Society and Oxford University for the last few years. He then turned his attentions upon us.

There were good times in those years but it was important – although not always possible – to keep things compartmentalized. Lucy and I were ecstatic with our new son, who was thriving. We had even added another room to our house in the heart of Mkomazi. Lighting was solar with an old generator to provide back-up. We had a fantastic view over the savannah and thick bush and could see Kilimanjaro for half the year when it wasn't in cloud or heat haze. Our beds and furniture were suitably rough and knocked up in our own workshops by an old and eccentric carpenter called Jumanne (Tuesday). We had a separate tent as a dining room and a small kitchen where Isaya and Emmanuel produced delicious food in glaring contrast to dear old Hamisi in Kora.

The front of the house was thirty-three foot wide, with big glass doors in slightly warped wood frames. We even had a proper loo and a tiny TV (no reception) with a video player. Curtains came later. On the sofa there was usually a small orphaned wild animal that we hoped would soon be joined, if not on the sofa at least in the reserve, by Nina, the friendly old elephant who had been living at the Mount Meru Game Sanctuary (zoo) in Arusha for the last twenty-seven years. We were already building her a compound. On the downside Harrie and Truus were being slowly muscled out of Tanzania, the court case with the Masai was looming and Marenga was a constant worry. In March we put all of that to one side so we could give Nina a new lease of life.

After years of preparation and persuasion we had managed to get all the many permits we needed to move an elephant and, more importantly, the right team and enough money. The Born Free Foundation had managed to borrow the skip truck for moving elephants that they had donated to the Kenya Wildlife Service a few years previously and Daphne Sheldrick had given us much useful advice. Daphne had been asked to take Nina to her animal orphanage in Nairobi but had foisted her on us, saying twenty-seven was a bit old for an orphan. When I said I knew nothing about elephants, she reminded me that I had known nothing about lions, leopards or wild dogs – a seal of approval for non-academics that I treasure, given the Sheldricks' magnificent track record in the care of wildlife. Tsavo would not exist without them.

Translocating elephants is notoriously hard as these behemoths of the African landscape are surprisingly delicate. They react badly to anaesthetics and cannot lie down for more than half an hour as the weight of one of their lungs crushes the other and kills them if they are left too long on their sides. Clem Coetzee is the world's greatest elephant translocater and very busy, but he flew in to help us make the move. Over many years, he has developed the drug doses that will keep an elephant conscious and standing but much subdued. The last member of the team was a quirky English actor called Martin Clunes, who was planning to film the whole episode. I'd never heard of him so had to ask some friends what he had been in before he came so I didn't insult him. I needn't have bothered – he's the least actory person I've ever met and has been a great mate and sponsor ever since. It took about sixty people and eye-watering amounts of cash to move just one elephant but the subsequent film was watched by thirteen million people on New Year's Day 1998 in the UK and has done more for the plight of African wildlife than years of slog that doesn't get publicity. And the results for Nina and ourselves were worth any amount of man-hours. Nina became part of the wider Mkomazi family and gave back so much more than we ever gave to her.

It took sixty people to get her into the crate and on to the low-loader, and then it was a grindingly slow eight-hour drive from Arusha to Mkomazi. The small, shady compound we had built for her at our camp was a wonder of engineering, making full use of the natural surroundings, including a massive rock for her to rub against. It looked like a sound stage for *Tarzan* by the time Nina arrived, with camera crews hanging from every ledge and Clunesy getting in the way all over the place. One and a half walls of the enclosure were of solid rock so she wouldn't be getting out in that direction. In fact, getting her out at all was something of a problem: after twenty-seven years in captivity she had a bad case of Stockholm syndrome. After a few weeks in her compound, I started rationing her bananas to make the outside world more attractive. Like Patty Hearst deprived of her Uzi submachine-gun, she shoved me up against the rock wall with her trunk and flexed her muscles. Well aware that she could crush me with just the slightest pressure she looked me in the eye and waited until I gave her another banana. It was my last attempt at rationing but I was damned if she was going to choose captivity over freedom.

Six weeks after we had moved her from Arusha, Clunesy and the film crew came back to film Nina's walk to freedom. They were to be sorely disappointed. With a great fanfare we opened the mighty gates of her enclosure and waited for her to emerge blinking into the sunlight. It was a very long wait, a full seven weeks, before, one morning, she just ambled out of the compound, said goodbye to everybody and charged off to the top of a mountain six miles away. It's been called Mlima Nina ever since. After all those years of captivity, she spent the next two months admiring the landscape and drinking in the view. The tallest mountain for miles around, Mlima Nina has wonderful vistas out over the plains east to Tsavo and north to Kilimanjaro. Nina then started cruising around Mkomazi and Tsavo, revelling in the freedom that she had been denied for her first three decades. She dropped in to see us every now and then before disappearing for another few months, a constant reminder of the fact that, even when times are bad, good things always happen. We adored her and she had us all taped.

There was catastrophe, too, in the middle of 1997. Harrie and Truus, who had done so much good work in the surrounding area, had, in support of us, managed to enrage all the wrong people. Their work permits were revoked and they were told they must leave the country immediately. There was so little wickedness in those two that it seemed crushingly unfair that they were paying the price while we evil sinners managed to hang on by the skin of our teeth. Harrie and Truus had adopted two children in Tanzania, built schools and clinics for children of all sorts. They were so good to everyone that they were defenceless when the powers of evil turned on them. The hunting lobby that we had so infuriated and whose tentacles stretched so far into the workings of the government took petty revenge, disregarding the fact that Harrie and Truus were doing such good for so many Tanzanians.

The Trust did everything it could for Harrie and Truus. Our new chairman, Brigadier General Hashim Mbita, went to see the minister for home affairs and had the decision to deport them delayed but it was reinstated the very next day and they had to leave for Holland immediately. We had angered the wrong people and they took revenge. Two transparently good people were thrown out of Tanzania, their lives in disarray. Their projects were dismembered and the people of the area once again cheated and disillusioned. We decided on the day they left that we would carry on their work in the area surrounding Mkomazi: we would continue to build schools and set up dispensaries on a much larger scale than we had ever intended. I think of it as vindictive do-gooding.

Amid all the grimness of Harrie and Truus's deportation and Marenga's harassment, our new chairman was a tremendous boon. Hashim Mbita is a former journalist, soldier, politician and civil servant, one of Africa's most respected elders. A close friend of both Julius Nyerere and Nelson Mandela, he was for twenty-two years the executive secretary of the Organization of African Unity's Co-ordination Committee for the Liberation of Africa during the apartheid era. He knows everybody and is respected by all. When Charles Dobie suggested we get him involved with the Trust, we were concerned that he would be too busy and would not be able to give us enough attention. We were not alone in being concerned. He vetted us thoroughly, coming down to

visit Mkomazi and analysing all our plans before he agreed to
lead us, and when he agreed, he did the job properly. I am so glad
that we passed his tests. We are honoured and proud to have him
in charge today, but back in 1997 my overwhelming feeling was
one of relief. If this great pan-African thought we were worth
wasting his time on then we were doing something right. A
marvellous man, he was a firebrand in the chamber and everybody's pal in looking for a peaceful settlement outside it. And
when Rose Lugembe – God bless her – agreed to join the Trust
a little later we knew that in the long term things would come
good.

For the time being, it was essential that we kept the momentum going on the rhino translocation. Building the sanctuary
was a massive civil-engineering project long before we could
let rhinos come anywhere near it, a point that was rammed
home to us when we received a surprise visit from an unexpected quarter. Some Germans involved with satellite imagery
translation for the government said they were curious about
the fenced area that they had seen from their satellites. Keen to
show off our work, I flew them over the compound, showed
them the rhino *boma*s and the many miles of fencing we had
been putting in over the last few years. I was proud of it. That
evening, looking a bit shame-faced, they told us that they had
actually been asked by NASA and the US government to find
out what was going on. The Americans were worried that we
were building a terrorist training camp! Considering that we
were now receiving funding and active support from the US
Fish and Wildlife Service it seemed very amusing that another
branch of the US government had to send some German scientists to check us out. All they'd had to do was ask! It's not just
Africa that can't do joined-up government.

Costa Mlay came to look at the rhino sanctuary that he had
been so involved in creating and we drove along the fence-line

together. Designed to keep rhinos in but allow free passage of smaller wildlife, many people were concerned that it was actually impeding the free movement of wildlife. That supposition was scotched on our journey along the fence when a vast bull eland – Africa's biggest antelope – jumped straight through the wire and almost landed on our bonnet. We had deliberately wired the fence to allow animals to wiggle through without hurting themselves.

Everything was ready for the big translocation but we had something to see to before then. Lucy had finally agreed to make an honest man of me and we had decided to have the wedding in Kora. Despite the national park status that George's death had earned it, Kora was still extremely insecure. The *shifta* were running wild and, in a cynical attempt to win an election, the ruling party was arming its supporters so they could intimidate the opposition. It was a very successful strategy but, more than a decade later, the country is still suffering the consequences. Pete Silvester put up a small camp for us near Christian's Rapids and was obliged to send in his trucks with an armed Kenya Wildlife Service escort. We got up there just before Easter – Elisaria, the Harries, the Runes, the Allens, the Masons, the Szaparys and the Silvesters. Maalim Shora came from Asako, and Charles Dobie stood up as my best man.

For two years there had been the most appalling drought but on the night before our wedding rain came in vast quantities, washing out the *lugga*s, streaming down the roads that Terence had built and testing Pete's safari-outfitting abilities to the height. In direct contrast to the wedding we might have had in England, rain on your wedding day in Africa is considered a great blessing. We were absolutely soaking blessed. RevCop Mike Harries – who has been a great support to Kora and Asako – did the ceremony for us as a group of bemused and bedraggled *shifta* watched from the other side of the river. Not your everyday vicar, Mike is also a pilot, farmer and windmill builder. The previous evening he said the customary 'few words' at George's grave. It was great to be able to think that the Old Man – and, yes, even Terence – were at our wedding. It was a glorious, happy day, which could only have been bettered by the rain allowing a few more of our friends to make it. Which is more than could be said for the honeymoon. We had one day on the coast at Kilifi before we had to get back to Tanzania and fight off the growing press campaign that was building up around the looming Masai court case. Our work permits had not been renewed and we were nervous that we would soon be going the same way as Harrie and Truus.

Back in camp, the wild dogs were on cracking form, mating like rabbits and keeping Sangito very busy. We were continuing with the inoculation programme at the same time as dividing the packs and allowing them to mate. We then did further separations to create more non-related breeding pairs. With extraordinary calm and patience, Sangito had come to know the dogs' pack structure and mastered feeding them – no easy task when they have such subtle differences and defer to each other in all they do. He had to learn and comprehend the complicated hierarchy existing within the groups or it would have been quite possible for some of the dogs to go hungry when the alphas and the pups were thriving. Pete Morkel and Mike Knight, who were invaluable throughout the rhino relocation process, were at Mkomazi when we returned home and we worked hard with them on yet more preparations before receiving another bolt from the blue.

In May a letter from the director of Wildlife landed on my desk. I quote it in full below:

*Subject Matter: Suspension of your Activities to Reintroduce Rhino to Mkomazi.
Point Number One: The Division is hereby suspending your activities of bringing rhino into Tanzania. Point Number Two: The Ministry is suspending the*

Memorandum of Understanding signed by Your Trust and the Ministry. Best regards. Bakari Mbano. Director of Wildlife

I didn't have much time to worry about this as I was about to set off on a fundraising trip to the UK and USA. Poor Lucy, who had only recently arrived from the more refined parts of Surrey and Sloane Square, had a terrible time, though. As I scrambled around the world looking for funding for a project whose future was now in serious doubt, she was stuck in England with a very sick Mukka who had caught malaria in Dar es Salaam on one of our endless visits trying to chase up our work permits. England is about the last place you want to be with malaria as the doctors don't recognize it and always say you have flu, a diagnosis that has killed many an African away from home.

Every week Elisaria would call from Arusha with profoundly depressing updates on how Marenga was harassing the staff members in camp and stealing from the few remnants holding out at the MERP scientific camp. I don't know whether it was because I was so worried about Mukka or because Brigadier Mbita inspired such confidence but there was something about this current setback that just didn't cause me too much stress. As always, I put my head down and kept everyone going – one step forward at a time.

Of course, we plotted revenge as well. When I told Martin Clunes what was going on, he came up with the idea of recording Marenga when he was ranting about getting rid of us. He and Neil Morrissey – with whom he was then starring in *Men Behaving Badly* – caused consternation in London's premier spy-equipment shop when they went in and bought a tiny recording device, which was then used against the official at a meeting with Elisaria. We caught him on tape vowing that he would get Elisaria 'frontwards or backwards' and would have the Trust out of Tanzania so that Mkomazi could go back to the 'sport' hunters.

It was fun to have got the recording but it wasn't that which did it in the end. Our opponents just hadn't bargained on Brigadier Hashim Mbita. It was impossible to besmirch a man of such sure integrity and he was the chairman of our Trust.

The period following 1994, the year of the Rwandan genocide when a million people were hacked to death in one of our neighbouring countries, was no time to be feeling sorry for yourself in Africa. It was a time for appreciating one's good fortune, as Lucy was reminded in Arusha one day. She was having tea with Brigadier Mbita at one of the hotels that served the Rwandan War Crimes Tribunal. He was working on the peace negotiations. They were discussing the pressures in Mkomazi while two men watched football on television at the other side of the room.

Those two between them had been responsible for hundreds of thousands of deaths in Rwanda, Brigadier Mbita told Lucy, as the men slapped each other on the back and cheered on their team. Let's keep a sense of proportion here.

Yes, we were having a horrible time but it was as nothing compared to our neighbours.

When the Brigadier and Rose Lugembe went to battle on our behalf, people knew that they couldn't get away with corruption and sly tactics. A few months after Mbano's suspension letter, we received another from the honourable minister for natural resources and tourism, Zakia Meghji. She confirmed her support for the Trust and for the rhino translocation. We were back on track.

Equipped once more with the full support of the government, we forged ahead with installing the communications equipment we had been given. Bakari Mbano, the director of Wildlife, had recently given the Trust permission to select its own security personnel to include a few Wildlife Division rangers and people from local communities who would then be under our command. With help from Brigadier Mbita, we took advantage of this singular privilege.

We identified and brought in some excellent retrenched military personnel who had been part of the invasion of Uganda that had overthrown Idi Amin. Hardened soldiers, I could teach them nothing about protecting themselves or Mkomazi's wildlife, but I could provide them with everything they needed to do a good job. We put in security posts for them, brought them the weapons they needed from the Wildlife Division Armoury and provided them with the best available radio network. All thanks to the Brigadier's influence and the support of Benson Kibonde, the highly respected warden of the Selous Game Reserve.

By the end of September, everything was ready to roll on the rhino relocation. Hall Martin in South Africa had given his final go-ahead after receiving the first 'donation' and Pete Morkel was back at Mkomazi to make sure nothing slipped in the interim. Even Nina popped in to check on everything after a long safari during which she had crossed to Tsavo with a herd of wild elephants and done a big circuit of Mkomazi. She was only one elephant but it was wonderful to see her enjoying her freedom, stretching her legs and horizons for the first time in her life. Clunesy flew in to film her in the wild and we had a fun few days before the rhino relocation took place.

We knew that having rhino in Mkomazi would be a huge boost to its status: once relocated, rhinos are hard to ignore so, politically, it was crucial to get them in. It would also help further in having Mkomazi gazetted as a national park, the highest level of protection for its inhabitants and a key part of our plan for the reserve's future. We were further convinced of the importance of bringing in the rhinos when Pilotlight tried to stop us. They were one of the non-governmental organizations (NGOs) behind the Masai court case against the reserve, and we knew they were getting desperate when they wrote to the South African High Commission, urging it to cancel the translocation. Too late. We had lengthened the airstrip at Mkomazi so it was now almost two kilometres long, one of the

longest bush strips in Africa. It was going to need to be. We had
chartered an Antonov 24, a huge Russian-built four-propeller
aircraft, to fly the rhinos directly into the reserve. Expensive, even
with BP covering the fuel costs, we figured that this was the safest,
quickest and kindest way to bring them in.

On 3 November Mkomazi was full of everyone who was anyone
in the wildlife business. Damian Bell, my old friend Pete Gilfillan's
stepson, made a beautiful camp for the VIPs, press and trust
members who had come to witness the culmination of our ten-year
project to bring rhinos back to the area. Hezekiah Mungure, who
had been so instrumental in the success of Mkomazi, was there, as
were Brigadier Mbita and Rose Lugembe. We even had Customs
and Immigration on the ground at our airstrip! Of course, after all
the years of planning something had to go wrong to keep it all
exciting. After years of drought, El Niño was upon us. The rains
that came with El Niño that year were unprecedented. Hundreds
of people died across the nation as rivers burst their banks, roads
were washed away and whole towns fell prey to rushing waters.
Our rhino-laden Antonov reached nearby Kilimanjaro airport on
the morning of 4 November, having overflown Mkomazi because
of the weather. Pete Morkel was on board, keeping the rhinos
lightly anaesthetized for they, like elephants, are perversely delicate
despite their enormous size.

We had no telephones back then – mobile or otherwise – and
were communicating by crackly HF radio with the plane on the
ground at Kilimanjaro. It had stopped raining at Mkomazi but
there was still 100 per cent cloud cover so the Russian Antonov
pilot didn't know where to land. Understandably, he refused to
move. I'm proud of my flying but there was no way I was capable of flying in those conditions so I gave the controls of my 206
to my friend Godfrey Mwella, who has more hours in his log
book than you could possibly imagine – at least twenty thousand
when we last counted. We flew into Kilimanjaro where the vast

Antonov loomed out of the mist, rain pounding its sides.

Pete was worried because he wanted to get the rhinos safely out of the plane; the pilot was worried because he'd never been to Mkomazi — it was a mud strip and there was zero visibility. A Russian, he lacked much basic English but he was not lacking in *cojones*. In the way of all English speakers the world over, Godfrey and I spoke slowly and loudly to him. On the third attempt, we managed to mime to him that if the strip dried out a little at Mkomazi, there would be no problem landing the Antonov. And he would be able to find the strip in the murky conditions because we would fly ahead of him and guide him in by sight. We set off for home, Godfrey pushing my 206 as fast as it could go, dwarfed by the much faster Antonov behind us going so slowly it was permanently on the verge of a stall. The disparity in engine sizes meant it was like a fighter plane trying to refuel in flight from a 747 — possible but requiring years of practice.

My last words to the Antonov pilot had been to land as far up the airstrip as possible because it's 'a bit muddy at the far end so you must land as close to the threshold as you can'. Those of us who had to dig out the plane later on that day felt it was a shame his English was so poor but when he landed and opened the cargo bay we had nothing but praise for him. We unloaded the crates from the plane, revived the rhinos and released them straight into their compounds. In a strangely moving ceremony, the South African high commissioner formally handed them over to Rose Lugembe. The Trust had owned them in flight; now they belonged to Tanzania, like all other wildlife in the country. Ten years after I had first come to Mkomazi, and millions of dollars later, we had something very large to show for it. Four northern black rhino were now back in the home of their forefathers, wallowing in rich red Tanzanian mud as the rain poured down on them. We didn't stop smiling for some time.

10. Homeward Bound

Having the rhinos back on their home turf was a tremendous boost for everyone working at Mkomazi. We had put so much work into building the sanctuary, fought off the hunters and the corruption, and here they were: four enormous northern black rhino that had to be guarded around the clock to protect them from poachers.

It was a shame they weren't a bit more interesting.

Rhinos do not give back like lions and leopards do. All the orphaned animals we have looked after over the years – Missie the caracal, Jipe the lioness, Tontoloki the bushbaby, Furpig the genet cat and so many more – have been affectionate even when very wild. We had discovered with Nina how important a part of our lives an elephant could become, but the rhinos were just rhinos. They like being fed and they like drinking and trotting around the place. There's a certain amount of recognition but really there's not much else, even with Semu, who spends his every waking hour with them. All this was initially a bit disconcerting but we soon realized that to expect gratitude or, indeed, anything back was to miss the point. This was their land that we had occupied. It was us that needed to fit in with them, not the other way around. And if anyone should have been showing gratitude in the relationship it was ourselves.

I'd spent thirty years devoting my life to animals, and the rhinos' complete lack of demonstrativeness was the definitive kick up the rear I needed to reassert my beliefs. George always told me that 'You must never expect more from an animal than it can give.' He was entirely correct. Animals should not be obliged to thank us for protecting their rights, to sing for their supper. And, in fact, as we gradually discovered, everything about the rhinos screamed out that they were at last living the lives of their choice. To this day they cruise around the sanctuary, nibbling at the trees they were born to browse, having the occasional fight, having sex and doing their rhino thing. To watch them live their lives free of interference is an enormous privilege and I thank them for that opportunity every day.

We settled down into a daily routine we had devised with Pete Morkel and his rhino crew from South Africa and Ian Craig from Lewa Downs. They taught our Tanzanian staff how to look after the rhinos, although they knew what to do instinctively anyway, and told them what problems to expect. But we didn't really have too many problems. The rhinos settled down happily and got on with their lives: they were home.

In the late 1990s Mkomazi at last started to take on a momentum of its own – one that wasn't a constant crisis – and allowed us to indulge in some of the things that we wanted to do, like reintroducing the wild dogs. We had put in an impressive infrastructure – it needed constant maintenance but it was all there. We had demarcated the borders of the reserve and we had water where it was required. Having the rhinos at Mkomazi was such a massive national event that we couldn't be pushed around, closed down and evicted in quite the same way as we had been before. Their very presence gave us legitimacy beyond anything we could have hoped for without them. That's not to say that our problems were over – we were about to face a spectacularly misconceived court case – but from this point on, whenever we were up against the worst of intransigent officialdom, we knew that things were different. The rhinos, their attendant security and development, cost $200,000 a year. Now if anyone wanted to take over Mkomazi, they would have to translocate the rhinos at great cost or watch them be killed off by poachers.

Guaranteeing the rhinos' safety gave us some small security of tenure.

Personal security of tenure was not really what we were looking for, however, so much as security for Mkomazi. While Marenga had concentrated all his efforts on getting rid of us, Mkomazi had paid the price: elephants were being poached, giraffe snared and he was taking bribes to allow grazing in the reserve. Our ultimate aim was to bring Mkomazi back to life and to earn it national park status, just as George's death had done for Kora. Getting the government to take full control of Mkomazi and to invest funds in protecting it was the only way to guarantee safety for the area and its wildlife, but we needed a strategy as I wasn't planning anything in the supreme-sacrifice line.

From the very beginning we had harboured the ambition of making Mkomazi into a park but had never dared to articulate it. Now I could. This overriding objective informed all our plans from this point onwards and kept us going through the bad times. Almost immediately after the rhinos arrived, when Project Officer Marenga came up with a new – and clearly insane – draft management plan for the reserve we were able to ride out the storm. The plan mentioned neither the rhino sanctuary nor the Trust; it advised demolishing the dog compounds, abandoning the security outposts and reintroducing 'sport hunting'. It wasn't quite water off a duck's back but we sent the proposal to our Tanzanian board with an incredibly detailed report and rebuttal written by Richard Lamprey, son of Hugh, who had founded the Serengeti Wildlife Research Institute. Then we let the trustees get on with things while we kept our heads down. New board member Costa Mlay, the ex-director of Wildlife who had supported us since we first came to Mkomazi, told us not to worry: 'I never told you Mkomazi would be easy,' he said. 'Just do what you do best while we on the board help protect it all.'

I took him at his word and got on with the rhinos. Giles Thornton had come down from Kenya to lend a bit of a hand, catch up with Sangito and Semu and see the doggies. Pete Morkel and his family came to stay and oversee the rhinos' release into the wider sanctuary. It was lucky that they did as I was in and out of hospital at the end of the year with malaria, septicaemia and all sorts of attendant ailments. Charlie (a female) was the first rhino to be released from the holding compounds, followed by Rose, Jonah and James. By the beginning of 1998 they had all settled down into their respective territories and then they even started to think about breeding. They didn't produce anything for years but at least they seemed to be having a good time.

Semu was doing wonders in the sanctuary, commanding a very diverse team of people from all over Tanzania as well as working closely with the autonomous security brigade who had been recruited with Brigadier Mbita's invaluable help. Once again Lucy and I were quite full of ourselves as we headed for England and the birth of our daughter Jemima on 26 January. We now had a proper family developing in Tanzania and had expanded the original one room at Mkomazi to include a bathroom, another bedroom and a separate office for Lucy. Lucy turned out to be a brilliant mother, managing to juggle two small children many miles from the nearest shop or hospital as well as taking on a lot of the work of the Trust. She did all the newsletters, kept in contact with our supporters, filled in all those damn forms and followed up after my marathon fundraising trips when I would update our supporters on our progress and enthuse them about the future. Lucy was now completely in charge of the wild-dog programme, calling me in only when grunt-work was needed, like blow-piping the dogs with darts she had prepared.

On top of the chronic difficulties with Marenga, we had the acute problem of the Masai court case. Whipped up by overseas NGOs, the Masai living around Mkomazi had brought a court case against the government, claiming that Mkomazi was their land and they should be recompensed for not being able to graze it. The government contended that the case was based on a great deal of misinformed research for which facts had been cherry-picked to fit in with a pre-planned conclusion. The plaintiffs' research had failed to turn up a very obvious fly in the ointment. The man who had negotiated, drawn up and signed the original agreements with the Masai and others was not a historical foot-note whose opinions could be surmised from slanted research: he was alive and well and in Cameroon.

David Anstey, Mkomazi's first warden, had been a lawyer and bureaucrat before he became a game warden. He came out from England and met with the Tanzanian government to discuss the case, prompting the Masai's lawyers to try to settle out of court. They had riled the government, however, which wouldn't allow them to drop the case and insisted that the matter be settled once and for all. David had to give nine hours' evidence in court during which he virtually demolished the Masai case. Following the court case, at the request of Tanzania's Wildlife Division, David and Lucy went through the report on which much of the case had been based. The government had found that in 'the above-mentioned document, both historical and current issues were corrupted to fit a particular viewpoint' and they wanted their views put on record so that the reports could not be used against them again. David and Lucy wholeheartedly agreed, but getting provisos added to already-published papers is impossible.

The Brigadier, Costa, Rose and Charles were doing a great job watching our backs in Dar es Salaam, but on the ground in Mkomazi, Marenga was enraged at his loss of face. The minister had told him off in front of his employees and he exacted his revenge upon us. 'A trap has been set for the *mzungu* by Marenga,' he told one of our employees on tape. 'He will get caught in the trap. He will get letters from Marenga. I will make him follow my orders or I will destroy him and his camp. This is now my place and nothing to do with the *mzungu* any more.'

The first salvo in his campaign came when he charged Elisaria, Lucy and me with 'violation of procedures'. We were obliged to stand trial in Same for Elisaria's alleged failure to turn on the interior light of a car when asked by a ranger at the Njiro entrance to the reserve; Lucy and I had not even been in the car in question; Elisaria was never asked to turn on the light; the car had no interior light. Just putting it down on paper reminds me of how very dark and mad that whole period was – the charge didn't even exist in Tanzanian law. A few weeks later Marenga arrested me and took me to Same jail late on a Friday night. Just as when I had been beaten up in Kora, the officer in charge refused to imprison me. A few weeks later, Marenga would not allow Bob and Gill Marshall-Andrews to visit us but was overruled by Dar es Salaam. All these humiliations were like death by a thousand cuts for Marenga. Every time he tried to get us, he was foiled and made to look yet more ridiculous. It wasn't easy being the butt of his ire. His hatred of us became ever more unhinged. And for the next nine months we had to go to court once a month where our case would be 'mentioned' and the usual paid-off witnesses arrayed against us. Elisaria, Lucy and I would fly into Same where our friend the district commissioner would pick us up and look after our babies while we appeared in court. We would stand in the dock with people we had helped to arrest for poaching while Marenga paid off his witnesses on the court steps in full view of anyone passing by. Angry as I was, I was able to laugh it off but it was no fun at all for Elisaria and Lucy. The magistrate was not enjoying it either. The obvious travesty of justice was demeaning his courtroom and wasting his time. And when he allowed us to play him the Martin Clunes-assisted spy-recording of Marenga vowing to 'get us', we knew we were going to be all right.

We could have spent our whole lives worrying about Marenga and the court cases but we had to keep the rhino and dog programmes moving forward and the Trusts had to keep them funded. Some of our trustees and donors, however, were understandably tiring of the endless shenanigans at Mkomazi. One minute we were asking for hundreds of thousands of dollars for rhino translocations, the next we were in court, fighting with the warden of the reserve. It all made sense to people like Bob Marshall-Andrews and Moritz Borman, our patron and chairman in the USA, who had been able to visit Mkomazi, but to those who hadn't, the project was beginning to sound dangerous with its court cases, the government's withdrawal of work permits and flying licences. Pete Brandon had been in the car with Elisaria during the incident that had sparked the current court case so he, too, understood but many others didn't. It was hard.

Funds became very tight, and some of the time we weren't able to use the vehicles we had been donated because we had no money for fuel. Feeding the dogs was not a problem as we were given tons of food by Gilbertson and Page, the British pet-food manufacturer. The rhinos were now browsing for themselves. Right when we were at our most broke we received the funds from the George Adamson Trust in the Netherlands to build a secondary school in Kisiwani. This major undertaking went on as we were scrabbling for money to pay the wages of the wild-dog keepers. It was a crazy situation but nothing new. We did what we could with the funds we had and pushed on with the school, which we hoped would stand as a monument to everything that Harrie and Truus had done in the area. Schools sound like an odd thing for an organization like ours to be building but education is a great way for Mkomazi and places like it to show they are of benefit to the communities on their borders.

The middle of 1998 was marred by appalling tragedy when the US embassies in Nairobi and Dar es Salaam were blown up in a simultaneous attack. Africa hosted the start of the 'war on terror' that was soon to engulf the world. Hundreds of people died –

none of whom we knew. But in October tragedy struck closer to home: we received news from Kenya that Giles had been murdered near Mombasa on the coast. His killers have never been found. It was no consolation that he had stayed with us in Mkomazi a few months earlier and seen how well the dogs he had found were doing. They had been long, happy days when Giles had flown around the reserve on his paraglider before jumping on his bike and roaring out of our lives. And it didn't lessen the sadness. Giles had brought a great sense of fun to everything he did and made even the smallest episode into an adventure. He would have loved the little lioness that came into our life just as he left it and she might even have kept him in the conservation business for which he was so well suited.

Some of Danny Woodley's rangers in Tsavo had found the cub close to a fire lit by pastoralists. They had waited in their car for twenty-four hours before deciding the mother must have died in the fire and picking up the cub. It was an amazing show of how thinking had changed since I had first come to Kenya. Before George's methods became widely known, a ranger would have scooped up the cub and driven away without a second thought as to where the mother was. We named the cub Jipe after the lake that lies between Tsavo and Mkomazi and started the long process of helping her to grow up in the wild.

I was electrified to have another lioness to look after. Nina the elephant was a glorious addition to our lives but having the chance to work with another lioness was an unexpected treat. The children adored Jipe and so did everyone else. She lived in the house with us for a short period, while Zacharia built her a compound, and formed special bonds with him, Elisaria, Fred and Ombeni. Warm and friendly from the very beginning, she reminded me of Lisa, the soppy but successful lioness who had been at Kora when I'd first arrived there. By December, Jipe had her own compound below the mess tent where she was looked after by Zacharia and Ombeni, both of whom had a wonderful way with her. She soon tired of mince with egg and milk and was on to solid bits of meat as she would have been in the wild. We took her for long walks around the reserve as we had in Kora and she soon made her first kill. I had almost forgotten how wonderful it was to walk through the bush with a lion by my side, seeing what was going on in a totally different way. It reminded me of those happy days with Christian, Lisa and Juma in Kora when I had first been learning about the bush. I was in heaven. But we had to hide her from Marenga by moving her, Zacharia and Ombeni to a tiny camp in the rhino sanctuary when she was eleven months old. We had the proper permissions but didn't dare take any chances.

The work in the reserve carried on as the court cases and controversies raged away. We had all sorts of academics coming to look at the rhino project and the wild dogs, many of whom were amazed by our success. Dr Rolf Baldus, who has done a huge amount of work at the Selous Game Reserve, said he was stunned by the efficiency of the rhino sanctuary and had thought he would never see its like in Tanzania. Our old friend Dr Rob Brett, who shares many of our views about his academic peers, came to do an assessment of the rhino sanctuary. Over dinner one night, we were discussing the world of conservation academia when Rob's face took on a sombre aspect. He said that there were two terribly depressing things about working in the rhino world, first, and most obviously, 'the imminent extinction of the species', but second, watching the Rhino Specialist Group of bearded academics dancing in a disco.

Because we were doing the dogs as well, we were involved with a whole different group of 'dog academics' although, happily, it is a much smaller field. In April there was a meeting of the Wild Dog Specialist Group in Arusha and it went surprisingly well. It was decided that we should carry on with our reintroductions. There was no disco. The very next day we had to attend court again in Same. As I had predicted from the start, but had often found hard to believe, the Wildlife Division had been embarrassed into withdrawing its case against us. Marenga was obviously sick in both head and body and had made the department look bad so they transferred him out of the reserve and threw him on the scrapheap. It was extraordinary how his departure put a new spring in people's steps. Although he had not worked alone, he had been the instrument of our persecution. His campaign against us had been wholly unpleasant, and for some quite terrifying, but it had strengthened us as a team. Elisaria had stood up in court to defend us outsiders against his own government and compatriots. Many others, too, including some of Marenga's officers, went out on a limb for us at great risk to themselves. I don't really do humble but was nonetheless incredibly grateful for how our team at Mkomazi supported us through those times.

Time had moved so quickly that we were amazed when in June Pete Morkel reminded us we had to change the transmitters in the rhino horns. This can be a major and expensive undertaking involving helicopters at a thousand dollars an hour if you want to minimize the risk to the rhinos. There's no distracting a rhino with a stick while you hold your breath and whip a collar round its neck as we had done in Kora with the lions. Like leopards, but more so, they don't have the right shaped heads for collars. What we do instead is drill a hole in their horns (which are just keratin and have no nerves in them), insert a battery-powered transmitter, then seal it with dental acrylic. To do this the rhino has to be completely knocked out, but the shorter and lighter the state of unconsciousness, the safer it is for the animal.

Pete had heard that a film crew was visiting in a helicopter so we took advantage of their presence. He darted the rhinos from the helicopter with a capture gun, then we landed nearby and did the business as fast as possible. We had a problem, though, with Jonah: he charged off into deep bush after we had darted him, a dangerous and possibly life-threatening thing to do. We had to act fast because he could fall and drown in the water nearby but there was nowhere to land the helicopter. Pete – calm and professional as always – guided in the helicopter, jumped thirty feet into the tree canopy, shinned down a trunk, fixed the transmitter and revived Jonah without batting an eyelid. Now that's my kind of academic.

In August we finished Kisiwani secondary school and Minister Zakia Meghji flew into Same to open it. It was wonderful to see one of our achievements being embraced so wholeheartedly by the government. A lot of work had gone into the school – US$100,000 raised by Aart Visee and the Dutch Trust, hundreds of hours of labour from Mkomazi and the Tanzanian Trust, but most of all the vision of Harrie and Truus who had done so much for the small community where they had lived. Our friend Richard Kipuyo Loisiki from the Masai steppe had come to stay with us a few weeks earlier and had met some of his fellow Masai elders. They blamed their court case against the government on the influence of foreign NGOs and were now showing their support for us by sending their children to the new school. Projects like the school – and, of course, the departure of Marenga – completely changed the atmosphere at Mkomazi and its environs.

And there was more good news to come. It was at the reception after the opening of the school that we first met Salum Lusasi, the new Wildlife Division project manager. After the horrors of Marenga we were very wary of what might happen next but were agreeably surprised. Lusasi was a real old pro who had worked at Headquarters for years. Now that he had been sent to the field, he made sure that he met all the old wardens who had worked in Mkomazi, and interviewed the rangers and the local government officials before jumping to any pre-ordained conclusions. Salum Lusasi worked with us rather than against us, and we had a great relationship for the next seven years. Almost immediately we started putting in a new road between his head-quarters at Zange and ours at Kisima. He provided the labour; Anthony Bamford and the English Trust provided the heavy plant. We put the fuel in.

By this time we really had a huge amount of equipment and could make a big difference quickly. Larry Freels sent us loads of kit from the States, we had a grader on hire purchase and we were receiving good funding again from people like Tusk. The key, however, to things working smoothly was incredibly mundane: good book-keeping. It was odd that I had never grasped this before. My office and workshop are both obsessively neat with everything labelled and in its place, but our accounts had always been a much-feared muddle.

Andy Mortimer went to school with me and has been on the Trust since the beginning, but in the mid-nineties he and his wife Georgina really took us in hand and showed us how to make the most of the money we were receiving. He guarded the Trust's money like a leopard looks after her cubs and ran the books like the chief finance officer of a large company. He gave us a monthly amount for wages, staff food, our grub and a few spares and made us keep a simple cash book. Andy paid all the big bills, had us audited and dealt with the charity commissioners as well as organizing obscure spares that I requested. He's still in charge of our finances. 'I don't like surprises,' he says, and we don't dare give them. Even before the Mortimers had come to see us, they knew where we were going wrong. They taught me about depreciation and how buying a new Land Cruiser might work out cheaper than constantly repairing a couple of wrecked Land Rovers. But by then, thank God, Lucy was here and could make sense of it all. I still do everything in my head. Without Andy and Georgina, it's fair to say we would have collapsed years ago, like so many other charity projects without strict financial controls. And we're still good friends, although I must exasperate the hell out of Andy. Bob Marshall-Andrews noted in his speech at the Trust's twenty-first anniversary at the Royal Geographical Society that he saw a letter from me to Andy that I had signed off, 'Yours, expecting a bollocking' and noted that it was an interesting relationship, seeing as Andy was only a couple of years older than me. But, then, you haven't met him.

As I've said before, it's fairly easy to get someone to adopt a wild dog or help buy a rhino from South Africa. They're tangible and you can see what you're getting. But with projects such as ours, there are always unforeseen emergencies that need money immediately, like fires, breached dams, rolled vehicles, broken windscreens and elephant ripping up pipelines. It is also difficult to raise money for the mundane but essential things – fuel, uniforms, batteries, wire, poles and the like. Everything Andy and Georgina did has set the Trusts on a much more stable basis. Of course we still have emergencies but they're no longer such nail-biting, shrieking crises as they used to be because we have planned ahead – maybe not for that *particular* emergency but at least for *an* emergency – and can react accordingly. The Mortimers completely transformed our accounting systems, forced me to plan ahead and to court more institutional funding.

Three of the institutions that have funded us allowed us to make fundamental changes to the way we work: the Suzuki Rhino Club, the International Fund for Animal Welfare and Bob Bishop's Swordspoint Foundation. IFAW in East Africa is headed up by James Isiche, the former warden of Tsavo West. He knows the pressures we work under, and introduced us to his boss, Fred O'Regan. Together they have allowed us to plan years rather than months ahead and, incidentally, have moved us on to more efficient Land Cruisers. The same must be said of Swordspoint, which helped us over a terrible funding crisis and continues to ensure the long-term safety of our rhinos. The Suzuki Rhino Club is our biggest donor.

Mkomazi is a good 1,300 kilometres away from Kora but both are very close to my heart. Even during the darkest days at Mkomazi, I was always keeping an eye on Kora and trying to do as much for it as possible, but in 1999 the Kora project had a major setback. Anne Spoerry, the marvellous doctor who had planned and spearheaded all our interventions in Asako, died in her sleep at the age of eighty. She had done many Flying Doctor clinics there and we had put in a new hand pump to provide the villagers with their first ever clean water. Without her forceful presence the board of her organization was not so interested in our partnership so we were going to have to think of new ways to help the village.

The fact that Kenyan foreign minister Stephen Kalonzo Musyoka was involved in the area was a great boon. He had pushed for a bridge to be built just above Adamson's Falls so now Kora and Asako were much more accessible to everything, including tourism, which could bring new life to the area if handled properly. And Prince Bernhard had come up with the cash to restore George's camp, burnt down by Somali raiders in the dark years. By this time the prince liked to fund things such as our Trust with personal cheques rather than making us go through his WWF's lengthy funding process.

We had great plans for Kora but commuting between it and Mkomazi was an expensive struggle. At least we knew it was being looked after by people who cared about it and progress was being made. Pete Jenkins's son Mark was now warden of Meru and Kora. Bitten as a child by the lion Boy, he had been brought up in Meru. He understood the area's wonders and was well aware of its problems. He was reclaiming it by taking the battle to the poachers – and winning. We got on well.

Throughout 2000 we made a concerted push towards getting Kora back on the map and Asako more into the twentieth century, if not yet the twenty-first. There was a real feeling of optimism in Kenya at that time. President Moi was still clinging on by his fingernails but he was going to have to stand down at the end of 2001, hoisted by a two-terms-only law of his own making. The government in waiting, with my friend Mike Wamalwa at its core, was running on an anti-corruption ticket and the whole country thought they had only a year left to wait before the good times started. Richard Leakey was the new head of the civil service and my old friend Nehemiah arap Rotich was in charge of the Kenya Wildlife Service. These were honourable people with whom our Trust could do business.

I managed to get a film company to finance most of the Kora trips that year because I was about to appear on celluloid – not as an actor, as I had for the Japanese, but as a character. Since George's death I had been approached by a wide variety of people wanting to make a film of George's life in Kora. I went with a Dutch Canadian called Peter Kronenborg, who gave me script control and agreed to film in Kenya instead of rushing off to South Africa. This provided four hundred Kenyans with jobs, which was a huge source of satisfaction to me.

They managed to get Richard Harris to play George and he was brilliant. I first arrived on the set in Shaba when they were filming a 'Joy visit' that I had written with the scriptwriters. The whole setting and the characters were incredibly realistic and made me feel very odd. Richard and I talked for twenty-four hours almost non-stop and he adopted all sorts of Georgeisms that I suggested to him. John Michie, who played me, became a good friend even if I thought he portrayed me a little bit too smoothly. Honor Blackman as Joy was terrific but they should have given her a bigger part. Geraldine Chaplin was great, and the African actors were well rounded and developed instead of being sidelined as usual. For once they weren't just the baddies: Fred Opondo was superb, as was Tonny Njuguna. It ended up being a strange mish-mash of a film and didn't do very well despite Richard's performance. Still, it provided me with a couple of opportunities to visit Shaba, where it was filmed, and Kora, and it wasn't the embarrassment that so many films turn out to be.

Back in Mkomazi we were having a relaxing year, for once, with most things going as planned. We had a chance to think about where we were going and do some more forward planning. We had seen how well security was handled at Lewa Downs in Kenya so we sent two groups of guards from the rhino sanctuary up there to see how they did their patrols. They came back enthused and invigorated, which was more than could be said for the rhinos. They had yet to produce any calves. We had re-entered negotiations with South Africa to bring in more rhinos and were also talking to Chester Zoo in England, fast becoming one of our key supporters.

Nina was a frequent visitor to the camp but, much more excitingly, she had been seen with a bull and close to a large herd that lived between Tsavo and Mkomazi. It is very rare for elephants kept so long in captivity to mate so this was great news. As with the lions in Kora, we knew we were doing well when Nina was feeding herself and controlling her own territory. And now she was mating. Jipe, too, had found a mate. We had moved her compound further out into the bush in the middle of the year where she lived with Zacharia and Ombeni. She had started to hunt from her tiny camp in the rhino sanctuary but the wildlife soon got twitchy and the rhino were due to start breeding. Her new camp had a wonderful high view towards the Kenya border, a wide-open *mbuga* (scrubland plains) surrounded by hills on three sides with a small double *kopje* on the open border with Tsavo West and Kenya. It was dry and dusty but there was plenty of game. Dust devils passed through, as did large herds of elephants. We called it the Supabowl and put in an airstrip there. Thus Jipe became the only lioness in Africa to have her own airstrip and, when occasion needed, a Flying Butcher!

There on the plains between Tsavo and the rhino sanctuary she was able to establish a territory for herself and become a proficient hunter. Most days I would manage to get down there to take her for a walk or help Zacharia feed her. They had formed a great bond, an important one since Jipe had no family to help her hunt. I wish George had lived long enough to meet Zacharia, who really was amazing; they would have got on so well together. I wish, too, that he could have met my children because in July 2000 Lucy managed to produce not one but two more – Imogen and Tilly. Lucy wanted to get rid of me after the birth so I went and had an operation similar to the one George had had just before he died, except mine was by laser and took just twenty-eight seconds on each eye. Not only did I now have four beautiful children but at last I could see the little buggers. We spent a quiet couple of weeks in England while Lucy got her strength back, then headed to Mkomazi with a family that we agreed was probably big enough by now.

Aart came out in August to do some more vaccination work with the wild dogs and look at the school that the Dutch trust had funded. Giles's original pack had now produced four litters and we were becoming very proud of what we had achieved – both on increasing overall numbers and on research. After a lot of trial and error we had discovered that wild dogs need three rabies vaccinations in quick succession for them to be effective. Aart had been working closely with Professor Osterhaus at the Erasmus University in Rotterdam and had written up his research in a series of papers. Our work had so impressed Save the Rhino that they were now indulging in a bit of cross-species fundraising and were giving us money for the dogs as well as the rhinos!

But then at the end of the year things went horribly wrong.

The wild dogs started dying. It began with the pups, then spread to the adults and there was nothing we could do to stop it. Some just went into their dens and didn't come back. Others got terrible diarrhoea and watery, light-sensitive eyes. They sneezed and whimpered, wasted away and then they died. We were all shattered, particularly Sangito, who had reared them from pups, as they died in the compounds below the house, moaning pitifully rather than chirping and twittering as before. Aart rushed out to Mkomazi immediately but could do nothing for them, except go back to Holland and try to pin down the disease. As more dogs died we had to report to him their symptoms, take blood samples from them, and then, much worse, brain samples. The virus jumped from compound to compound until forty-nine of the fifty-two dogs were dead. The three remaining dogs called all night every night for the whole of January.

Our work in the field continued but it wasn't being helped by the Wildlife Division rangers who were behaving badly. They had been at Mkomazi for many years longer than Lusasi and were brilliant at playing the game. They knew how everything worked, and they knew how they could take a bribe to turn a blind eye to illegal grazing or sneak off to Same when they should have been patrolling. When we picked them up on anything, they would accuse us of spying, illegal mining or some other strange activity that would require another investigation to put the rumour to rest. There was an ever-growing animosity between our professional and efficient security team of retrenched soldiers and the slovenly rangers with whom they were obliged to work. They didn't like my work in the air or our guys on the ground.

We were able to raise these problems when Erasmus Tarimo and the director of Wildlife came in with our new MP John Singo. They were all supportive but the problem with the rangers was chronic, not helped by Tanzania's employment laws,

which meant they were almost impossible to fire. It was great
to meet our new MP: a former headmaster of one of Tanzania's
top schools, he was enormously respected and seemed to know
everyone who was anyone as he had either taught them or their
children at some point in his long career.

We have many great visitors at Mkomazi but in early 2001 we
just had too many. At times it was almost like Kampi ya Simba
in those days before George's death. All our nerves were on edge
with the still unexplained deaths of the dogs and the growing
problems with the rangers. It was very difficult to be gracious
with our guests even when one of them turned out to be Deng
Xiaoping's daughter. One with whom I had no problem, though,
was Fred Lwezaula, whose visit gave us a big boost. Now retired
and living in Mwanza on Lake Victoria, it was Fred who had
given me the pick of his game reserves when I was on my uppers.
It was thrilling to be able to show him the rhino sanctuary, the
road network we had built up, the dams we had dug and the
communications systems we had put in. He was genuinely
impressed by how much we had managed to achieve in the last
ten years and, based on long experience, had some sage remarks
to make about the problems we had encountered with rumours,
politics and corruption.

In an entirely selfish way, my trip to the Netherlands in March
was gratifying: Prince Bernhard awarded me the Golden Ark for
Conservation, a great honour that cheered me up at a grim time.
'I should have done this years ago,' he said, as he pinned the medal
on my chest at the Soestdijk Palace.

'That wouldn't have done your reputation much good,' I
replied.

'Do I look like a man who would care about that?' said the
prince, before dragging me into the corner and insisting that I
write to him direct for funding for the George Adamson Wildlife
Preservation Trust.

It reminded me of the funny day in Kora when I had first met him. He had insisted on being photographed with George, sitting on our elephant-jaw loo seat. He had then given us enough money to build a ranger station in Asako. He was a good man, Prince Bernhard.

I followed up the award ceremony with a visit to our Trusts in the UK and US. We were trying to reach out to more main-stream donors and, as I'm sure Prince Bernhard was aware, my award impressed a great many of them. One who didn't need impressing was the B in JCB, Anthony Bamford, who had already done so much for us. He gave us a Fastrac tractor. And Hilla and Moritz Borman, who head our US Trust, said they would help start a fund for school fees. This was something that Pete Brandon and the Marshall-Andrews family had done on a less formal basis a few years earlier, with startlingly successful results. They had clubbed together to fund Elisaria's son Zakaria through university and law school. Zakaria is now the attorney general's deputy in Arusha.

There was good news back at Mkomazi. Our surviving alpha female wild dog was pregnant and two female stranger wild dogs had been visiting the holding compounds where the three survivors were living. The visiting females were fit and in good condition, but we had to think hard about what to do. We needed some new blood but were still worried about what had killed the old dogs. It had been distemper but of a virulent strain that had overcome their vaccinations. Could we ensure that any new dogs would not succumb to the same thing? While we decided what to do, our alpha female gave birth to a litter of eight pups and died.

We had to hand-rear the pups while Aart consulted with his fellow veterinary experts over what to do about the two visitors. Towards the end of August we came to the joint decision to try to capture them so we could restart the breeding programme. We only managed to get one, by the sophisticated method of leaving a trail of meat leading to the open door of one of the compounds, then pulling it shut with a string when hunger and curiosity got the better of her. The other was a lot more wary and it was another month before we managed to dart her from the back of a moving quad bike. The two formed the basis of all our later dog work.

As the world rocked from the effects of 9/11, there was a sympathetic feeling of togetherness in Kenya and Tanzania. We had suffered this sort of terrorism before – and from the same source – when the US embassies in Nairobi and Dar es Salaam had been bombed a few years earlier. Even out in the middle of the bush, the attack on the Twin Towers felt much closer to home than it might have done in another country. However, it is astonishing how quickly that feeling dissolved following the invasions of Iraq and Afghanistan.

Simultaneous with the terrible news from abroad, happier events closer to home started to catch up. Suddenly and unexpectedly the Wildlife Division issued a permit for us to bring in a further four rhinos from South Africa. BP again agreed to cover most of the fuel costs and within days we were gearing up for another translocation.

Minister Zakia Meghji said that she would officiate at the ceremony when the rhinos arrived. This added greatly to the complication but was an honour we wouldn't have missed for the world. At the same time as fixing the holding pens and getting everything prepared for the rhinos we had to learn all sorts of complicated protocol to ensure that Mkomazi didn't let down the minister who had supported us through so many hard times.

Three days before the rhinos were expected to arrive, our manager Elisaria was driving back from Moshi on the back road into Mkomazi. Many miles from anywhere he found a car angled across the road that looked as if it had broken down. A woman stood beside it, peering into the engine. As soon as Elisaria stopped, bullets tore into his car and he was dragged from the front seat. He was pistol-whipped and badly beaten before being driven into the middle of the reserve, roughed up some more, tied to a drum of fuel and abandoned after they threatened to set fire to it. The bandits had torn the car to pieces but Elisaria didn't have what they wanted – the monthly wages that came in by air. He had just driven to Moshi to sort out some last-minute arrangements for the rhino translocation.

Bleeding and concussed, Elisaria managed to untie himself, then walked ten kilometres in the dark to Salum Lusasi's office at the main gate. But it was too late to catch the kidnappers. Fred and I flew all over the reserve, the police searched and put up roadblocks, but they had disappeared. The gang went on a long spree and were eventually gunned down in Arusha a few months later. Bruised and battered though he was, Elisaria was lucky to have survived.

The incident gave the press something to talk about as they waited at Mkomazi for the new rhinos to arrive. Given the scarcity of rhinos in Tanzania and the presence of the minister, the relocation was a major news event so Elisaria was the centre of attention. For months afterwards people would come to his house and say how sorry they were about the attack. We all were. It left us badly shaken that something so nasty and potentially lethal could have happened right in the middle of the reserve. We knew that the car must have passed through a very quiet roadblock on the back road – yet, scarily, the rangers manning it had no recollection of the car's number plate and couldn't describe the people in it. Luckily, with the arrival of the rhinos, we didn't have much time to think about it.

Once again a vast Antonov landed them on the airstrip by the rhino sanctuary. This time it wasn't raining but that was about the only thing that didn't go wrong. South Africa had given us the wrong measurements for the vast gaping maw of the Antonov's cargo bay. This meant that there was a two-foot drop between the lip of the door and the base of our trailer – a logistical nightmare: you can't just fling around rhino crates and hope for the best. You have to keep the rhinos lightly sedated and get them in and out as quickly as possible or they dehydrate. But if you worry too much about sedating them and instead drop them two feet into a trailer, you can easily injure the animal or the trailer.

Lucy worked wonders by whisking all the 150 guests and dignitaries off for lunch while we worked away with the JCB and the tractors, putting in ramps and inching the tightly packed crates out of the cargo bay. There were all sorts of speeches up at the camp and all the right people were there: Lucy managed to pluck the available triumph from the jaws of the Antonov while we attempted to avert disaster. We managed it with no mishap but it took ages. That one wrong measurement meant it took six hours to offload the rhinos. It was with some relief therefore that we had a last check of them, put the empty crates back into the Antonov and watched as it took off into the setting sun, scattering buffalo from the airstrip with the roar of its four mighty engines.

One of the rhinos – called Badger – was very young and could be hand-fed by the children when he first arrived but there was always something wrong with him. The other three adapted well to the holding pens but Badger, although charming, was never on completely top form. We tried all sorts of veterinary tests but couldn't work out what the problem was. The dogs, too, were subjected to a barrage of tests. Aart came in to see the new breeding pairs and the eight new pups and everything seemed to be going well.

Soon after the rhinos arrived we set off for a fundraising do in England that friends of the Brandons had managed to persuade

Jeremy Beadle to host. Earlier in the year I had met one of my heroes, David Attenborough, in bizarre circumstances. I had been dragged kicking and screaming to the Glyndebourne Opera Festival to see our old neighbours Gus and Imogen Christie. Gus had been a wildlife cameraman in Tanzania before inheriting the family opera house and Imo was a great friend.

'I always knew one day that I'd meet Tony Fitzjohn but I'd never in my life thought it would be at Glyndebourne,' said Attenborough.

We beamed happily at one another as Imo said, 'You'll never know what it took me to set this up.'

It was a great day and I even liked the singing. A quiz night, however, was a little more my style – even if it was with celebrity backing. Beadle did a brilliant job and made us a fortune. Despite being regularly voted the most hated man in Britain he was incredibly kind and good fun. We were sad when he died a few years later.

Rage was closer to what we felt when we returned to Tanzania. We had problems with Immigration at the airport, which should have been an augury of things to come. We spent much of 2002 trying to have our work permits renewed but always came up against strange reasons why they were being delayed. Despite the efforts of our wonderful new trustee Bernard Mchomvu, we were passed from ministry to ministry on endless trips to Dar but we never received more than a month's extension. Both Bernard and Rose Lugembe are former permanent secretaries who have worked in many ministries yet they came up against an immovable object. This lack of legitimacy was a constant nagging worry and wasted a huge amount of time in what was a very busy year.

We now had eight rhinos living in the sanctuary, all named, I should add, by their former keepers in South Africa. One of them, Elvis, spent his whole time either picking fights or looking for them. Badger was not at all well and, despite many visits from Pete Morkel, we still couldn't work out what was wrong with him. We had wormed him, given him antibiotics and special food, but he was still failing to digest properly and was fast losing muscle condition. Our main concern with the rhinos, however, was their security. The Wildlife Division rangers with whom our security teams were obliged to work were becoming ever more slack and manipulative. They had stopped wearing their uniforms, often didn't turn up for work and were always disappearing with the keys to the sanctuary gate. Sadly Lusasi seemed unable to recall them to their duty. Once when Pete Morkel – whom they all knew – flew in from South Africa to check Badger, the Wildlife Division guards at the rhino sanctuary refused to let him in. The atmosphere was ever more unpleasant.

When we heard news from Danny Woodley in Tsavo that their poaching problems were increasing we became extremely worried. There is no fence between Tsavo and Mkomazi so if the well-trained paramilitary anti-poaching teams in Tsavo were losing rhinos to poachers, then our ill-trained and badly led Wildlife Division rangers would be no match for them. It was a great credit to our security teams that they managed to maintain security in the sanctuary and protect the rhinos from the ever-present threat. We've not lost one to poachers yet but it remains a worry.

Another worry was more personal. We now had four children running wild in Mkomazi. There are risks to living in the bush, like snakes, disease and skin cancer, but they were living a wonderful life of adventure and fun. Like the rhinos, they were free to roam within certain boundaries and were always watched over by our extended family. Dickson, Isaya and Happy Ndaskoi all took time to watch out for them and taught them how to do whatever they were up to. We decided, however, that they were going to need more if they were ever to survive in the world outside Mkomazi. By the age of four Mukka could make and shoot an excellent bow and arrow and he spoke two languages but he needed some more formal education. Gill Marshall-Andrews, ever the educator, put an advertisement for a tutor in the *Times Educational Supplement*. It started, 'Looking for Something Different?' And it produced excellent results. Over the next seven years we had six sets of teachers who managed to get the children up to a standard at which they could start boarding school at nearly nine in Kenya.

We were thinking ahead on that front too. My education had been incredibly important to me – an opportunity to do something different and surprising with my life. We decided early on that, although we would love to have them with us throughout their childhood, it would be cruel not to give our children the best chance we could. Palle and Caroline Rune had given us a wonderful wedding present of a plot in Naivasha near where I had first met Joy. It was the only thing in the whole world that we owned and we love them for it. Even more brilliant, the plot was just a few miles from an excellent school where the kids could go from seven to thirteen. We were already used to having to drive thousand-kilometre round trips to buy spare parts and Parmesan so an 1,100-kilometre school run would be child's play. Bob and Gill Marshall-Andrews offered to build two houses on our plot, one for them and one for us. It would be a joint company in trust for all of our children. Over the next couple of years our plot above Lake Naivasha was furnished with houses for both families, and a tasty garden has come up where buffalo still roam. And we can take the kids out from school whenever we want.

Bob and Gill came out to make plans for the houses in the middle of 2002 and came down to Mkomazi with some friends. Princess Michael of Kent came out shortly afterwards and she didn't bat an eyelid, flying around in my rather battered old aircraft. The princess was wonderful at enthusing people about our projects. They were all happy to see how well everything was going. The rhinos, except poor Badger, were thriving. Nina was in and out of camp whenever she felt like it, and Jipe had become a brilliant hunter, capable of taking down oryx and eland as well as easier game, like impala. We were all worried, though, by the mixed signals emanating from parts of the Wildlife Division. The permanent secretary had written to us to say what a great job we were doing but at the same time we were being given no help with our work permits and, of course, the Wildlife Division employees in the reserve were appalling. It was ever more important that Mkomazi was raised to national park status. This would offer a much higher degree of protection and we hoped that TANAPA – the national parks authority – would be much easier to deal with.

Bob and I put together an advocacy campaign. We would work and push for national park status for Mkomazi while diverting some of our efforts towards Kora and its reconstruction. After all, we were the George Adamson Wildlife Preservation Trust. It seemed like the perfect time to do it. At the end of 2002 there was a new government in Kenya and a new ambition to reclaim the country from the bandits and thieves. We would take advantage of it to help Asako and Kora, the places George had loved most. And some significant advantages had just come into play. My great friend and trustee Stephen Kalonzo Musyoka was a key member of the new government and, even better, my old friend Mike Wamalwa was vice president. But would the two of them be able to help us with our ambitions for Kora?

11. No Free Parking

My old partner in the Mateus Rosé venture Mike Wamalwa never managed to serve Kenya as he would have wished. Aged only fifty-eight, he died in a London hospital just eight months into his vice-presidency. Heartbreaking as it was, it was important to celebrate his life and achievements rather than bemoan his early departure. It was magnificent that Mike had managed to achieve the ambition he had professed to then Vice President Daniel arap Moi when we had met him in Parliament all those years ago. 'I'm after your job,' Mike had said to the professor of politics. And he got it. I was very proud of my old drinking partner and I resolved to make him proud of me by concentrating more of our efforts on the Kenya we both loved. At the same time as pushing for Mkomazi to become a national park, we would work on restoring Kora to its former glory. Keen to help me in that goal was my other great friend in Kenyan politics, Foreign Minister Stephen Kalonzo Musyoka.

Now a trustee of the George Adamson Wildlife Preservation Trust, Steve was as anxious as I to get Kora up and running again. I took full advantage of the goodwill that his interest stimulated. And this was a time of great goodwill, with the whole Kenyan population believing that the dark days were over. Policemen soliciting bribes at roadblocks were beaten up and stripped by angry drivers chanting, 'Corruption is over.' If only it had lasted.

In those early months of Kenya's new regime, we put in a lot of hours on the plane, flying up and down to Kora. Thank God, Fred Ayo was always meticulous when looking after it. Early in the year I had good reason to thank him for his professionalism. It is obligatory in East African countries to have your aircraft checked by the authorities every seventy-five flying hours or ninety days, and because we were so remote Fred always went over the plane both before and after we sent it off to be checked. When I was flying the plane back from its January Check III tests I noticed a vibration while I was in the air. Fred stripped back the cowling as soon as I landed and started poking around in the engine to see what was wrong; I thought maybe there was a loose engine bearer somewhere. He soon discovered that the mainte-nance facility had failed to tighten all the nuts when putting the propeller back on. Once again Fred had saved the day.

When you are living in the bush, such obsessive checking and rechecking is not always life-saving but it is still very important. Fred is inherently meticulous and he caught the rest off me. It's one of the great lessons I'd learnt from Terence and George in the early days at Kora. When you live in a tiny camp built on sand where there are snakes and scorpions under everything, silverfish to eat all your documents, rats to steal the food, leaking roofs, lizards and thieving fan-tailed ravens, it makes sense to keep everything neatly in tin trunks or metal boxes. Terence only had one suit, which he would seal up by soldering it into a four-gallon paraffin container. On the rare occasions that he needed it, he would break it out with a hacksaw then weld it back in again the next day, clean and ready for the next funeral.

If you weren't careful, everything in the workshop at Kora used to fall into the sand and get lost. Springs would fly out of automatic pistols during maintenance so I always spread sheets out when I was cleaning them. It was at Kora that I started nail-ing the lids of screw and nail jars to the underside of shelves so they could be undone by turning the glass bottom and were always where I could find them. The diaries I used to write this book only survived because I sealed them in a tin trunk where

56. Death of Badger

57. Breeding gets going –
Rose and her second
calf, Daisy

58. The rhino sanctuary takes off

59. Jabu – home at last

60. Elvis the fighter gets operated on after a bad goring by James and Jonah

61. Martin Clunes accompanies Nina into Mkomazi and falls in love

62. Anyone for bananas?

63. Nina brings Jonny Wilkinson to meet us

64. Jipe has a bottle on an evening walk along the airstrip

65. Emmanuel, myself and Jipe

66. Jipe brings us one of her cubs

67. Friends for seven years

68. Jipe, myself and Zacharia Nasari at the edge of the Supabowl

69. A lesser kudu became Jipe's first kill

70. Putting on Jipe's collar: Ombeni Kitomari, myself and Zacharia

71. Jipe admires Anthony Bamford's JCB

72. The new Kampi ya Simba, Kora, 2010

73. Meeting with Asako elders on my return

74. Tana river bridge, which links Kora and Meru National Parks, 2009

75. Kenya Wildlife Seminar on Kora, 2009: Mark Cheruyiot, Kora warden, in the centre in black trousers, on his left, deputy director, Kenya Wildlife Service, Joacim Kagiri

76. At Buckingham Palace, 2006: *from left*, Bob Marshall-Andrews, Lucy, me, Andy Mortimer, Brigadier General Hashim Mbita

77. Elisaria, Fred and Semu Pallangyo, the Trust's senior managers in Mkomazi

78. Jemima, Mukka, Kenya's Vice President Stephen Kalonzo Musyoka EGH, Saada, his youngest daughter, and myself

79. The family returns to Kora, 2009: *from left*, Mukka, Jemima, Imogen

80. Lucy and Missie, our orphaned caracal

81. Tilly and two baby ostriches, Kora

82. Our family, Mkomazi, 2009: *from left*, Jemima Mukka, Lucy, me, Tilly and Imogen in front

they languished for decades. As we were given ever more sophisticated equipment it was important both to look after it and to make sure it didn't stray. In Mkomazi we have six airtight shipping containers with racks and shelves where everything has its place. There are stencilled crime-scene outlines round every tool so you can see where something belongs or if anything is missing. Even with the most cursory of glances I notice if something is not where it should be, and if one of the mechanics needs a tool I can tell him exactly where it is.

A few years ago, Lucy was in England and I was at home listening to a World Service programme on which Tony Benn was being interviewed. I have no idea what he was going on about but I did hear the interviewer drawing amused attention to the fact that everything in his office was labelled. We were meant to join with the presenter to laugh *at* the veteran politician but when he said he couldn't live without his Brother labeller, I got on the phone immediately and asked Lucy to buy me one. Now everything I own has been Benned so I always know which phone I'm using, when the car needs servicing or what a dusty drawer contains. I have the same problem with rubbish. Stanley Murithii, my predecessor with the lions at Kora, was killed beyond the rubbish dump, Shade the lion got Terence in the dump and almost my last sight of the world was the very same rubbish dump when Shyman tried to kill me. I now recycle or burn everything in a huge pit, then bury the remains really deep.

Kampi ya Simba was filthy when I started going back there regularly. There were tins and bottles lying all over the place, a vivid example of how rubbish doesn't just go away but hangs around for generations. The first thing we had to do when we started rebuilding was clean up all the garbage and dispose of it outside the reserve. I now had two full-time jobs – one in Kora, the other in Mkomazi. Life at Mkomazi continues, and although Lucy takes a lot of work off my hands, it is still the major project demanding most of my time and funding. Lucy handles all Mkomazi's administration, the newsletters and the dog programmes, and we now have a staff of forty-five to help us out. Nevertheless, there is always as much work as you have time for. There were at least some new members of the Mkomazi family to remind us of what we were doing there. Zacharia had seen Jipe mating a few times and we knew that she was pregnant but we were not sure that she would reach full term as she had aborted a litter the year before. In January 2003, however, she gave us all a great treat. She had three tiny, still spotted cubs each about the size of a domestic cat. Two were playful and brave but, sadly, the smallest female died almost immediately.

Jipe had become very well known in the area around Mkomazi and after she gave birth the most unlikely people would offer us their congratulations just as they had when our kids had arrived. Shopkeepers in Same and Arusha would say, 'Well done,' as though we had done something clever. It was charming but also a sea change in people's attitudes. Very soon after she had given birth, Ombeni led me to Jipe, who collected her cubs and dumped them at my feet. Still with their blue eyes closed, they were in pretty poor condition but they were feisty and lively. We were inordinately proud of her. We cured the cubs of mange and immediately treated them for worms, which would give them a much better chance of survival. They were feeding well and in much better health than Freddie the lion had been when I'd first seen him all those years ago in the army mess at Garissa so I had plenty of confidence. Jipe, though, was going to have to do a lot of work on her own. Solitary lionesses struggle to bring up their cubs as it is both dangerous to leave them when hunting and hard to hunt alone. Jipe, however, was a great hunter and, with a lot of help from Zacharia and a bit from me, she took it all in her sinuous stride. The cubs soon began to grow and thrive.

The new life in Mkomazi seemed to symbolize our greater

ambitions for the reserve. Jipe was not the only lioness breeding there. The lion population was recovering from the terrible effects of the 'sport' hunting and elephant numbers were going up too. We kept on pushing for Mkomazi to be elevated to a national park and were gratified to be receiving plenty of support. The Tanzania National Parks Authority (TANAPA) – like the Kenya Wildlife Service – is a vibrant organization with proper management and clear lines of command. In Tanzania, national park status offers the highest level of resource protection available so it was logical that this should be our goal. In addition, we did everything else we could to keep Mkomazi at the top of the conservation agenda. I was particularly pleased to hear that Mweka College of Wildlife Management was now teaching a course about our work at Mkomazi. We had been hosting each class of students for years. Every term they would come out to Mkomazi so I could give them my 'Make mistakes and learn from them' speech, but for them to be teaching our methods was a signal honour. Since I had first arrived in Tanzania, I had always encouraged our guys to make mistakes and own up to them so that we could all learn from them. It was incredibly flattering that, twelve years later, I could leave Elisaria to host the Mweka students – I hear he gives them pretty much the same speech as I do, if with a lot less cursing.

Elisaria has always been integral to our work in Mkomazi but, more and more, he was becoming crucial to the Trust's work outside the reserve. He had built up the outreach programme to a point at which he was helping to upgrade dozens of schools. We decided about this time that we also needed to be doing things another way. If we could bring the school children into Mkomazi, like the students at Mweka, they would have a much better and less abstract understanding of what we were doing and how that could help the country. It is always a surprise to outsiders how few Africans visit game reserves and national parks; it is a tiny percentage of the population. We were slowly coming to realize that one short visit to Mkomazi would be ten times as effective as one long lecture in a classroom many miles away.

Another part of our strategy was trying to make Mkomazi pay. Of course, it paid for itself in preservation of wilderness and species terms but there was no reason why it shouldn't also have a cash income. After all the years of trying, we still didn't have very much tourism. A few intrepid visitors came every month but Mkomazi just didn't have the facilities to attract larger groups. It was hard to get to and not very rewarding for the kind of travellers who just wanted to tick off the Big Five and move on. We had a great discussion about the problem with Pete Silvester and the local MP, John Singo. Pete had recently set up the much-needed Kenyan Professional Guides Association and thought it would be a good thing to have in Tanzania. We talked about setting up a guiding school and study centre at Mkomazi and even got to the stage of deciding where to put it. Seven years later we haven't pulled it off but we're still trying. We always try anything that might bring in revenue for the government and raise our profile both within and without the country. It always pays off in increased recognition and respectability but sometimes achieves even more.

In early 2002 the collaborative artists Olly and Suzi came in to paint the wild dogs. It was the fifth time they had come and was a perfect example of how it's always valuable to put ourselves out to raise the profile of our projects. Olly and Suzi don't mind getting their hands dirty and have done some wonderful work with the dogs, producing fabulous paintings that capture the very life force of their subjects. They have become close friends as well as seriously raising the dogs' profile with their beautiful two-handed paintings. They have painted together for years and have not painted a solo canvas since art college. Extremely famous and successful, they have exhibited work done at Mkomazi in London and New York, and have invited me to talk with them at the Royal Geographical Society, the Royal Institute and the Natural History Museum. It has been a lot of fun, but also a great way of disseminating the importance of our work to a completely new sector of society, one with which we had no previous contact at all.

While they were staying I was asked to go to Arusha by a friend to give a talk to a group of car dealers from Holland. I thought that might be pushing friendship too far so, as I drove the five hours to Arusha, I was feeling a bit put upon and 'Why me?' Nevertheless, I gave them a talk and was about to drive home when their leader, Ted van Dam, gave me a cheque for 15,000 euros. I couldn't believe it. And since that time the Netherlands Suzuki Rhino Club has covered almost all the running costs of the rhino sanctuary as well as giving us some wonderful cars and quad bikes. We now have little Suzukis that are not only fun to drive but they go anywhere for half the running costs of the big Land Cruisers and Land Rovers that we use to move more people or heavy equipment. The dealers and staff of the company have been immensely supportive and are keen to make sure the project works. It saves me a lot of running around the world looking for funds. This was a telling example of how it behoves us to get out and spread the word that the world's wildernesses require protection. We can't just sit there and enjoy them on our own. The rewards are not always as spectacular, and we don't expect them to be, but every time we have a chance to tell someone about the perils faced by the world's wildlife we should do so.

It's not just in the rich world where these messages are important. If anything, it is more important closer to home. When people in Tanzania – who have to live with dangerous animals on their doorstep – don't appreciate their worth, our projects face a constant battle. Initially a sceptic, John Singo MP helped us a huge amount with getting our message across to as many

Tanzanians as possible. By encouraging us to publicize our donations to communities living near Mkomazi he has helped to safeguard its future. We used to assist local schools by giving them cement or helping them to build dormitories and classrooms. It was just something we did for our neighbours rather than something we shouted about. John persuaded us that we should do both. He started giving rousing speeches whenever we did something for a local school or church. When we helped build a new secondary school in Same, we all went along to the opening and the minister for natural resources and tourism, Zakia Meghji, gave a great speech about George, about the Trust's work in Kora and Mkomazi and how we were bringing jobs and money to the area. Elisaria and Lusasi were happy to see that our work was being appreciated, that there were only a few bad guys trying to make life hard for us and that most people thought we were doing a good job.

Another way of getting the word out within Tanzania was when rangers from other parks came to see how we did things at Mkomazi's rhino sanctuary. Even though we hadn't known much about rhinos when we started, we had managed to create a sanctuary that is used as a model in Tanzania and beyond. The professional interaction with other rangers and wildlife guardians was just as useful as the visits from Mweka College that had been going on for so many years. In 2003 rangers visited from the vast Selous Game Reserve and, even more excitingly, a few months later the national parks authority sent in twelve of their rhino rangers from the Serengeti – the very people we wanted to come into Mkomazi. This was recognition and appreciation on a wholly different level.

It remains hard to surf the wave between travelling to spread the word and actually getting things done. I was lucky to have such a good team at Mkomazi that I could do things like visit the Czech Republic, as I did that year, 2003, secure in the knowledge that everything would carry on without me. There was a zoo there with East African black rhinos and I spent years persuading its board that they should come home to Mkomazi. There was already a lot for our staff to look after. Badger was still in very poor condition and Pete Morkel could not understand what was wrong with him. There was a possibility that he couldn't masticate his food properly so Pete flew in a horse dentist from Zimbabwe who filed his enormous rhino teeth down. Badger had to be lightly sedated, sat upon by six men to hold him steady then worked on by the resolute horse dentist. It was a horrid job for all concerned – particularly Badger – and sadly made little difference. Badger was fading. Semu had to organize people to be with him twenty-four hours a day and we were spending a fortune on feeding him supplements just to keep him alive.

One of the aspects of helping animals that I try to get across when I give speeches and meet people is that it's not always fun. It's wonderful being in the bush but queuing for permits and listening to academics at conferences is torture. Even trying to help Badger was hard work and ultimately not very rewarding. The same can also be said of caring for Spike, the serval cat, a beautiful long-legged cub that our friends Charlie and Serena Mason gave us after he was orphaned on their farm. We always stay with them when we're in Arusha and they come to Mkomazi when they can. Spike was no purring kitten that liked having his tummy rubbed. Indeed, he had been called Spike only because he was so difficult. He hissed at anyone who came within twenty feet but we couldn't let him free until he was old enough and large enough to look after himself.

Dickson Kaaya, who was helping to raise our children, was put in charge of Spike's welfare and devoted many hours to him, including feeding him two large birds a day – in vain. Spike hated Dickson even more than he disliked the rest of us. He was a spectacularly effective killer but he needed a bit of help at the start. Once he had got the hang of catching and eating his own food, he played with his prey then dismembered it with a peculiarly sinister relish. His room, which was also our bathroom, came to look like a voodoo torture chamber with blood and feathers daubed all over the walls, viscera and fur on the floor. One morning I stepped gingerly over the threshold to brush my teeth, expecting to be pounced on by the hissing ball of rage. I was relieved to see a Spike-shaped hole in the mosquito mesh. He had gone without a backward glance. We saw him a few times over the next couple of years but never if he saw us first. He hated us way too much.

Spike's nemesis, Dickson, was absolutely brilliant at looking after the kids. It was always embarrassing that when we took them for walks they would return covered with cuts and bruises. With Dickson no harm ever befell them. But he had it pretty easy compared to the guys out in the reserve where elephant, rhino and lion roamed. We had a very nasty shock in August when Mollel, one of the rhino-sanctuary team who had been with us from the beginning, was attacked by a buffalo. The poachers had been hard at work in Mkomazi and the buffalo's testicles had been ripped off in a snare. Understandably this had driven it mad with rage. Mollel was badly gored but we managed to fly him to Moshi in time and he made a remarkable recovery. He fared much better than the poor emasculated buffalo, who was put out of his misery by one of our security team.

Dramas like the one with Mollel are inevitable when you are living far out in the bush, surrounded by nature at its most red, but they became a lot more easily manageable over the years as our communications systems clawed its way into the modern world. From the days when we used to have to drive to Arusha to use the telex machine things had moved on apace. We now had a radio linked up to a phone in a friend's office sixty miles away. It meant that we could make phone calls without driving to Same, and when Mollel was hurt, we were able to alert the hospital that we needed to be met at the airport by an ambulance. The improvement in communications made us feel much better about having the kids with us, although I'm not sure Lucy agreed on the day we discovered a spitting cobra in the schoolhouse.

My flying had been significantly helped by technology too. We hadn't realized quite how invaluable the global positioning system all pilots were now using had become until America and Britain invaded Iraq in 2003. Rumours circulated around the flying community that the GPS system would be turned off or made inaccurate so as not to 'give succour to the enemy'. It's astonishing to think how much my life has been changed by the GPS: I would literally be lost without mine, although I always have a map as a back-up.

Just before Saddam Hussein was captured in December, Badger had another incident. His back legs gave way as he was drinking and he collapsed into his water trough. For two whole days the staff down in the rhino sanctuary had to try to keep him upright with ropes. Pete Morkel – who was now based with his family in nearby Ngorongoro Crater – flew in to have a look at him but didn't hold out much hope for his recovery. Sadly he was right. Two months later Badger collapsed again at that grimmest of all hours, four o'clock in the morning. He had fallen over, been pulled up again with ropes, then immediately fallen over again. In the cold darkness he gave up after his long struggle with illness and died with his head in Semu's arms at eight thirty a.m. The only consolation was that he had died on home soil, but it was a miserable end for a lovely and trusting animal that had struggled so bravely with years of illness. I remembered the happy day when he had first arrived and the kids had been able to feed him by hand. Indeed, some of the sanctuary staff continued to do so until his death.

Pete came in and did an autopsy where Badger had died in the middle of the sanctuary. The top rhino vet in the world, he was worried that the autopsy needed to be done as quickly as possible, so instead of messing around waiting for the right equipment, he did the whole thing with a Leatherman pocket-knife. There are so many prima donnas in the wildlife world who wouldn't dream of doing things the rough and ready way, but if Pete hadn't done the autopsy then, we would have been unable to do it at all. We at Mkomazi and Kora have been incredibly lucky to have people like Pete and Aart coming out to help us over the years. And when, later in the year, Aart resigned from looking after the wild-dog programme, Pete immediately took his place. Now Pete has moved to a home in Namibia and has a roaming rhino practice but before he left us he worked with the capable Tanzanian vets who have taken his place.

In the course of Badger's alfresco autopsy, Pete discovered trauma to his spinal cord that was likely to have been caused by an injury sustained while he was in South Africa. He felt that this was probably behind all Badger's mysterious illnesses over the years. Pete had been unable to save him – but if he couldn't save him then nobody could. I wish we had been told early on that Badger's mother had been killed by an elephant and that Badger had possibly been injured at the same time. We might not have saved him but it would have helped in our diagnosis.

As always happens in the natural world when it is sufficiently protected, new life soon replaces the old. Nina had disappeared almost a year earlier and we had all given up hope of ever seeing her again. After six years of freedom, her radio collar had long ago been dumped or fallen off and we hadn't been able to track her down despite my flying all over Mkomazi searching for her while checking on illegal activity for Lusasi. There were all sorts of threats to elephants in Mkomazi and in neighbouring Tsavo. We thought that she might have succumbed to the drought or to the increase in poaching on both sides of the border. Nina had become a great part of our lives since that monumental move in 1997 and we all missed her. Then, just as Badger was facing his final illness, and after nearly a year away, she strolled into camp and came up to the workshop to say hello. She was looking fat and healthy although there was still plenty of room for the children to feed her a few bananas. Just a couple of days later we discovered why. On the night before England won the rugby world cup, Nina put her trunk through Elisaria's window at four in the morning and encouraged him to come outside. There, between her legs, was a newly born calf. She had come home so that she could have her son in safety. One memorable drop goal later, we decided to call him Jonny Wilkinson in honour of England's cup-winning fly-half.

It felt good to be alive that day. It had been the combination of rugby and wildlife that had first brought me to East Africa when I hitched a ride on the Comet from Malawi to see Middlesex Rugby Club play in Nairobi. For years many of my old school rugby friends had been on the board of the Trust. Now we had performed the impossible. Even Daphne Sheldrick – one of the world's elephant experts – had thought it unlikely that Nina would assimilate enough to mate and have a calf, but Nina had proved everybody wrong. She had taken her time and had a great holiday in the bush with her friends but now at the age of thirty-three she had come home to the safety of Mkomazi to have her first calf. We felt greatly privileged that she had chosen us, and everyone was proud that an expectant mother should have seen Mkomazi as the right place to have her calf in safety. She was not the only one producing young either – the wild dogs were producing litters at a heady pace and we now had a viable population that we would soon be able to start reintroducing to the wild.

Amid all the drama of the dogs and the rhinos, it's hard to imagine that we have anything approaching a routine at Mkomazi. We do, however, have the occasional normal day and it usually

starts before daybreak with the World Service and a cup of tea.
Then in comes Elisaria, followed by a long line of others. '*Hodi*,'
he says, the Kiswahili for 'I'm outside, may I approach?'

'*Karibu*.' Draw near, or welcome.

'The elephants destroyed three wild dog *boma*s last night. Most
of the Lendenai dogs are out and we're out of new poles.'

'The old *dungu* [Bedford lorry] lost a front wheel last night on
the way back from taking water to Kifukua and is stuck near the
southern end of the rhino fence-line.'

'The alarm has packed up on the Kilo Mike to Kilo Tango
section.'

'The water pump on the big storage tank has packed up. Didn't
we have a spare somewhere? Fred's on leave and I'm not sure
where it is.'

'Helena's sick. I think it's malaria and she should go to hospital.'

'The regional labour officer wants to come in. When would
be a good time?'

'We're out of potatoes and rice. When's the next vehicle going
out?'

'TANAPA HQ just called. They can't make the meeting on
the third in Dar es Salaam. When can we reschedule?'

'Kilo Echo says they need water for all the outposts and the
rhinos.'

'We need to re-roof the generator house. The sun has destroyed
the asphalt sheeting. What shall we try next?'

'George at Zange [the park HQ] has just been on the radio.
Can he come over and discuss help with moving stone for the
new road signs and washaways? Helima wants to come too and
talk about new water projects.'

'I just heard that District Commissioner Mwanga is coming in
with a group. Can you give them a talk and show them the rhinos
this afternoon?'

'Eliudi just called on the radio. He's blown a hydraulic pipe on the grader on the new line and his compressor's not working.'

'Can the tracking team have new alarm report and sighting sheets? They also need new uniforms.'

'Sorry, Mzee, my child is very sick at home. Can I have a few days off?'

'Mama Lucy, Mnygatwa has asked if he could have a history of all the Trust's work in Mkomazi over the past twenty-one years.'

'There's a fire over the back of Kisima Hill. Shall I go and check it out? I think the repeater battery has died – I'll change it on the way back. Can I take your quad bike?'

'Can we do a group of elders on the next school trip rather than the schoolkids? I think it's about time.'

'I need a list of equipment for the next Kora trip. Shall we take the welding machine?'

And the tea's not even cold yet . . .

The complications of working in a game reserve started to become a problem again in the course of 2004 but somehow we managed to keep going. Lusasi's rangers continued to run rings around him, and although we had great support from the government and within the ministries, problems continued to manifest themselves on the ground. Poor Lusasi did his very best but he had no way of disciplining the rangers. They absolutely hated me, particularly my flying. It gave their boss Lusasi an aerial picture of what was going on, which made it much harder for them to be up to no good. With twenty minutes of flying, I could monitor more of their activities than Lusasi could in a month. I reported back to him the minute I saw any cattle incursions or poachers' camps, helping him to force his rangers to take on the poachers. My bird's-eye view meant he could ultimately use them to arrest the trespassers on the basis of my intelligence.

In the areas surrounding Mkomazi there were five cattle barons and three commercial meat-poaching gangs, who relied on paying off the rangers for their profit. So when I reported what was going on to Lusasi, the rangers were infuriated. They couldn't take bribes from people they were being forced to push out of the reserve. By way of a retaliatory smokescreen they used to write endless letters to the wildlife authorities and ministries accusing us of selling ivory, mining, spying and dealing in rhino horn – all of which, of course, had to be investigated. I was praying that the rangers would be removed and replaced with some goodies, but we don't live in a perfect world so we worked even harder to impress the director and staff of the national parks. It was crucial that Mkomazi was gazetted as a park.

In the interim, we had to keep working with what we had and there was tragedy stalking close to home. I was on a fundraising trip to the US when Lucy called me as I changed planes in Phoenix. Jipe was dead. I could hardly breathe and my eyes were so full of tears that I could scarcely see. The cabin crew were nervous about letting me on to the plane because I looked so weird. I had to tell them there had been a death in the family and I suppose it was true: she really had been family. Jipe had reopened an old part of my life and made me feel as if I were twenty-seven again. Walking in the bush at Mkomazi with Jipe and her cubs had been such a very special and unexpected bonus. She had such a gentle character but had been a tough, efficient killer when she needed to be. She had looked after her family and made sure they always had enough to eat. I still miss her terribly when I'm out on the plains where she used to come and greet me.

I found out when I got home that she had been poisoned by some stockherders who had left bait around their cattle camp – just as someone had killed Squeaks in Kora. Both animals would have died very slowly and in blinding agony. After a radio signal showed Jipe had gone across into Kenya, Fred and Zacharia had gone out looking for her, following a faint bleep from her radio collar. It led them to an active Tanzanian cattle camp just inside the Tsavo border where they found her body – skinned, decapitated, paws cut off and all her teeth smashed out for tourist trinkets and witchcraft. Jipe's radio collar had been shattered and buried with her but to no avail. It continued to work even from the grave, a credit to AVM Instruments but not much consolation to Fred and Zacharia who had feared the worst but hoped for the best. They called in reinforcements, ambushed the grazers when they returned that evening and dragged them to Zange to be formally arrested by Lusasi and his rangers. I don't think Zacharia has ever recovered from the grief. Seven years of looking after Jipe had forged an extraordinary bond between them. He was completely devastated by her death and indeed asked to resign some months later, saying Mkomazi was not the same without her. We didn't try to persuade him otherwise as we understood his grief and, in any case, his elderly dad needed looking after. He's still on standby for the next lion . . .

Jipe and her relationship with Zacharia were so well known around Tanzania that her death made the national news. We received condolence letters from all over Tanzania and there was a genuine outrage that such a thing should have happened. When Zacharia went to report the incident and take the prisoners in with some rangers he had collected on the way he was confronted by a sobbing policeman, a hard Special Branch cop, who had already heard the news. The minister wrote to us to express her sadness. And, significantly, so did scores of ordinary people. Of course it was awful that Jipe had been killed but we consoled ourselves with the fact that she had achieved a great deal in her life. All those people who had heard about her, the visitors who had been to Mkomazi, the school children to whom Elisaria had spoken as part of our outreach programme, all now put a value on preserving wildlife rather than killing it. In her short life she had achieved what so few of us can manage: she had changed the way people think. It was very similar to the effect that *Born Free* engendered when it had been published fifty years earlier. Before the story of Elsa, lions were seen as big game to be hunted and killed by rich white hunters. After *Born Free* lions became wildlife to be protected and conserved. We hoped that Jipe's story would have a similar effect in rural Tanzania. And there was some good news: her cubs had survived. They had not eaten the poisoned bait and towards the end of the month they came back to see Zacharia. It was the first time he had smiled for weeks. The cubs went on to thrive in Mkomazi and, indeed, become parents themselves.

Animal tragedy is one thing, but human tragedy is something completely different. Soon after Jipe died, Jacobo Mbise, our grader driver for the past eight years who had done so much to build the rhino sanctuary, was killed when he inexplicably drove up a completely undriveable hill, stalled and then rolled the huge CAT grader. A father with young kids, his death was a terrible thing to happen in our close-knit community and we were concerned about how to provide for his family. We need not have worried. As ever, my old school-friends in the UK Trust showed their depth of understanding and compassion. They put together a fund, with Elisaria as signatory, that would see the children through school, take care of medical bills and ensure they were looked after.

Another big blow in 2004 was the death of Costa Mlay, the former director of Wildlife, who had gone on to be one of our trustees. It was a huge loss on a personal and professional level. Costa had stood with us through thick and thin when it seemed that the whole world was trying to get rid of us. He had taken great weights off our shoulders by quietly fighting battles for us in the corridors of power and always had a calming word to put our minds at rest. I went to the funeral at his home in Marangu where he was buried. A great many people were there, showing their respect for the man who, like Richard Leakey in Kenya but with a lot less money and publicity, had brought Tanzania's wild-life back from the very brink of disaster. We really missed him as a man and, in just a few months' time, we were destined to miss him as a trustee.

Government systems the world over are such that tiny grains of sand can bring entire administrative machines to a grinding halt. We have found almost since the first day we arrived in Tanzania that, however much support we had from the ministers and directors, it needed only one small cog in the government machinery to be against us to put us into real trouble. And it all started happening again in 2004 and 2005. On the one hand we knew that our efforts to gain national-park status were being treated favourably at the very highest level – they had even reached the president's office – but on the other we were unable even to get our work permits renewed. The latest problem in a very long line was that we were being investigated by the Anti-corruption Squad for illegal mining. It reminded me of the mad days in Kora when I was accused of spying. In Mkomazi we were now nervous of dredging the dams in case one of the rangers reported we were looking for gold.

At the beginning of 2005 I was once again on a fundraising trip when our trustee and friend Charles Dobie rang Lucy to say she had to be ready to leave Mkomazi, the country and our whole lives in two hours. The Anti-corruption Squad had decided that we were, in fact, illegal miners and not conservationists: the rhinos were a blind. It was now when the chips were down that we saw the mettle of our Tanzanian friends and trustees, mettle we had never doubted but that we had never needed quite so much before. Immediately we missed Costa Mlay because our chairman Brigadier Hashim Mbita was away in Zimbabwe where he was now ambassador, but Bernard Mchomvu and Charles worked the corridors of power and were able to postpone disaster while we tried to work out what was going on. Some even laid their careers on the line to support us. Two thousand and five was a time of great importance in the terrible decline of Zimbabwe; we couldn't expect our problems to overshadow Brigadier Mbita's work yet he flew back to Tanzania and went to see the president without us even asking. He told President Benjamin Mkapa that he was willing to resign his post as ambassador if his integrity was doubted over Mkomazi. The brigadier didn't even tell us he had done this and we didn't find out until months later.

Even with all this support we still had difficulties. But at least in March we discovered whom we were up against: it was the hunters again. One of the great and continuing scandals of the wildlife world in Tanzania is that there are hunting blocks adjoining the Serengeti. For years they have been no-go areas to most Tanzanians. Men of enormous wealth fly in to slaughter the wildlife using a variety of weapons, from machine-guns to hunting rifles, and fly out again without ever setting foot in the real world of Tanzania and Tanzanians. These people have so much money that they feel they can do what they like. They fly in and out and bring in their own helicopters, Hummers and Range Rovers. It was at times such as this that we missed President Nyerere, who would never have allowed such an attack on Tanzania's sovereignty. Pretty nearly untouchable, they cannot, however, manipulate everyone: when a group offered our local MP John Singo an envelope of cash and asked him to withdraw his support for Mkomazi becoming a national park, they made a terrible tactical mistake. John's vision for his people was the creation of a national park. He not only rebuffed the bribers, he exposed them too.

John asked them to put their offer in writing and so arrogant were they that they did. We still have the letter from the hunting group promising a never-ending supply of euphemistic 'money for local communities' in exchange for Mkomazi as a hunting block. John rejected them out of hand. This had far-reaching consequences. The Tanzanian Parliament had already said that Mkomazi should not be a hunting block and had even agreed in principle to its becoming a national park. Tanzania's patriotic citizens – including the district commissioner in Same and those in power in Dar es Salaam – were utterly enraged at such treachery. The whole episode smacked of neo-colonialism and encouraged many people who had been indifferent to hunting to adopt our stance of total opposition. Hunting continues in Tanzania today but there is an ever-increasing groundswell of opinion that is firmly against it. Our troubles were by no means over but at last we understood why we were having so many difficulties: we were up against people who had no conscience and to whom money was no object.

Hunting was once the preserve of royalty but, these days, most royals know better. In 2005 Princess Michael of Kent became patron of our UK Trust, thus bestowing on us a level of respectability I could hardly have imagined when I first started work at Mkomazi – sad, bruised and exhausted after George's murder in 1989. The princess had been to visit us before and had been wonderfully helpful in broadening our fundraising base, but actually having her on the writing paper was a huge boost for us, as well as being a great honour. She is a dedicated and hard-working animal lover and became a good friend. The knowledge that we were gaining new supporters and increased respectability elsewhere gave us greater confidence when we faced the threat of expulsion in Dar es Salaam.

We were still very uncertain of our future at Mkomazi when we decided that we must at last send Mukka away to school. He was almost nine, and although he had his younger sisters to play with at Mkomazi and had received a varied education from their many tutors, we knew that he needed the stimulus of other children. We managed to get him into Pembroke House, the boarding school near our little house on Lake Naivasha that we

had looked at a few years earlier. Many of our friends, some living
in similarly remote outposts, sent their children there and we
knew he would make friends. We dropped him off for the first
time at the beginning of the spring term and moped for days. We
were utterly devastated by his departure – but our sadness was
put firmly into perspective when Laurence, the son of our beloved
friends Serena and Charlie Mason, was killed in a car accident.
We all missed Mukka because he was away for a few weeks but
Laurence had gone for ever. It was impossible to imagine how
they must feel. Only a few days before he died, we had been
thinking of Laurence because we had seen his friend Spike, the
angry serval, by the kitchen. Laurence was only eleven when he
died yet there were more people at his funeral than many adults
four times his age could have brought together.

Much of that summer was something of a blur, with Lucy and
the kids spending a lot of their time in Arusha with the Masons,
while I charged up and down to Kora. Events carried on regard-
less of the losses we faced elsewhere. Prince Bernhard had joined
a funding consortium for a windmill at Asako, which Mike
Harries – who had married Lucy and me – was going to erect.
This would bring proper running water to Asako at last.

In Mkomazi Nina, too, wanted water. She spent a lot of time
around our camp that summer, flirting with a huge male she had
befriended and taking advantage of the available water. Of
course, little Jonny Wilkinson was never far from her side but
we wished at times that she was a rather less indulgent mother.
Jonny was a feisty little bugger who was always charging at everyone around the camp. His tiny little trunk made the sweetest
noise but, cute and cuddly as he was, even the smallest elephants
are by definition elephantine: large, clumsy or awkward. Pete
Silvester had discovered, at the cost of a broken back, that it is
unwise to herd even the smallest of elephants so we put in some
special measures to ensure that no one got hurt. After a bit of

experimentation, we dug a ditch round the edge of the vehicle workshop so even if Jonny Wilkinson chased us out in the open, we had a good chance of jumping the ditch and making the safety of the workshop before he could catch up. Jonny screeched and trumpeted at all hours of the night and became a total menace, but we loved him and he was a shining symbol of Mkomazi's future.

At the end of June Mkomazi was blessed with an even more exciting youngster: Rose, one of the first batch of rhinos from South Africa, gave birth to a calf called Suzi. She was almost immediately attacked by the female Charlie, whom Pete Morkel describes as the most aggressive rhino he has ever come across. Charlie was a classic bloody-minded and unpredictable rhino, unlike Badger, who had actually seemed to like us. Despite twice being hit so hard that she did a complete somersault ten feet up in the air, Suzi thrived. This was more than could be said for Elvis, who was just as aggressive as Charlie but rather more stupid. Rhinos love to fight and sometimes kill each other when doing so, but instead of taking on small calves, Elvis insisted on fighting with big bulls, often two at a time. He had to be sedated and sewn up more than once in the course of the year.

The wild dogs were rather less combative than the rhinos but their fertility far surpassed them. After the disasters of 2001, when all but three had died of canine distemper, we managed to get the numbers back up to fifty. It was a personal triumph for Aart, who had done so much work for the dogs in his eleven years as chief vet of the wild-dog programme. Soon after, we moved four brothers from their compound below our house to freedom in the rhino sanctuary. Wild dogs require an enormous range to be truly free but getting them out of their compound and into the forty-five-square-kilometre compound was a great start. They killed an impala almost immediately we let them free, then started hunting successfully almost every day. It was amazing to see how they adapted so quickly to life in the wild, having been born and bred in captivity, another example of how wild animals only need to be helped to reintegrate – they don't need to be taught anything. It's mainly instinct and inherited knowledge. We just act as surrogate mothers for a while, providing protection, care, attention and play until they come of age.

In mid-October, we drove up to Kenya to collect Mukka for half-term. He had adjusted well to boarding school and was enjoying his time at Pembroke, but the rest of us still missed him every day. We were very lucky that we had all gone up to see him as Jemima kept having stomach-aches, which would have been hard to treat in Mkomazi. Midway through Mukka's half-term I took her to hospital in Nairobi where she had her appendix removed an hour later. What with Jemima's convalescence and all the other little everyday dramas of life at Mkomazi we had almost forgotten about our long campaign to have the reserve gazetted as a national park. It was therefore something of a surprise when a friendly local journalist called us up and read us the front page of the *Daily News*, Tanzania's government newspaper: 'Mkomazi Reserve to be National Park,' it said.

At last it was official. Mkomazi would gain its final level of protection and TANAPA could replace the corrupt rangers who had caused so much trouble over the years. To say we were overjoyed would be greatly understating the case.

12. Back on Track

Mkomazi becoming a national park was a huge triumph for all of us. For Lucy and me, for our Trusts in Germany, Holland, Kenya, the UK and the US. But most of all it was a victory for all the Tanzanians who had worked with us over the years – our trustees, Elisaria, Fred, Semu and Zacharia, Hezekiah Mungure and Salum Lusasi. With all the work we have done on education in the past few years, we are sure that there will be more of their calibre to come. Thinking back to my earliest days there, when I had slept in my Land Rover cursing my luck and missing George, I couldn't quite believe how far we had come. We still had the wonderful old tractor for which my friends in England had guaranteed the payments; we even had the horrid old Bedford that had come down from Kora. And right next to them we now had two JCBs, a digger and a massive Fastrac tractor. Big, yellow, impressive and all operational, thanks to Fred Ayo. We had a workshop that could house an elephant – indeed, that had been its original function. Instead of a tool roll in the back of my pickup, we had lines of containers full of specialized wrenches, radio equipment, telemetry gear and goodness knows what bits of rubbish Fred and I had squirrelled away over the years. If all of that was anything to go by, we were indeed worthy of becoming a real game park.

The real reason why the National Parks (TANAPA) wanted to take us on was positioned next to the airstrip: our pride and joy, the rhino sanctuary, in which nine northern black rhino were now living and breeding in the land where they belonged. And there were more on the way from the Czech Republic too: the Dvur Kralove Zoo – with lots of prompting from Pete Morkel's

Back to Africa organization – had decided that Mkomazi was the most suitable place to send their extra northern black rhinos. Pete and his team had to do a great deal of pre-move planning to get them used to their crates as Dvur Kralove is a very long way from home. Our captive breeding and reintroduction wild-dog programme was the only one in East Africa and was doing well. We had big plans for more releases and for building up more packs on the Tsavo/Mkomazi border. Elephant numbers were up, as were the numbers of beautifully horned kudu, eland antelope, fringe-eared oryx and the long-necked gerenuk that had suffered badly for their heads during the slaughter of the hunting years. We had reasons to be happy with what we had achieved but, as ever, there was no room for complacency. There would always be more trouble around the corner.

The occasion of our triumph came tinged with sadness. Costa Mlay had died the year before, and now, in quick succession, two other close friends and mentors, Prince Bernhard and Keith Eltringham, followed him. Keith had chaired the UK Trust from the very beginning when Bob Marshall-Andrews and Ant Marrian had first formed it. He had always been a source of great advice and direction through the backbiting, tunnel-visioned academic world of conservation and zoology. A great pilot and a pioneer of aerial survey work when he worked with elephants in Uganda, Keith had also been a respected Cambridge professor. Whenever we were attacked for our lack of academic credentials Keith came out fighting for us in his gentle, highly informed and respectful manner – so much more effective at silencing our would-be saboteurs than antagonistic and arrogant sniping would have been. He monitored our fieldwork, corrected reports and told us when we had to do things differently to be taken seriously. As we moved ever closer to institutional donors and started working with big international players, his advice became ever more relevant and valued.

Prince Bernhard – PB, as he liked to be known – had been a

steadfast supporter of everything the Trust had done from the day I'd first met him in Kora. He had paid for dreary things like housing for the rangers and, most recently, had given money for the windmill at Asako and for the rebuilding of Kampi ya Simba. When he awarded me the Most Excellent Order of the Golden Ark for my 'outstanding work in the field of lion and leopard rehabilitation in Kenya and reintroduction of rhinos and wild dogs in Tanzania', it gave me much-needed ammunition against the academics, and respectability in those still hard-to-access corridors of power. Given that he only pinned the Ark on three hundred people, I felt I was in good company.

From the start of 2006 we experienced a strange and prolonged lull while the Wildlife Division rangers made as much money as they possibly could before TANAPA took over. We longed for a swift changeover but these things always take aeons. For the time being, the reserve filled with cattle and there was a great deal of poaching for bush meat, even if it was well below the damaging levels of yesteryear. Lusasi did his very best but everyone knew that TANAPA was coming and they would no longer be able to use Mkomazi as a vast store cupboard. We concentrated our efforts on our existing programmes and indeed had a very rewarding year. I was flying every day in support of Lusasi, and when I was on the ground, I was working hard on the wild dog and rhino programmes. Early in January we released four male wild dogs into the sanctuary and they started hunting immediately. It was incredibly gratifying to watch – as if they had been born and brought up in the wild. The sanctuary fence proved no barrier to them and they were soon out in the reserve and, indeed, further afield. Excitingly, a male wild dog from a local pack came to see the females in the compounds. We made a swift decision to collar and release two females – a successful strategy. After all those years of long, seemingly never-ending, veterinary programmes, we were off.

The rhinos were doing well but Elvis continued to pick fights with both James and Jonah; his aggression was beginning to take its toll. In late February he had a massive ruckus, which ended with him flat on his back, his two opponents laying into him like muggers in a subway. Pete and Estelle Morkel spent more and more time with us, sewing up the increasingly battered Elvis, until we were obliged to build a separate section for him. We had left it too late: James and Jonah had done too much damage and Elvis never really recovered. At the end of March Semu called me on the radio and said he thought Elvis had only a few minutes left. We sat with him and watched in silence as he breathed his last, the heavy, dulling weight of sadness descending on us yet again. We were distraught – both Badger and Elvis dead. Elvis had at least died doing what he loved best – fighting – but our rhino birth rate was only just keeping up with the death rate and Elvis had been a lovable if crazy old brute.

It wasn't until the late summer that the Trust managed to sign a new agreement with the Government of Tanzania and it was December before we were given another year's work permits. Bernard Mchomvu, the brigadier, Charles Dobie and Rose Lugembe had been working closely with Elisaria to ensure that we were going forward on the right basis, but all the bureaucracy had been a tremendous waste of time for everyone. All the trustees had much better things to be doing and it seemed as if Elisaria was hardly ever in Mkomazi doing his real job any more. We contributed to his absences when we sent him to Lakipia in Kenya to do a training course on environmental education. The education team at Chester Zoo had come in to assess our work and had been so impressed that they had volunteered to fund the course and advise us on how to do things. They were hugely impressed with Elisaria and had lots of great new directions for our education work.

If only we could have come up with a similar solution for our own children. At the beginning of the school year, we lost another to Kenya when we sent Jemima to join her brother at Pembroke. Mukka was doing well academically and loving rugby. The Trust was working on education at Kora, too, where Gill Marshall-Andrews had set up the Trusts for African Schools to support and assist Asako primary school as well as schools closer to her new home at Naivasha. It seemed sometimes that we spent more time on education and administrative work than we did with the animals but they were flourishing too. I just wasn't doing it myself – something for which I was thankful when Evans, a top rhino tracker, got tossed in the air by Charlie, one of the females to arrive in the first translocation from South Africa. She and her newly born calf had been sleeping in thick bush when Evans almost tripped over her. We had a nasty few days while Evans lay in hospital with a punctured lung but he made a full recovery and is still working in the sanctuary today.

So many of our staff at Mkomazi have been with us for years that I feel we must be doing something right or they would all go and work elsewhere. It's not as if we pay better than anywhere else and we do keep people a long way out in the bush, away from their homes and families. Evans has two cousins working at Mkomazi and they have all been with us for more than fifteen years. All the key people – Elisaria, Semu, Fred and Sangito – have been with us for at least twenty years. Increasingly they are working not just at Mkomazi but helping train staff at Kora, too. It's a source of great pride that we have managed to hang on to them for so long. Highly skilled and experienced, they elicit much envy in other conservation and government organizations. I always wish I could do more for them but with nearly fifty staff it is difficult.

A similar source of pride are the extraordinarily generous people who have helped us as Trustees over the thirty-five years since we first set up the Kora Trust at Bob and Gill's house in

Richmond. In December 2006 we held a big supporters' dinner in London and just before it I was awarded another medal. Amazingly, I had been given an OBE in the Queen's Birthday Honours List, another punch in the eye for the nay-sayers, which gave me enormous satisfaction. George had always been quietly proud of his MBE; I now knew the feeling. Brigadier Mbita flew over for the ceremony at Buckingham Palace where he, Lucy and I were shepherded by Andy Mortimer and Bob Marshall-Andrews – both of whom are much more used to such hallowed ground. I wished my parents had been around to see it. They had worked hard to get me into Mill Hill and here I was, fifty years later, still so close to two of my school-friends that we could all go to Buckingham Palace together.

Aart Visee and Ally van der Lught, and Ted and Catrien van Dam came over from Holland for the trustees' dinner and the next day we had a fabulous time driving around London on a big red open-topped tourist bus. It was one of those freezing cold but gloriously sunny winter days and took me right back to the tourist boat in Paris where I had bumped into Bob, after my first few years at Kora. Back then I had been sad and alone, staring into the abyss of an empty future. I felt extraordinarily blessed to be sitting next to my loving, hard-working and wonderful wife, surrounded by good friends who had helped to fill my past by contributing to the plight of Africa, its animals and its last few wilderness areas: the Marshall-Andrewses, who had built us a house and set up the first trust for George and me; Aart, who had given us Arusha the lion and many years of his veterinary skills; Brigadier Mbita, who had offered his resignation to the President of Tanzania for us; Ant Marrian, who had helped to save me from drinking myself to death and had been on the Trust since day one; Andy Mortimer, who had taught us how to make our money work harder. I'm sure George and Terence were there somewhere, too, harrumphing in a corner and complaining about the cold. It was a wonderful, happy day when all our problems receded into the distance and we lingered smugly over our successes.

We went home with renewed vigour, keen to do our best for Asako and to help TANAPA make Mkomazi into a national park worthy of the name. I was soon off to Kora again where I hoped to work similar miracles. In Kora, however, I had no official status, no agreement with the authorities. I was just an interested party trying to help the area that George and I had loved. I hadn't spent any time in the main town of Garissa for more than twenty years. The last time I had been there, I had been handcuffed in the back of George's pickup and we hadn't stopped. It had changed a great deal. In the 1980s it had been a three-street town. Now it looked like Khartoum after a sandstorm. I didn't know where I was. Ant Gross and I were trying to open a bank account for the Trust for African Schools and were told at the bank that we needed an account-holder of long standing to vouch for us. I racked my brains, then remembered the Bayusufs.

Five minutes later we walked through the Wild West doors of the iron-grilled shop I remembered from all those years ago. Fahim walked out of his office, a little tubbier, a little greyer, but the same Fahim who had always looked after me. 'Tony, you're back. *Allahu Akbar.* I pray to Allah you come. I have seven sons. I show you five now. I see you on the satellite TV on Discovery Channel and BBC and I tell everyone, "That's Tony . . . He is coming back one day . . ."'

I remembered the times when his family made sure I had tea and something to eat in the mornings, the way he had helped me to buy things, to find things, even to pay for things. It was great to be back.

'How can I help?' he asked.

He picked up the phone and dialled. 'I'm on the board of the bank, now!' he said. 'Manager – Tony and his friends, give them anything they want. I'll sign everything in the morning. Thank you.'

As I left the shop, two menacing-looking Somalis were walking down the middle of the road: age indeterminate, thin as rakes, straggly beards.

'Hello, Tony,' said one.

I felt goose bumps all over me. The baddies knew I was there.

On my way back to Mkomazi I heard that Father Nicky from Kyuso was in Nairobi. I tracked him down and dragged him home with me. It was great seeing my old friend again, the man who had kept us going with his supply runs into Kora. He had some great ideas for projects the Trust could do around Kora and we started again just where we had left off. He had always found peace in the natural world of Kora and our work, and I had found peace in his simple sermons to the Wakamba beneath a shady tree on the simple choice that we all had between good and evil. Nicky had been in Rwanda after the horrors of the genocide, and I knew the healing and building of the spirit he was capable of, even after the worst human atrocities. He had now been posted back to Kenya. We will not fall out of touch again.

We had a new pet in Mkomazi, a scared and timid aardwolf with a wonky back leg. Aardwolves are neither wolf-like nor hard. Nocturnal termite eaters, they have just four peg-like teeth and are very shy. Gizmo spent her day sleeping behind the sofa and was much beloved by the children, who used to feed her treats of hand-caught termites. She spent the evenings happily pottering around the house but as soon as we let her out her legs went wrong again and she couldn't do anything – completely paralysed from the middle of her back downwards. We had become very attached to her over the months she had lived with us and we all howled when I decided I had to put her down. The twins were beside themselves but there was nothing else we could do. It's so hard to know what to do with all the orphans who have lived with us over the years. Many of them are alone because their mothers deserted them – they can't bring up disabled or sickly young. I never know precisely why they've been abandoned but, having almost been there myself, I find it hard to let nature take its course.

One afternoon at Mkomazi, I was having a peaceful siesta when the door opened and a complete stranger walked in. This never happens at Mkomazi – we are thirty miles from the main gate and no one is allowed in without prior approval. I was pretty rude to the stranger and told him to go away.

'But I've come to help you and the project,' he said.

And so he had. He was Nick de Souza from the World Society for the Protection of Animals (WSPA) who gave us a car and funded our new de-snaring team for the next two years. It was incredibly fortuitous. I had decided that if we waited for TANAPA to take over, there wouldn't be much wildlife left for them to protect by the time they arrived. We had no powers of arrest but we could at least confound the poachers who were denuding the park. I set up a virtually silent bicycle-borne de-snaring team who pedalled around the reserve like Vietnamese Special Forces. They looked for snares, dismantling them when they found them, and also provided great intelligence on cattle movements. They were not expensive teams to run and were highly effective, but they did get a lot of punctures and they did need to be paid.

Education was our main theme for the year, though, both at Kora and at Mkomazi. We put a lot of thought into education and outreach because school children and local communities are the future custodians of the environment. Tusk and Save the Rhino had done a fundraiser for us at one of the guildhalls in London – I had given a PowerPoint presentation on huge screens. At the end of the night we had been pledged enough money to build an education centre and to fund a bus that would ferry children in and out. We set the education centre on a glorious

site in the middle of the rhino sanctuary. It is bordered by forested
hills and overlooks the plains, reaching out towards Tsavo. We
put the car park at the bottom of a hill so that the children would
have a short walk up to the top, taking in the incredible view
that rewards them for their climb. The bus had been built to our
specifications with big windows so the kids could look out of
them, with extra-strong suspension for our roads and painted
panels on the sides. I managed to find a great *tinga-tinga* artist to
paint it. I told him roughly what I wanted – the rhinos, the water
projects and the wild dogs. He said, 'Yeah, man. I know what
you mean.'

And he did. He smoked a big joint and painted exactly what
I wanted. His work captivates the visiting children from the very
moment they see it.

The wild dog introductions carried on apace, and in doing
them we came to realize why the species had veered so close to
extinction. Man was the main problem. With a range as big as
1,350 square miles, they were bound to come up against someone
who didn't like them and would poison them but they didn't help
themselves. We released another group into the rhino sanctuary
and they soon developed a habit of resting under the same tree
every afternoon. A leopard noticed this and killed one of the dogs
after waiting for them in the tree one afternoon. We regarded
the first loss as a misfortune but when they rested there three days
in a row with predictable results we began to think they were
being careless.

The Trust has survived by an adherence to rules and procedures
that is endlessly frustrating but holds its own against even the
most concerted opposition. I have never got used to the office
procedures that are such a deadening contrast to the enterprising
people who deal with them – they're always keen to go out of
their way to help and explain to us once more the Byzantine
processes we must follow. Kenya, these days, has disposed of

many layers of bureaucracy, and working there is much easier than in Tanzania but, as always, it is people that are important. Just as Mkomazi had been blessed by Hezekiah Mungure when we first arrived, our new ventures back in Kora would be blessed by its warden, Mark Cheruyiot. Mark is tough and keen, with great natural authority and an enthusiasm for Kora that infects all who meet him. On first meeting him, I knew he was a man that the Trust and I could do business with, and I immediately committed to refurbishing George Adamson's camp in Kora, keeping it maintained, opening up the road networks and paying for the casual labour gang to do the work.

In June, Mark and I met up in Kora to start working on a plan to resurrect a broader area. I went back to Kampi ya Simba and set up camp there for the first time in twenty years. The chicken wire and hessian huts had all been burnt down with the chain-link fences, but most of the wire was still usable, and from the rocks above camp you could see the outlines of how it had been before. I looked down at the shadows of my former life and resolved to restore it to the way it had been. That night, I slept on the top of the car in the ruins of the camp, surrounded by friendly ghosts. I heard lions in the far distance down by Boy's Lugga and the next day went down to pay my respects to George. Kora was still a front-line state, but in its new warden it had a man who was not only dedicated to his job but was also dedicated to Kora. Mark was genuinely committed to Kora's rehabilitation and seemed to love the place – which is odd, because it's still boiling hot, inaccessible, thorny, remote and incredibly hard work.

Kora had suddenly become fresh and new again for me. I racked my brains for ways that the Trust could be of more use there. Excited, I went to Asako to research what they needed, then back to Mkomazi to work on a scheme for our thrust back into Kenya. Although we had no plans to leave, there was a valedictory feel to a lot of our work in Tanzania at the time. It was emphasized by a great OBE party that Philip Parham, the British high commissioner, gave us in Dar es Salaam. Steve Kalonzo Musyoka flew in for the party in the middle of his presidential campaign, all our Tanzanian trustees came, and friends who had supported us with tools, workshops, beds, advice and money. It was wonderful to be able to say thank you to them for all the work they had done over the last two decades.

At Mkomazi, Nina had come to visit us. This was always a treat as she had been going off for ever longer safaris over the years and we missed her. She was limping slightly but had Jonny Wilkinson with her; she seemed ready to hand him over to a big bull among the several escorting them. It was great to reflect on how we had improved Nina's life from her days at Mount Meru, entertaining the tourists and staring at the same unattainable view every day on the main road to Dar es Salaam. At Mkomazi she had stared from the top of mountains, then walked to wherever she wanted – to Tsavo in Kenya, to the water-pans by the rhino sanctuary, the Dindira Dam in the north and many miles into the south of the park. She had joined up with and been accepted by herds of elephant that had lived together since birth; she had mated and had a calf. I'm glad she came to say goodbye.

I smelt her first. After all her hundreds of miles of roaming, Nina had come back to camp to give birth to her second calf. But she had died while delivering. The smell and the buzzing of flies guided us to the spot where she had died. The calf had been wrongly presented and had become stuck in her birth canal. Poor Nina – she wasn't old in elephant terms and had had many years of roaming left in her. We could have done nothing for her but it would have been nice to be with her as she died or even to put her out of her misery. Semu and I did a quick autopsy – our tears washing away the blood amid the stink of death. However many times an animal that's been close to you dies, it's always shockingly painful. I have never mastered the ability to be unaffected by it and I don't want to. It's part of what keeps me going. Nina was an individual to us – we knew her habits, her funny ways, when she would compromise and when we shouldn't mess with her – but the death of any elephant upsets me. There are not enough of them left for me to be able to look lightly upon even one. That evening, Lucy and I walked down to the airstrip in the evening, both of us feeling sad, as though a part of our lives had been taken away. We watched as thirty elephant crossed silently in front of us and I vividly recalled the day George and I had watched a herd cross the Tana from Kora and pull themselves out on the Meru side. He had asked me then how long I wanted to stay at Kora. I should have replied, 'A lifetime.' It was what I'd felt even then.

There was no time for reminiscing, though, or moping over the loss of one of our friends. We had given Nina a good life and we had problems with the wild-dog reintroductions. With the perversity we had observed in them before, they were soon leaving the safety of Mkomazi to raid goats in nearby villages. They had discovered a taste for them as a result of illegal grazing but that argument held little water with the pastoralists on our borders. We pleaded with them not to put down poison and, with Salum Lusasi, agreed compensation terms but the dogs were soon killed. Since then we have done all our releases on the Kenyan border – in the middle of the protected areas of Tsavo and Mkomazi – but wild dog roam so widely that all we can do is hope for the best. So far, so good.

Overall, I suppose a little more than half of our wild-dog reintroductions have been successful – not much of a success rate for all the effort but a lot better than nothing and comparable to survival rates in the wild. There are so few ecosystems in Africa that remain good for wild-dog packs, but Mkomazi/Tsavo is one of those areas so we are obliged to try to help them. We breed them, vaccinate them, patiently wait a year until the first-born group of pups helps raise the next litter, translocate them to holding *bomas* on the Kenya border, then reintroduce them to the wild and help them if they need feeding. It sounds simple but the work behind doing that is enormous and can be very wearing. We saw that when all but three of the first batch of dogs died. And trying to find an effective vaccination programme had almost been Aart's life work. When – through brilliant detective work and close collaboration with Erasmus University and Professor Osterhaus – he pioneered a new method, it took years to get permission to bring the vaccines into Tanzania.

Just before Christmas I did another of my talks with Olly and Suzi at the Royal Geographical Society. It was a really interesting evening with the two artists talking about endangered animals from their perspective and me talking about the harsh realities of trying to keep the dogs alive. After all the fundraisers that Tusk had organized for us in Kensington Gore I had become almost blasé about addressing the RGS. Nothing, however, had prepared me for dinner that evening. I jumped into a cab after my talk and raced off to Kensington Palace for dinner with Prince and Princess Michael of Kent, the Queen and Prince Philip. As you do. It was nice to be able to thank the Queen in person for my OBE as it had been Prince Charles who had invested me on that memorable day at the other palace.

We had good news at Christmas when our old friend Erasmus Tarimo was made director of Wildlife. He had supported us from the very start of the Mkomazi project, warning us of trouble ahead and ensuring that we did everything correctly. He had helped Elisaria on his endless quests for agreements and work permits for Lucy and myself. We had our turkey that year with Pete and Estelle Morkel, quietly satisfied about how things were going in Tanzania but horrified at the news from across the border. Kenya was going up in flames after an incredibly divisive election in which politicians had whipped up their supporters to attack each other on the front lines between different tribes. It was very unsettling – not the kind of thing that's meant to happen in Kenya. We observed from a safe distance, horrified, as pictures of places we knew and loved were relayed across the world – on fire and in ruins. Then, of course, the kids got sick and we had to fly them straight into the eye of the storm.

As everyone who could afford to was putting up the shutters and hunkering down until the unrest died away, I had to drive right into the centre of it with Imogen and Mukka. They were puking so much they could scarcely move. Nairobi was empty – no traffic, few people, the occasional scared-looking passer-by or unruly mob. I put the children in hospital and headed out to Pete and Julianna Silvester's house in the suburbs. I drove down the usually heavily congested Ngong Road at 150 k.p.h. It was just like the 1960s when you could drive that fast everywhere. There were lots of young guys on that side of town who gave me the thumbs-up as I drove past, amazed to see a *mzungu* on the roads at such a volatile time. The start of 2008 was a very disturbing time in Kenya. After forty-five years of peace and stability, the country teetered on the very brink of civil war, only pulling back under enormous international pressure from the likes of Kofi Annan and George Bush. The kids turned out to be fine but we had become nervous after Jemima's appendicitis the year before.

Back home at Mkomazi, 2008 was a time of consolidation spent continuing to prepare for the handover to TANAPA and getting the education programme working properly. It was sad that Salum Lusasi would not be there for the long-awaited handover: it had taken so long that he came up for retirement before it happened. Although his rangers had been a constant thorn in our sides, Lusasi had been a great man to work with, yet more so after the horrors of Swai and Marenga. We missed him when he went into retirement although he still had a house in Same and we caught up occasionally.

Lusasi had been particularly supportive of our environmental education programme that was launched shortly after his departure. You have to be careful when arranging outreach and education that it doesn't take away from the bigger picture. Elisaria was our operations manager, but over the past few years he had spent way too much time in Dar es Salaam dealing with bureaucracy and yet more working on the education programme. We were very fortunate that Chester Zoo was able to help us arrange the programme more effectively and efficiently. Chester is renowned for its education programme, which is planned on the well-known premise that children have a very brief attention span. The plan we devised was all short sharp shock – ten-minute lessons and nice activities, lunch for all the kids, a ten-minute DVD, a quick, well-thought-out game, meet the rhino trackers for ten minutes, see a rhino and then go home. Elisaria and I were mightily relieved that we could do an effective programme for eight hundred children a year without it becoming a burden.

In Asako, too, education was in the ascendant. Gill Marshall-Andrews's Trust for African Schools had agreed to assist Asako's secondary school in Garissa. This meant that children born in Asako would attend a well-funded primary school in Asako and could then go on to Garissa to continue their education; the Trust was also helping with bursaries – attending school a hundred miles from home is not cheap.

After a lot of rushing around in the early part of the year I managed to break my collarbone in several places by falling off my motorbike on the way back from a picnic. After all the wrestling with lions and relocating rhinos, I managed to do myself serious damage trying to avoid a rabbit! In serious pain, I had to be medivaced to Nairobi and operated on immediately. It was by far the worst injury that I had endured since I was chewed

up by Shyman in the seventies and eventually took three operations to put right. For the rest of the year I had to wear a sling
and was unable to pick things up with my left arm. The guys at
camp hated it because I was always in and out of the workshop,
tidying up and, for the first time in years, focusing on rebuilding
the camp and bringing it back up to the standards of the rhino
sanctuary.

They were much relieved when we went on a family holiday
for the first time in years. My great friend Rick Anderson of
AFEW, who had helped us so much in Kora and Asako, lent us
his beach cottage at Malindi and we spent long hours swimming
in the sea, lounging around the house and going for long walks
on the beach. Malindi is now very much in the twenty-first
century but it has retained the charm that so drew me to it when
I used to camp out on PA and Agneta's sofa, swim out to the
break with Attila the surfing dog and pick up girls on the beach
in the evenings. And it was in Malindi that I had had the fateful
call from George asking if I'd like to come and help him at Kora.

Despite the constant pain in my shoulder I was much refreshed
when I returned to Mkomazi and a similar call from Mark Cheruyiot, the warden in Kora. Mark had been down to visit earlier in
the year and had looked at what we had achieved in Mkomazi.
He must have been impressed because when he returned in
September with Robert Njue, a senior officer, it was an official
visit on behalf of the director of the Kenya Wildlife Service. On
the night before he left, we had a long chat by the campfire outside
the mess tent and Mark asked Lucy and me formally if we would
move back to Kora and continue the work I had left off in 1989.
I was dumbfounded. And quietly excited.

The excitement grew when the invitation was backed up by
the director – in person. Lucy and I went to see Julius Kipn'getich
at his headquarters in Nairobi. He repeated it, and we went on
to discuss rhino sanctuaries, outreach programmes and the thing

I really wanted to do: lion and leopard reintroduction. It truly looked as though a return to Kora might be on the cards. They even wanted to put up a statue of George and start a museum at our old camp.

We had dinner with Steve and Pauline Kalonzo Musyoka, who were just as keen for us to return. Steve had just become vice president so his ever-present support was now even more valuable. There was, however, a lot to think about. Lucy and I were very happy in Mkomazi. We had brought all our kids up there. It was safe, we had good friends and we had built up a wonderful team. On the other hand, although we had been there for almost twenty years, it remained pretty stressful living under insecure conditions, always facing mysterious delays with our work permits and memorandums of understanding with the wildlife authorities. We knew TANAPA would be better for Mkomazi and its wildlife – but would TANAPA be better for us?

We would soon find out for during September the handover finally took place and Mkomazi at last became a national park. It was just around the time that Barack Obama – a fellow exiled Kenyan! – became President of the United States. It was as if the whole world had turned over a new leaf. The TANAPA rangers soon started patrolling and the Wildlife Division rangers were moved out. The new rangers were immediately effective and by the end of the year there were hardly any cattle in the park. It wasn't all perfect, though. In fact, in many ways it was a total disaster. In September the Tanzania Revenue Authority (TRA) changed its rules overnight in a way that could well have bankrupted the Trust. We were not alone – the TRA targeted every charity and non-governmental organization working in Tanzania – but that didn't make it any better. Until 2008 we had been granted a tax exemption on any equipment we used to help the government restore Mkomazi. Since tax on imports is extremely high in Tanzania, this made a huge difference to our operations.

Withdrawing our exemption meant that we suddenly had to pay tax on gifts. Right then we had two extremely expensive gifts just arriving at the port in Dar es Salaam, the two rally-built Suzuki Vitaras that I had seen and been given by the Suzuki Rhino Club in the Netherlands the previous year. They were worth a fortune: to pay tax on them would cripple the Tanzanian Trust.

Elisaria and our trustee Bernard Mchomvu were in and out of government offices trying to obtain an exemption since the cars had been given to us long before the tax laws were changed while they were on the high seas. The problem was made doubly difficult and urgent since the port authorities wouldn't release the cars until the tax had been paid. They charged us port fees for every day we left them there. We despaired of ever sorting the problem out and, indeed, it was another four months before we did. In the end, the government agreed to pay the tax but we had to pay the port fees. It's lucky they turned out to be such fabulous cars for all the trouble they caused! Ted van Dam's mechanics will come out in 2010 to check them and train Fred.

The Suzukis were not the only financial problem we had. Like everyone else in the world, we have been seriously affected by the recession that started to bite at the start of 2009. Many of our donors were having problems. Expansion seemed even more daunting: some of our longest-standing supporters have been obliged to reduce their funding or pull out completely. On the whole, though, we have been pretty fortunate since we now have institutional donors, like the International Fund for Animal Welfare (IFAW) and US Fish and Wildlife.

Lucy and I were still not sure what to do about the Kora question. I desperately wanted to go back to the place I loved but I was very torn as I loved Mkomazi too and I had responsibilities as a husband, a father and an employer. I couldn't just cut and run as I had in 1989. In March we took the children up to Kora to see if it would help us decide. Imogen and Tilly were nine and just about to go off to school as well, so we wanted to spend some time together as a family before Lucy and I were left alone. A lot of people don't 'get' Kora – it's as hot as hell and never easy or gentle. Thank heavens the children did. We had a wonderful safari, camping under the stars. I showed them where Christian and I had slept away the afternoons down by the river. I took them to the places I had lived with thirty lions and ten leopards. We visited Kampi ya Chui where I had stayed with Squeaks and Bugsy. We went to George's grave and slept at the foot of Kora Rock where I had spent so many happy years. I really think at last they understood me a little better as the strands of their child-hood stories came together.

It became much easier for them to imagine my life when I was in my twenties and thirties after they had seen the place where Shyman had tried to kill me and they had driven up the hill towards Kampi ya Simba, aiming the car's bonnet at the three great rocks that you can see from miles away. I hope, now they understand a bit more, they can forgive me for being the oldest father at the school gates. Jemima was doing brilliantly at Pembroke and was soon to run in the Kenyan national stadium. We would miss the twins terribly but we knew that Jemima would look after them at school. But who was going to look after Mukka? I had bumped into the headmaster of Stowe, the English public school, at a friend's house a few years earlier and he had told me about the bursaries offered there. Mukka had done his bit and passed Common Entrance and now he was about to go to school five thousand kilometres from home. I don't know who was more upset at the prospect – me or Lucy. Mukka, though, took it in his stride and is now doing brilliantly at the world's most beautiful school. There was two foot of snow on the eight-eenth-century palace when we sent him back this time, unaccompanied on the plane from Dar es Salaam.

Our visit to Kora helped us make a lot of decisions. We would get Kora going again and we would try to start another lion and leopard project there but it would not be at any cost to Mkomazi, which was in the best of hands while we were away. We would do both. Lucy and I were going to need a hell of a lot of help but we would get there – one step at a time. On our last night at Kora we spent the evening with three of the guys who, we knew, would help us – senior warden Mark Cheruyiot, Kora warden Joseph Nyongesa and Kenya Wildlife Service pilot Samwel Muchina. All three were from different tribes and different areas. High fliers all, they were on their way up. And they weren't afraid. They shared a love of their country and a commitment to making it a better place that transcended any tribal barrier. We discussed the political situation and they told us of their plans for their own futures and for the future of their nation. And my family sat there with them, flipping back and forth between fluent Swahili and English, accepted and welcome in the place where I had grown up. My God, I was proud of them.

We've made great strides forward since that holiday in Kora, but that was the turning point. We've completely rebuilt George's old camp and we're well ahead with our plans for a visitors' centre and study camp. The chain-link fence that I was worried would not be strong enough to keep out the lions has stood the test of time. The camp has been burnt down and abandoned, rained on and scorched by the sun, but the wire still holds. We just put up some more posts, buried the wire three feet down, curled it over with rocks on top and stapled it back on. Bob and Gill have given us a set of encyclopedias just like Terence's old ones, and Fred and I rebuilt the huts using Terence's old method of chucking cement at a sheet of hessian. We've made another elephant-jaw loo seat like the one Prince Bernhard loved and I've even found the same ugly vinyl tablecloth that we used to have. The only visible difference is the seating arrangements. Now I sit in George's chair! And it still feels a bit weird!

The work we are doing in Kora, though, is not just cosmetic and retrograde. Lucy and I decided that a simple return to Kora was pointless. If we were going anywhere we must be moving forwards, not backwards. Fred and I have put in a solar system under the antiques; we have a water filtration plant instead of the old diatomite candles, and a container for a workshop. We're fixing the roads and making plans to build an historical education centre at the proposed tourist camp. We need to put in a radio network for our own security and see if the Kenya Civil Aviation Authority will make it easy for us to bring the aircraft back and forth from Tanzania. At the moment we have to apply well in advance for permission to fly into Kenya, then fly over the Pare Mountains and land at Kilimanjaro International to clear Customs. We get airborne again and fly on to Nairobi between Mounts Kilimanjaro and Meru. We land at Nairobi where we have to clear Customs again and pay our dues. Then we fill in more forms and fly on to Kora, past Ol Donyo Sabuk and over the Tana hydro dams, the dryness of Ukambani. It takes most of the day and is exhausting.

We need to employ full-time staff and temporary labourers to work on the road and camps at Kora. We have to involve nearby communities, provide employment and make people love and believe in our projects as we do. Mark Cheruyiot is spearheading the effort from the Kenya Wildlife Service side, and we're making huge progress. In Asako we're mending the windmill that Prince Bernhard paid for and digging a little deeper to where the fresh water is. Trusts for African Schools have put a new roof on the school and built good housing for the teachers to make sure they stay in the area and don't go off to the towns eighty miles away. The elephant are back in Kora too. The other day I flew down the river with my old friend Mike Harries (the priest who married Lucy and me). We'd been checking the windmill in Asako and attending a trustees' meeting at the school in Garissa with Maalim

Shora. As the sun started to weaken at the close of the day, we flew low along the twisting Tana and surprised a large herd of elephant playing on a sand bar not far from camp. We saw lion tracks by Christian's Crossing and there were plenty of waterbuck, lesser kudu, gerenuk, bushbuck and dik-dik. It's taken a terrible thrashing over the years but Kora now has a warden who cares and we're going to help him every step of the way.

Things are looking good in Mkomazi too. We've had more births in the sanctuary and in mid-2009 we brought in three more rhino from the Czech Republic. Ted van Dam and the Suzuki Rhino Club in the Netherlands sponsored the translocation but even he balked at paying the Tanzanian government $60,000 in Customs duty on priceless endangered animals that we were giving to the nation. This time we took it to the top and explained to the commissioner of Customs that the rhinos had no financial value. Erasmus Tarimo, the director of Wildlife, reminded Customs it was illegal for them to charge on endangered species on CITES permits. The exemption was granted and came through four days before the translocation but we thought we'd better cover ourselves anyway. We paid the $340 import tax on their meat value!

It was a great and happy day when the rhinos arrived, this time by truck from Kilimanjaro airport, Pete Morkel as ever jumping about on the crates, keeping the rhinos just sleepy enough to do themselves no damage. Brigadier Mbita and Rose Lugembe flew into Mkomazi to greet the director of Wildlife, our trustees and the director general of TANAPA. Mkomazi is now a fully operational national park and the Trust has a great relationship with TANAPA. Just the other day I met some of their board members and asked them if we had a future at Mkomazi or if they wanted us to look for an exit strategy.

'Tony,' they said, 'the board of TANAPA are very happy with your investment here in Mkomazi and we would like you to continue for as long as is practical and possible.'

It was great to hear it said out loud. Over the twenty years we have been at Mkomazi we have had all sorts of problems with individuals but the central relationship between us and the government has always been good. The authorities have always let me get on and do the job in the field. They trust us and the Tanzanians who work here to do the best we can for the wildlife and the area. I am extremely grateful to them for giving me the chance. Brigadier Mbita has announced his intention to step down as chairman as soon as the agreement with TANAPA is signed so they can take as long as they like: we don't want to let him go.

The great thing about both our projects is that they are vibrant and flourishing and moving forward. The wild dogs continue to breed, we continue to vaccinate, wait a generation and then release them. The rhino sanctuary is a going concern with a viable population from various gene pools. The rhinos are breeding, there's no fighting and they browse happily away – being rhinos in the place where they belong. More importantly, we have trained up an entire team of people at Mkomazi to know how to run a game sanctuary, look after the most valuable animals in the world and bring a species back from the edge of extinction. I'm not redundant yet but I'm working on it.

Of course I'm desperate to have some more lions or leopards in Kora and it will come. Julius Kipn'getich told me the other day I have his blessing. And we are going to train up a new team in Kora. I had some great people working for me in George's day but I didn't manage them as well as I should have done. I didn't give them enough chances to make mistakes and I didn't help them to exceed their expectations. I'm so proud of my team in Mkomazi – Elisaria and Fred at Headquarters and Semu and Sangito with the animals. And they have brought on teams of their own too. I want to do the same again in Kora and I know George will be watching over me as I do.

In earlier days, my constant urge to keep going forward may

have prevented me from reflecting enough on the past. Now I try to do both. I was asked by a film crew the other day why it had taken me so long to go back to where George had been killed. I was with Ibrahim Mursa, a Kenya Wildlife Service game scout from Asako, who was the driver of the first vehicle on the scene after the ambush. The reporter asked why I was writing a book and taking so much time to look back when normally I only looked forwards. I didn't know how to answer for a while but then said that I felt I had to reflect on the past a little more responsibly. They asked me what I'd learnt or found out. I recalled the carefully prepared words of Winston Churchill that George had once read out to me: 'Success is not final,' he said. 'Failure is not fatal, it is the courage to continue that counts.'

I have found that courage.

ACKNOWLEDGEMENTS

As I reach the end of this book I feel as if I should embark on an Oscar-winner's speech of thanks. There are so many people I need to thank and so many debts to be paid but I'll never manage it. All of you, all over the world, who have helped me so much over the years know who you are and I couldn't have done it without you, and whether it's been a bed for a night, a tractor, a year's running costs or pure moral support, my gratitude is immense. Thank you, all. This book is for you as well.

I also know that without George's guidance I would never have succeeded in half of what we have done. George devoted his life to the wildlife of East Africa and he showed me how to walk with lions. I miss the Old Man every day as I try to live up to his beliefs – working to give animals a chance to live with dignity in their own land. I know there'll be problems ahead but I also know that Lucy and I will be able to find a way around them. If we continue to care enough and 'keep going forward one step at a time', we'll walk with lions again.

And this book would never have taken off, let alone been completed, without the friendship, professionalism and sheer lunatic energy of Miles Bredin, my co-author. An accomplished journalist and author, he 'got it' and was often way ahead of me on this journey of reflection and adventure. I was amazed at both his perceptions and feelings, and the historical context that he provided as background was invaluable.

Eleo Gordon at Penguin worked tirelessly and with formidable and enormous enthusiasm to make sure that the book was a fitting tribute to both George and all the animals. The way she steered the project across continents and still allowed us to be able to continue with our work was a coup of some genius. It was always a great pleasure when we got together in London, but even I almost crumpled at the pace!

Without my wife Lucy no one would have had anything to work from. She produced three hundred pages of chronology from both our diaries and was critical at the end stages when I didn't quite get it right or went a bit overboard. But that's just work. She has been an amazing friend and companion in two of the more remote areas of East Africa under, at times, some very trying and difficult conditions, and managed to raise four lovely children at the same time as doing all the field administration of the project. It's all We now, not Me, and without her love and support there would have been a very different story. Many men have said it before, but love is all you need . . .

KORA FAMILY TREE

1st generation

BOY
Born 1963
Arrived 1970
From Scots Guards, Kenya
– Mascot with Girl
Born Free actor
Kills Stanley Murithii
Shot by
George Adamson 1971

KATANIA
Born 1970
Arrived 1970
From Maralal
Taken by crocodile 1970

CHRISTIAN
Born 1969
Arrived 1970
From Ifracombe Zoo. Sold to
Harrods, to Ace and John,
World's End, King's Road.
Surrey. Kora, Kenya
Last seen 1973

SUPERCUB
Born 1971
Arrived 1971
From Nairobi.
Flown to Kora in a
Supercub plane
Killed by wild lion 1971
Terence, then
George Adamson buried
next to him

2nd generation

LEAKEY
Born 1972
Arrived 1974
From Nairobi fairground.
Orphanage
'Henry Kissinger'
peacemaker
Crossed Tana with
Freddie 1976
Last seen on the way
to Meru Park 1978

FREDDIE
Born 1974
Arrived aged four
weeks 1974
From Wajir. Garissa
Exchanged for a
Temptations tape
Crossed Tana
with Leakey 1976
Last heard with Leakey on
the way to Meru Park 1978

GIGI
Born 1974
Arrived 1974
From Nairobi
orphanage
Crossed the
Tana 1980

ARUSHA
Born 1973
Arrived 1974
From Blijdorp Zoo,
Rotterdam, via
Aart Visee,
the vet there
Crossed the
Tana 1980

GROWLIE = **DANIEL I**
Born 1974   *Born* 1972
Arrived 1974   Crossed
From Nairobi   Tana with
orphanage   Oscar and Kora
Last seen 1980   Last seen 1977

3rd generation

GROWE = Wild lions = GLOWE

Numerous cubs

DANIEL II
Born 1977
Attacked stock
Shot by warden
with his brother
Shade, 1981

SHADE
Born 1977
Mauled Terence
Attacked stock
Shot by warden
with his brother
Daniel II, 1981

4th generation

Numerous cubs   3 cubs

5th generation

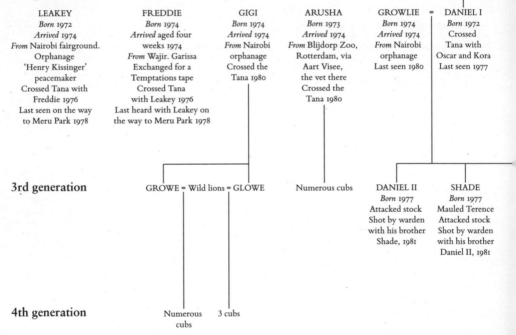

Note: Adapted from my family trees, produced
in George Adamson's book *My Pride and Joy*

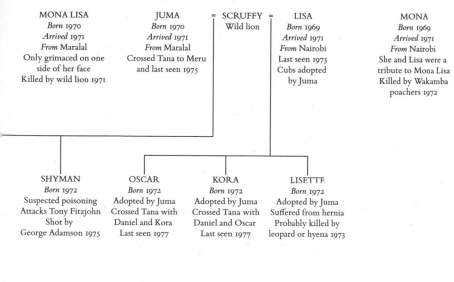

MONA LISA
Born 1970
Arrived 1971
From Maralal
Only grimaced on one
side of her face
Killed by wild lion 1971

JUMA
Born 1970
Arrived 1971
From Maralal
Crossed Tana to Meru
and last seen 1975

= **SCRUFFY** =
Wild lion

LISA
Born 1969
Arrived 1971
From Nairobi
Last seen 1973
Cubs adopted
by Juma

MONA
Born 1969
Arrived 1971
From Nairobi
She and Lisa were a
tribute to Mona Lisa
Killed by Wakamba
poachers 1972

SHYMAN
Born 1972
Suspected poisoning
Attacks Tony Fitzjohn
Shot by
George Adamson 1975

OSCAR
Born 1972
Adopted by Juma
Crossed Tana with
Daniel and Kora
Last seen 1977

KORA
Born 1972
Adopted by Juma
Crossed Tana with
Daniel and Oscar
Last seen 1977

LISETTE
Born 1972
Adopted by Juma
Suffered from hernia
Probably killed by
leopard or hyena 1973

KORETTA
Born 1977
Had many cubs
Had a long life
A real star!
Moved away to
Asako 1987

Numerous
cubs

SULEIMAN
Born 1975
Arrived 1977
From Ken Clarke
at Galana Ranch
Attacked
George Adamson
Killed by hippo 1978

SHEBA
Born 1976
Arrived 1977
From Ken Clarke
at Galana Ranch
Killed by Somali
poachers 1978
Ken murdered
soon afterwards

KAUNDA
Born 1975
Arrived 1976
From Nairobi orphanage
Very friendly
I think I saw him at
1st Eastern Meru Park
signpost cairn

JOJO
Born 1975
Arrived 1976
From Masai Mara.
Bill Woodley at
Aberdare Park
Killed attacking
Somali stock 1981

LUCIFER (Bugsy)
Born 1985
Found Komonyu
aged 3-4 weeks 1985
Best friend of
leopard Squeaks
Last seen 1987

NAJA
Born 1977
Had three litters
of cubs
Last seen 1984

Numerous
cubs

Index